IDENTITY AND RELIGION

International, Cross-Cultural Approaches

Edited by Hans Mol

 SAGE Studies in International Sociology 16
sponsored by the International Sociological Association/ISA

For information address

SAGE Publications Ltd
28 Banner Street
London EC1Y 8QE

SAGE Publications Inc
275 South Beverly Drive
Beverly Hills, California 90212

International Standard Book Number

0 8039 9890 2 Cloth
0 8039 9891 0 Paper

Library of Congress Catalog Card Number
77-93700

First Printing

Printed in Great Britain by
Biddles Ltd, Guildford, Surrey

IDENTITY
AND RELIGION

CONTENTS

Each chapter is introduced by a critical abstract by the Editor

---

INTRODUCTION

Hans Mol
McMaster University, Canada

There are a number of reasons why the ISA research committee on the sociology of religion has sponsored the following project. Since the beginning of the seventies a dozen or so sociologists in as many countries have carried out research on religion and identity, usually independent from, and unbeknown to, one another. Clearly, research coordination was necessary, particularly because there is hardly a tradition of research of this kind. Just as important was the strong fructifying potential of the identity model for the sociological theory of religion. In addition the editor, who happens to be the president for the 1974-78 quadrennium of the committee, has a personal interest in international comparisons of this kind (Mol, 1976).

It seems worthwhile, therefore, to do some international detective work and bring the efforts of all these scholars together in a volume for the Sage international series in sociology, tailor-made for this kind of enterprise.

The following international collection of contributions presents an interesting harvest. It represents the kind of crop that farmers do not particularly care for. They would grudgingly admit that it is all of one kind (wheat rather than barley or oats), but they would be rather critical about the variety of strain. As I am not a farmer, but a sociologist, I would like to defend the view that both unity and diversity have their separate merits.

On unity: all authors link two variables, religion and identity. They do so because to them it seems the almost natural outcome of their research to associate the two. They are almost all young scholars and they all did their work recently (since the beginning of the seventies).

Generally the authors use 'identity' in the sense of stable niche rather than in the sense of something to be negotiated or performed according to circumstance as the social psychologists tend to do. The authors in this volume tend to follow the usage of the psychiatrist

Wheelis (1958: 200) when he says that 'identity is founded . . . on those values which are at the top of the hierarchy — the beliefs, faiths and ideals which integrate and determine subordinate values' or his colleague de Levita (1965: 131) who defines identity amongst others as 'the most essential nucleus of man which becomes visible only after all his roles have been laid aside'. In sociology a similar definition is the one by Bellah (1965: 173): identity is 'a statement of what a person or group is essentially, and as it were, permanently'.

The main reason for this conceptual usage is that it fits better with the integrating religious element. Natanson's journeying self (Natanson, 1970); Goffman's performing self (Goffman, 1959); Berger and Luckmann's role-playing self (Berger and Luckman, 1967); Lifton's protean man (Lifton, 1967); and Orr and Nichelson's self as process (Orr and Nichelson, 1970) all direct the attention to the façade rather than to the niche-constructing self. This leads to an underestimation of the boundary construction of social, group, and personal identity which most of the authors in this volume feel to be salient for the understanding of religious phenomena.

On diversity; it is awesome! Not so much because good and bad, sophistication and naïveté are mingled together, but because legitimate perspectives differ considerably.

There are those with a historical bend (e.g. Abdullah and Thurlings). They trace the intricate link between identity threat, defense, and confidence through the history of Minangkabau Islam and Dutch Catholicism. They find that the place of organized religion varies according to the resistance it meets from either secular forces or competing religious organizations. Yet both infer that traditional religions have a pivotal role to play in the consolidation of regional or group identity.

Then there are those with primarily a philosophical bend (e.g. Gopalan). He traces the intricate link between identity and Dharma (Hinduism). His chapter suggests that originally there was a considerable synonymity between our two variables.

Others veer more towards the psychological side of sociology (Jones, Hardin and Kehrer) and relate conversion within both sectarian and more secular groups to identity of self in England and West Germany. Their chapters suggest that an unsatisfactory personality integration leads to the search for a new personal identity.

On the other side of this pole are sociologists such as Assimeng, who discusses Ghana as the new symbolic mother figure, and Moodie, who expressly limits himself to the association between Afrikaner Calvinism and national identity in South Africa.

Yet Assimeng's frame of reference (which is broader than most of the other contributors) also allows him to pay detailed attention to group identity. He sees modern sects taking the place of African tribal groupings in moral regeneration.

Other sociologists who focus on group rather than personal or national identity are Lewins, Shaffir and Gordon. Lewins is interested in ethnic identity and attempts to answer the question as to how the Catholic Church in Australia has contributed both to its formation and maintenance. Shaffir describes the identity consolidation of the Luba-vitcher chassidim in Montreal and Gordon the segregating and integrating buffer roles of two Jesus People groups in a large American Midwest city.

To complete this picture of diversity, Manju and Braj Sinha and Mol concentrate entirely on the ways (mechanisms of sacralization) of reinforcing Hindu and Maori society, respectively.

The diversity of this book is also its attraction. It represents the variety of approaches possible within sociology, even if the focus is as narrow as the relationship between two specific variables. After an initial attempt at closer meshing of chapters I felt it would be better for the quality of the symposium to leave things alone. Too much co-ordination would have done an injustice to the integrity and level of interest of the authors.

Yet this does not mean that I decided to leave the contributions as just an interesting but diverse harvest. In the remainder of this introduction I will present what I feel to be an overarching theoretical frame of reference which ties together both the variety of contributions and, more importantly, the major approaches in the sociology of religion.

However, before doing so I must spend a few paragraphs on the work of those colleagues who have written about religion and identity and are not represented here. Some of these (such as Robert N. Bellah) will be represented in the companion volume dealing with the cross-disciplinary, theoretical issues, as against the cross-cultural, descriptive ones of this volume.

Others, however, were unavailable because of work pressure or change in research interest. I think that some of their ideas should be summarized here before I embark on the description of an identity model of religion.

Very interesting work on religion and identity has been done by Christian (1972). In his research on a valley in Northern Spain it struck him that there was a rather close correspondence between shrines and 'the levels on which people form a community, or have a sense of identity (nation, region, province, vale, village barriada)' (Christian, 1972: xii).

In Japan Morioka and Shimpo (1971) detected a similar correspondence between Buddhism and family identity, Shinto and communal identity and Christianity and personal identity.

Interesting work has also been done about rituals reinforcing family, ethnic group, class, and national identity by communism both in the Soviet Union (Ugrinowitch, 1977) and in Italy (Kertzer, 1975). This, of course, is only a fraction of the literature on ritual reinforcing identity (Mol, 1976: 233-45).

In Ceylon Obeyesekere (1976) has written on the effect of charisma on the stripping of an old identity and the welding of a new one.

In the US Dashefsky (1972) has investigated the usage of identity in relation to religio-ethnic background. And there is probably other work which has not yet come to our attention.

I now want to sketch a model for understanding religious phenomena using identity in the above sense as a basic variable. In the course of the description I want to compare the model with the major classics in the scientific study of religion.

It is probably best to start with the most general of contexts, Darwin's, or rather Spencer's, 'survival of the fittest'. I interpret it to mean that a *change* within a biological unit is more likely to be genetically implanted when survivability in the relevant ecosystem is thereby advanced. The division of labor between white and red corpuscles in the blood enhances the capacity of the human body to cope with intruding germs and thereby advances survival.

Yet the less emphasized but equally necessary and almost opposite proposition follows from the first: in order to survive the biological unit must integrate and harmonize its internal diversifications. This means that stabilization of function is just as necessary for survival as change and adaptation. The body needs reliable, stable, and consistent functioning of heart and liver to survive.

This leads to a third basic proposition: optimal functioning is the result of unresolvable tension or constant dialectic between change and stability, or differentiation and integration. Progress seems to depend on each side of the dialectic maximizing the functions and minimizing the dysfunctions of its side without actually succeeding, because that would mean that the opposition has atrophied. And that would have the direst of consequences! Integration without differentiation, or stability without change is as doomed as differentiation without integration, or change without stability!

This most basic dialectic seems to be just as much part of man's non-biological, psychological or social existence. A primitive tribe would survive better in its ecosystem through a division of labor whereby the hunter best at scouting could coordinate his efforts with those best at running, aiming or brute strength. Here too differentiation of function must be counterbalanced by integration or stabilization of function. For the first division of labor is as necessary as conformity to expectations is a prerequisite for its subsequent success.

The emergence and elaboration of signs, symbols, and language appear to fit in this general outline. Some of them denote and thereby facilitate a more intrinsic division of labor and mastery of the environment. Yet precisely because signs and symbols make for greater flexibility and more efficient change than genetic mutations they have to be counterbalanced by other signs and symbols which represent the opposite: stability, conformity and security. Acts of mastery and conquest appear to be doomed unless they take place in a context of legitimacy, emotional support, and confidence. This most basic distinction between concepts which deal with mastery, instrumentality, and differentiation and those which deal with integration, stability, and expressiveness Langer (1951: 113) calls the distinction between discursive and non-discursive symbols.

There are historical precedents for related distinctions. Even before Confucius Chinese philosophers categorized the natural world in two interacting elements: yang and yin. Yang is roughly present in such disparate items as change, motion, life, activity, procreation, fire, masculinity, summer, and the sun. Yin, on the other hand, predominates in stability, quiescence, death, rest, harmony, darkness, femininity, winter, and the moon (Toynbee, 1946: 51, 63, 65; Watts,

1963: 54 ff.). Toynbee finds the yang-yin or differentiation-integration or challenge-response dialectic in such diverse sources as the Biblical stories of the Fall, Job, and Goethe's *Faust.* Each of this primordial pair is both conflicting with, and complementary to, the other. Lévi-Strauss (1963: 89) similarly finds in the principles of yang and yin, united in the totality of *Tao*, the most general model of Totemism. The latter too turns opposition from an obstructor of integration to a constructor. Yang and yin have also been seen as the basic model for the opposition between war and peace (Heraclitean Ionism), striving and loving (Empedocles) and even the sickness and well-being of acupuncture (Durkheim and Mauss, 1969: 80; Lyall Watson, 1973: 148).

Plato often contrasts *logos*, containing more rational, skeptical elements, with *mythos*, containing more expressive elements (Aall, 1968: 71, Gorgias 523A, Protagoras 320C, Phaedo 61B). James (1902: 365 ff.) describes the conflicting and complementary characteristics of aggressive strength and gentle saintliness. Hegel contrasts *Begriff* (philosophical, rational understanding, abstract differentiation) with *Vorstellung* (representation, religious expression) (Coreth, 1967: 988). Weber (1958: 332) opposes restlessness to peace; Arapura (1972) anxiety to tranquillity. Husserl contrasts objectivity and scientific rationalism with subjectivity and human expressivity (Poole, 1972: 69, 84).

There hardly seems to be a major discipline of scholarship in which the same dialectic is not present in some form or other. In the physical sciences and economics (Maruyama, 1953: 174) it is sometimes described as morphogenesis (structure generation, deviation-amplification, the second cybernetics) versus morphostasis (structure stabilization, deviation-counteraction, the first cybernetics). In biology and anthropology (Róheim, 1930: 381) it is described as the tendency towards fission versus the resistance to fission. Some historians use differentiation-integration (Toynbee, 1957, II: 287), but others (Bryce, 1901: 216-62) write about centrifugal versus centripetal forces. Sometimes the dialectic is described as change versus continuity (Firth, 1963: 209 ff.), or dynamics versus statics (Comte, 1858), or homogeneity versus heterogeneity (Spencer, 1896: 371), at other times as innovation versus continuity (Lenski, 1970: 63).

There are considerable differences between these dichotomies. Yet they have one thing in common: one of the pair fits in the instrumental-rational-scientific sphere, the other in the integrative-expressive sphere.

The dialectic relation between these two spheres is characterized by both conflict and complementarity. Usually complementarity is clearly noted, but the references to the conflict are few and far between.

Where does religion fit in this basic dialectic? Langer has put religion, as well as music and art, on the non-discursive, or what we have called the integrative, side of the dialectic. So have numerous others. Yet there is much more. Customs, habits, rules, culture patterns, and similarities of acting and reacting, as well as such minor matters as routines at work or at home, contribute to integration. And vice versa, conquests, disaster, discoveries, injustices, conflict, overchoice, war, culture contacts, skepticism, technical reason, and rationality, as well as such minor, personal matters as a new job, a win in the lottery, sickness, promotion, frustration, and diffidence, contribute to the opposite, change and differentiation.

Maybe we can isolate the specific contribution of religion to the integration side of the dialectic by suggesting that it sacralizes identity (or a system of meaning, or a definition of reality) by means of at least four means or mechanisms (Mol, 1976). The first we may call 'objectification' (the projection of order in a beyond where it is less vulnerable to contradictions, exceptions, and contingencies − in other words, a rarified realm where major outlines of order can be maintained in the face of temporal, but all-absorbing, dislocations of that order). The second is commitment (the emotional anchorage in the various proliferating foci of identity). The third is ritual (the repetitive actions, articulations, and movements which prevent the object of sacralizations being lost from sight). The fourth is myth (the integration of the various strains in a coherent, short-hand, symbolic account).

Some of the postulations we have advanced so far can be summarized in the following schematic outline (Figure 1). The arrow in between the two diverging lines *AD* and *AI* represents the historical dialectic between integration and differentiation; abstraction and complexification; and sacralization and secularization (Becker, 1950; Fallding, 1974: 210). It represents the uneasy balance between basic, opposing, but also complementary forces which guarantees both progress and order by preventing the petrifaction of order and the berserk of progress. It represents what Lévi-Strauss (1967: 226) calls the reconciliation of binary oppositions in primitive myths (closer to A in the figure) or the sin-salvation dialectic in sectarian Christianity (further away from A).

Figure 1

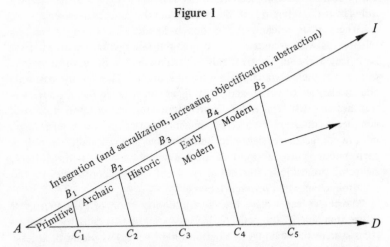

Differentiation over time (increasing complexification and secularization)

The line AI diverges in an upward direction primarily because of the objectification mechanism which tends to further transcendentalization and abstraction in order to be able to straddle the increasing complexification represented by the line AD. It was the direction of the various points C (C_1, C_2, C_3, C_4, C_5) to B (B_1, B_2, B_3, B_4, B_5) which Karl Marx tended to emphasize. Or to say the same thing differently: the line AI was to Marx an epiphenomenon of the line AD which deals with mastery and economic advance. '(A)ll the different forms in which Christianity was conceived . . . were brought about by wholly empirical causes in no way dependent on any influence of the religious spirit' (Marx, 1974: 139). To Marx religion was self-alienation (Marx, 1974: 43, 44), although at least one of his prominent interpreters (Birnbaum, 1973) credits him with also thinking of religion as an antidote to alienation. This is what the line AI represents: a resolution of the very marginality and alienation produced by AD.

This was, of course, what Weber was interested in. In most of his work on religion he tended to stress the opposite: the effect of AI on

AD, or the effect of the various *B*s on the corresponding *C*s. In *The Protestant Ethic* (Weber, 1952) he specifically said that he only intended to deal with one side of the causal chain. In our schematic outline this is represented by the direction $B_4 \rightarrow C_4$. In his other books too (Weber, 1952a, 1958, 1964a) his concern was primarily with the effect of *AI* on *AD*, although one should be careful not to overestimate Weber's theoretical intent. Yet it is true that Weber studied religions to see how far they possessed the Archimedean point for facilitating economic change (Mol, 1968). On the other hand, in his later work Weber (1964: 107-12) takes the line which Nietzsche (1956) took before him and all those who adhere to a deprivation theory of religion (Barber, 1965: 509; Glock, 1973: 213; Talmon, 1965: 530) took after him, namely that theologies of salvation and predestination result from destitution in the mundane. And this argument deals almost exclusively with the primary effect of *AD* on *AI*.

Our scheme also allows us to reinterpret Bellah's fructifying work. In his important article on the evolutionary approach to religion in 1964 (republished in 1970) Bellah traces the increasingly differentiated religious symbolism over time. From the hovering closeness (p. 27) of the world of myth to the actual world (represented by the closeness of the line *AB*, to *AC*, in our scheme) mythical beings become more objectified in Archaic religion. In Historic religions transcendental assertions, universalistic notions of salvation, appear (represented by the trapezoid $B \ B_3 \ C_3 \ C_2$) and in subsequent phases of development the independence of the self and personal faith became increasingly more salient. Missing in Bellah's scheme is the dialectical tension of the identity preserving religious forces with the differentiation producing secular elements. Yet in other work (1965; 1970: 257) this dialectic is beginning to emerge in embryonic form.

In order to accommodate the other classics in the scientific study of religion we have to make a further postulation: that the basic dialectic (conflict as well as complementarity) between integration (identity) and differentiation (change) takes place on a variety of levels. In a simplified form these levels may be placed on a continuum from personal identity to group identity to social identity. And these kinds of identity may in turn be both conflicting and complementary. When Jehovah's Witnesses refuse to salute the flag they thereby question a national (social) identity and enhance their own (group) identity. And yet they also contribute to social cohesion by reinforcing social responsibility and reliability. Self-assertion may reinforce personal identity but take away from group identity. In Maoist China the national identity is strongly advanced at the expense of the historical family identity. In all these examples there is good evidence that transcendental projections, commitments, rituals and/or belief systems reinforced one identity as against another.

Luckmann (1967: 109-10) justifiably calls the themes of the autonomous individual, self-expression and self-realization, 'the central topics of the modern sacred cosmos'. This has obviously made nonpersonal forms of identity more precarious. Erikson (1962: 254) contrasts an optimum ego synthesis to which the individual aspires with an optimum societal metabolism for which societies and cultures strive.

These ideas too can be represented in a diagrammatic outline as is shown in Figure 2.

Figure 2

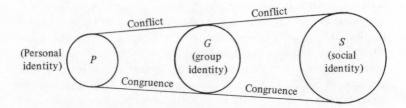

It would be wrong to assume that identity-integration or identity-disintegration are entirely consonant with the patterns of conflict or congruence at other levels of identity. There are forces internal to each level (e.g. need for order, and 'being on a similar wavelength') or external to all levels (e.g. disaster or modes of skepticism). Yet the patterns of conflict and congruence are not unimportant. The conflict of filial piety and national ideology in China is obviously enhancing S and diminishing G. One may even speculate that in history times of great change have tended to shift the emphasis from S to G (e.g. the vitality of sects at the fall of the Roman Empire) or from S to P (Western society), but that in times of consolidation the movement was in the reverse direction. Cargo cults and revitalization movements

(Wallace, 1966) in primitive tribes also are clear examples of a shift from S to G in times of change. In military terms one may speak of withdrawal in order to take over when disintegration of S advances.

With this further elaboration we can now locate most of the other classics in the scientific study of religion. Durkheim was obviously primarily concerned with S. One can actually say that he was almost exclusively concerned with S in the *Elementary Forms of Religious Life* (1954). Yet in his article on dualism (1964) he certainly emphasized the congruence rather than the conflict between S and P. In addition he tended to stress the last two of the sacralization mechanisms (ritual and myth) at the expense of objectification (Weber paid more attention here) and commitment. Particularly when the emotionally anchoring aspects of the commitment concept are stressed not only Durkheim, but Weber and many other sociologists of religion underrated commitment as an increasingly more prominent functional equivalent for the other mechanisms of sacralization. The entire secularization debate hinges essentially on the controversy between those who define religion narrowly (insisting on the supernatural) and those who define it more widely. Only in the latter case does one's conceptual strategy allow for question-asking about a possible shift from the saliency of transcendence to commitment.

Like Durkheim the earlier functionalists in anthropology such as Malinowsky (1936, 1954) and Radcliffe-Brown (1948) tended to stress S and the congruence with G and P. Yet there is interesting evidence of conflict between P and S in the celebrated attack by Radcliffe-Brown (1939: 35, 29) on Malinowsky's anxiety theory of ritual. The former said, as the reader will remember, that if it were not for the rites the individual tribesman would feel no anxiety and that instead of anxiety being resolved it was produced by the rites. In actual fact both anthropologists are speaking about different things in terms of our outline. Malinowsky is thinking about the individual's enhanced confidence or about ritual reinforcing personal identity, whereas Radcliffe-Brown thinks in terms of ritual sacralizing social identity. The latter kind apparently exercises restraint on (or is in conflict with, as we have postulated) the individual. Homans (1951: 330; 1962: 192-201) makes a similar point.

Freud and the psychoanalytic school did the reverse from Durkheim in our outline. Instead of stressing S, they stressed even more exclusively *P*. Instead of emphasizing the congruences, they spoke about the conflicts. This is, for example, very much true for R. D. Laing's *The Politics of the Family* (1971) in which the integration of the individual is so much at the center of the analysis that other, competing kinds of identity, such as the family, are analyzed in terms of their failure to contribute to this central goal. It is also true for most of Fromm's work. To him authoritarian religion (which to us is primarily the sacralization of group or social identity) is vehemently rejected as it leads to bondage. Yet humanistic religion (which to us is primarily sacralization of personal identity) is good because it is centered around man and his strength (Fromm, 1957: 36-37; 1965: 283).

A similar emphasis on *P* at the expense of *S* can be found in Feuerbach for whom God was 'nothing else than the projected personality of man' (1957: 226), 'nothing else than man's highest feeling of self' (p. 284). Here too the emphasis is on conflict with *G* and *S*. To Feuerbach man becomes alienated from his true self when God becomes objectified, or as we would say, 'when God also reflects group or social identity'. 'Only he who thinks is free and independent', says Feuerbach (p. 39). All this is rather reminiscent of Descartes for whom the thinking self also was at the center of reality and for whom individualism worked for the good of others. It is often forgotten that he qualified that observation by adding '(if one lives) in a society where moral customs are not corrupt' (Descartes, 1956: 320).

The oversimplifying, underestimating, Feuerbachian notions about religion are repeated almost verbatim in existentialism (Nietzsche, 1954: 569-70; Sartre, 1960: 141; Heidegger, 1962: 220) and humanism. A waft of it can even be found in such an astute sociologist as Peter Berger who objects to reified religious ideas which desacralize full individual self-determination (Berger, 1967: 81-101).

Although Troeltsch's three categories of mysticism, sect, and church are rather culture-bound, Western categories, they are readily translatable in our outline. To Troeltsch mysticism was closely bound to the personal (Troeltsch, 1931, II: 993); sects fit rather well in our sacralized group-identity; and churches generally reinforce social identity (Troeltsch, 1931, I: 331-43). Yet, as we have done with the other classics, here too we can put Troeltsch's typology in a more comprehensive, cross-cultural frame of reference. We could, for instance, postulate that *all* universal religions both mute and motivate individuals; constrain and coopt groups; and reinforce and reform society and culture.

Niebuhr adapted Troeltsch to the North American environment. But why was frontier religion so often sectarian in the sense of revivalistic, enthusiastic, rather than church-like, reserved and dignified? Niebuhr (1957: 141) attempts to account for frontier sectarianism through the pathology of loneliness. 'The isolation of frontier life fostered the craving for companionship, suppressed the gregarious tendency and so subjected the lonely settler to the temptations of crowd suggestion to an unusual degree.' Apart from the bias of this pathological explanation it does not accord too well with the emergence of sectarian religiosity in situations where loneliness was not a factor. We are probably somewhat closer to the truth when we hypothesize that the anomic tendencies of the kind of individualism flourishing on the frontiers of North America (numerous are the references to intemperance, profanity, gambling, and licentiousness; Sweet, 1950: 231) did not square too well with the social and kinship responsibilities emerging from a more enduring kind of settlement. The frontier necessitated the creation of a new identity and it is for that reason that the new settlers so often rejected (as was the case in the Maritime Provinces of Canada; Clark, 1948: 83) the respectable Anglican and Presbyterian Churches which served as agents of English and Scottish cultural preservation. Charismatic movements are eminently equipped for this task through their capacity for emotional stripping and welding. The charismatic sects contributed strongly to the formation of this new identity. As Clark (1948: 88) points out, 'the evangelical movements are essentially movements of social reorganization or social unification'. We may add that it was no accident that frontier sectarianism (and other 'sectarianisms' as well) made such a sharp distinction between the sin of selfishness and self-indulgence, on the one hand, and redemption through surrender to Christ, on the other.

On the other hand, once the creation of this new identity had taken place it also seems inevitable that these sects then turned into denominations intent upon maintaining the status quo. The metamorphosis of sects into denominations which has understandably drawn so much attention on the North American continent (where it was and is a recurring phenomenon as is well described by Niebuhr) is in the last resort typical only for changing, mobile societies. It is in those societies that one can most clearly observe the relevance of sects for the forging of a new identity and the relevance of denominations and churches for maintaining its identity once formed.

So far we have neglected one of the prominent classics (James, 1902) and one of the prominent contemporary scholars in the scientific study of religion (Geertz, 1973). Maybe that is the way it should be. Dittes (1973) typifies James as anything but a systematizer. And the more Geertz and Bellah have moved away both in age and distance from mother-hen Harvard and father-figure Parsons the less interested they seem to have become in high level theorizing rather than astute observations. Maybe this is the end of good scholarship: to let a cloak of 'preposterous postulations' hang rather loosely, inevitably guiding one's observations and protecting oneself against the coldness of chaos, yet keeping enough air in between to ventilate the sacralizations.

REFERENCES

AALL, Anathon (1968) *Geschichte der Logosidee*, Frankfurt: Minerva.

ARAPURA, John G. (1972) *Religion as Anxiety and Tranquillity*. The Hague: Mouton.

BARBER, Bernard (1965) 'Acculturation and Messianic Movements', in William A. LESSA and Evon Z. VOGT *Reader in Comparative Religion*. New York: Harper & Row, pp. 506-9.

BECKER, Howard (1950) *Through Values to Social Interpretation*. Durham, N.C.: Duke University Press.

BELLAH, Robert N. (1965) 'Epilogue: Religion and Progress in Modern Asia' in Robert N. BELLAH (ed.) *Religion and Progress in Modern Asia*. New York: Free Press, pp. 168-229.

——, (1970) *Beyond Belief*. New York: Harper & Row.

BERGER, Peter L. (1967) *The Sacred Canopy*. Garden City, New York: Doubleday.

BERGER, Peter L. and Thomas LUCKMAN (1967) *The Social Construction of Reality*. London: Allen Lane Penguin Press.

BIRNBAUM, Norman (1973) 'Beyond Marx in the Sociology of Religion', in Charles Y. GLOCK and Philip E. HAMMOND (eds.) *Beyond the Classics? Essays in the Scientific Study of Religion*. New York: Harper & Row, pp. 3-70.

BRYCE, James (1901) *Studies in History and Jurisprudence*. New York: Oxford University Press.

CHRISTIAN, William A. Jr (1972) *Person and God in a Spanish Valley*. New York: Seminar Press.

CLARK, S. D. (1948) *Church and Sect in Canada*. Toronto: University of Toronto Press.

COMTE, Auguste (1858) *The Positive Philosophy*. New York: Blanchard.

CORETH, E. (1967) 'Hegel, Georg, Wilhelm, Friedrich', in *New Catholic Encyclopedia*, VI. New York: McGraw-Hill, pp. 987-90.

DASHEFSKY, Arnold (1972) 'And the Search goes on: the Meaning of Religio-Ethnic Identity and Identification', *Sociological Analysis*, 33, (4) (Winter): 239-45.

DE LEVITA, David J. (1965) *The Concept of Identity*. New York: Basic Books.

DESCARTES, René (1956) *Correspondence*, VI. Paris: Presses Universitaires de France.

DITTES, James E. (1973) 'Beyond William James', in Charles Y. GLOCK and Philip E. HAMMOND (eds.), *Beyond the Classics? Essays in the Scientific Study of Religion*. New York: Harper & Row, pp. 291-354.

DURKHEIM, Emile (1954) *Elementary Forms of Religious Life*. Glencoe: Free Press.

––, (1964) 'The Dualism of Human Nature and its Social Conditions' in Kurt WOLFF (ed.), *Essays on Sociology and Philosophy*. New York: Harper & Row, pp. 325-40.

DURKHEIM, Emile and Marcel MAUSS (1969) *Primitive Classifications*. Chicago: University of Chicago Press.

ERIKSON, Erik H. (1962) *Young Man Luther*. New York: Norton.

FALLDING, Harold (1974) *The Sociology of Religion*. Toronto: McGraw-Hill Ryerson.

FEUERBACH, Ludwig (1957) *The Essence of Christianity*. New York: Harper & Row.

FIRTH, Raymond (1963) *Elements of Social Organization*. Boston: Beacon Press.

FROMM, Erich (1957) *Psychoanalysis and Religion*. New York: Bantam Books.

––, (1965) *Escape from Freedom*. New York: Avon Books.

GEERTZ, Clifford (1973) *The Interpretation of Cultures*. New York: Basic Books.

GLOCK, Charles Y. (1973) 'On the Origin and Evolution of Religious Groups', in Charles Y. GLOCK (ed.), *Religion in Sociological Perspectives*. Belmont, California: Wardsworth.

GOFFMAN, Erving (1959) *The Presentation of Self in Everyday Life*. Garden City, N.Y.: Doubleday.

HEIDEGGER, Martin (1962) *Being and Time*. New York: Harper & Row.

HOMANS, George C. (1951) *The Human Group*. London: Routledge & Kegan Paul.

––, (1962) *Sentiments and Activities*. Glencoe, Illinois: Free Press.

JAMES, William (1902) *The Varieties of Religious Experience*. New York: Modern Library.

KERTZER, David I. (1975) 'Participation of Italian Communists in Catholic Rituals: a Case Study', *Journal for the Scientific Study of Religion*, 14 (1): 1-11.

LAING, R. D. (1971) *The Politics of the Family and Other Essays*. New York: Random.

LANGER, Suzanne K. (1951) *Philosophy in a New Key*. New York: Mentor.

LENSKI, Gerhard (1970) *Human Societies*. New York: McGraw-Hill.

LÉVI-STRAUSS, Claude (1963) *Totemism*. Boston: Beacon Press.

——, (1967) *Structural Anthropology*. Garden City, New York: Doubleday.

LIFTON, Robert J. (1967) *Boundaries: Psychological Man in Revolution*. New York: Random.

LUCKMANN, Thomas (1967) *The Invisible Religion*. New York: Macmillan.

MALINOWSKI, Bronislaw (1936) *The Foundations of Faith and Morals*. London: Oxford University Press.

——, (1954) *Magic, Science and Religion and Other Essays*. Garden City, New York: Doubleday.

MARUYAMA, Magoroh (1953) 'The Second Cybernetics: Deviation-Amplifying Mutual Causal Processes', *American Scientist*, 51 (June): 164-79.

MARX, Karl (1974) *On Religion* (arranged and edited by Saul K. PADOVER). New York: McGraw-Hill.

MOL, Johannis (Hans) J. (1968) *The Breaking of Traditions*. Berkeley, California: Glendessary Press.

——, (1976) *Identity and the Sacred*. Oxford: Basil Blackwell (or 1977 New York: Free Press). Some sentences of this introduction have been taken verbatim from this book.

MORIOKA, Kiyomi and Mitsuru SHIMPO (1971) 'The Impact of the Physical Movement of Population on Japanese Religions after the World War II', in Jacques VERSCHEURE (ed.), *Acts of the 11th Conference of the C.I.S.R.*, Lille, France: C.I.S.R., pp. 184-211.

NATANSON, Maurice (1970) *The Journeying Self*. Reading, Mass.: Addison-Wesley.

NIEBUHR, H. Richard (1957) *The Social Sources of Denominationalism*. New York: Meridian.

NIETZSCHE, Friedrich (1954) 'The Antichrist', in Walter KAUFMANN (ed.) *The Portable Nietzsche*. New York: Viking, pp. 565-656.

——, (1956) *The Genealogy of Morals*. Garden City, New York: Doubleday.

OBEYESEKERE, Gananath (1976) 'Personal Identity and Cultural Crisis', in Frank E. REYNOLDS and Donald CAPPS (eds.), *The Biographical Process*. The Hague: Mouton.

ORR, John B. and F. Patrick NICHELSON (1970) *The Radical Suburb: Soundings in Changing American Character*. Philadelphia: Westminster.

POOLE, Roger (1972) *Towards Deep Subjectivity*. New York: Harper & Row.

RADCLIFFE-BROWN, Alfred Reginald (1939) *Taboo*. Cambridge: University Press.

——, (1948) *The Andaman Islanders*. Glencoe, Ill.: Free Press.

RÖHEIM, Géza (1930) *Animism, Magic and the Divine King*. London: Routledge & Kegan Paul.

SARTRE, Jean-Paul (1960) *The Devil and the Good Lord*. New York: Vintage.

SPENCER, Herbert (1896) *First Principles*, New York: Appleton.

SWEET, William W. (1950) *The Story of Religion in America*. New York: Harper & Row.

TALMON, Yonina (1965) 'Pursuit of the Millenium: The Relation between Religious and Social Change', in William A. LESSA and Evon Z. VOGT (eds.), *Reader in Comparative Religion*. New York: Harper & Row, pp. 522-37.

TOYNBEE, Arnold J. (1946) *A Study of History* (Abridgement of Volumes I-VI). New York: Oxford University Press.

— —, (1957) *A Study of History* (Abridgement of Volumes VII-X). New York: Oxford University Press.

TROELTSCH, Ernst (1931) *The Social Teaching of the Christian Churches*, 2 Volumes. London: Allen and Unwin.

UGRINOWITSCH, Dimitrov M. (1977) 'Das Wesen und die sozialen Funktionen von Brauchtum und Ritual in der Sozialistischen Gesellschaft' *Deutsche Zeitschrift für Philosophie*, 25 (1): 15-24.

WALLACE, Anthony F. C. (1966) *Religion: An Anthropological View*. New York: Random.

WATSON, Lyall (1973) *Supernature*. Garden City, New York: Doubleday.

WATTS, Alan W. (1963) *The Two Hands of God*. New York: Braziller.

WEBER, Max (1952) *The Protestant Ethic and The Spirit of Capitalism*. New York: Scribner.

— —, (1952a) Ancient Judaism. Glencoe, Ill.: Free Press.

— —, (1958) *The Religion of India*. Glencoe, Ill.: Free Press.

— —, (1964) *The Sociology of Religion*. Boston: Beacon Press.

— —, (1964a) *The Religion of China*. Glencoe, Ill.: Free Press.

WHEELIS, Allen (1958) *The Quest for Identity*. New York: Norton.

1

RELIGION AND ETHNIC IDENTITY

Frank W. Lewins
Australian National University, Australia

Lewins' main interest is in the interaction between religious organization (Catholicism) and ethnic identity (Italian and Ukrainian). Following social psychological practice he attempts to answer the question as to how religion contributed to the formation *of identity. And so he perceptively describes how, as a result of Australianizing pressures, Catholicism tends to encourage the formation of an Italian identity as against a regional identity in Italy.*

Yet towards the end of the chapter he takes up the same question which occupies most of the contributors of this book: how does religion reinforce *identity? Here he investigates how Catholicism reinforces Ukrainian identity by means of the mechanisms of sacralization.*

This chapter suggests that further systematic research is necessary about the similarities and differences between religious function and organization.

My general purpose in this chapter is to assess the relationship between religion and ethnic identity. Two factors prompt this assessment: the inclusion of religion in discussions of ethnic subcultures; and the recent emphasis on 'ethnicity' and 'ethnic identity' in the sociological literature. With regard to the former it is well recognized that religious affiliation is a significant aspect of ethnic subculture (see, for example, Lenski, 1963: 288-89, 362-63; Gordon, 1964: 27; Abramson, 1971: 359-88; and Lewins, 1976b). However, it is not clear whether religion is significant in an organizational sense to the extent that ethnic communities can be regarded as 'socio-religious' subcommunities (Lenski, 1963: 363), or whether religious orientations actually influence ethnic identity.

Concerning the (re)emergence of 'ethnicity' and 'ethnic identity' in the literature the treatment of these concepts by a number of scholars, such as Bell (1975), Glazer and Moynihan (1975), Horowitz (1975), and Isaacs (1975), implies a complex and varied role of religion vis-à-vis 'ethnicity' and 'ethnic identity'. A closer examination of the recent discussions concerning the latter concepts is necessary to illuminate the significance of their relation to religion.

A convenient starting point is Beals's paper 'The Levels of Identity' (1978). In presenting three levels of identity — culture, society and self — which closely resemble those levels of identity on Mol's continuum (1978), Beals argues for a 'law' of identity allocation. As he says,

> when the most general level of participation is below the societal level, alternative identity foci will arise which register, subsume and interpret the abstract or coercive societal relationships.

As an illustration he points to the sect in relation to 'church' religion, where the sect makes its religious identity the only valid form of commitment and meaning. Beals adds that ethnic identity may perform similar functions. Given the proximity of religion to ethnic subculture, does religion reinforce ethnic identity? Or is it, in an organizational sense, *another* focus of identity?

In this chapter I argue that religion reinforces ethnic identity to a varying extent depending on the particular ethnic group. This variable influence is closely related to the relative contributions of cultural and situational interest factors which shape ethnic identity and group formation.

Recent literature on 'ethnicity' and 'ethnic identity' stresses, in varying degrees, the salience of situational interest factors in shaping ethnic identity. While Glazer and Moynihan (1975: 19) point out that ethnicity is 'not *only* a means of advancing interests' (their emphasis), they lay considerable emphasis on the relatively new role of ethnic groups as interest groups. They note that

> One of the striking characteristics of the present situation is indeed the extent to which we find the ethnic group defined in terms of interest, *as an interest group* (their emphasis). Thus, whereas in the past a religious conflict, such as that which is tearing Northern Ireland apart, was based on such issues as the free and public practice of a religion, today it is based on the issue of *which group shall gain benefits or hold power of a wholly secular sort* (my emphasis).

Similarly,

> Language conflicts – as in India – today . . . have more to do with *which*
> *language user shall have the best opportunity to get which job* (my emphasis)
> (1975: 7).

While Glazer and Moynihan argue that one 'should not make the
distinction too sharp' (1975: 7), that religion and language, as such, are
influential in these conflicts, they conclude that the weight of these
kinds of conflicts has changed,

> from an emphasis on culture, language, religion, *as such*, it shifts to an
> emphasis on the *interests* broadly defined by members of the group (1975:
> 7-8) (their emphasis).

In the light of their depicting group interests as political and material
interests how does this affect our understanding of religion in relation
to ethnic identity? Before we conclude from the above that ethnic
identity and religion are merely aspects of a Marxian superstructure it
will be useful to explore what Glazer and Moynihan mean when they
say that ethnicity is 'not *only* a means of advancing interests' (1975:
19) (their emphasis).

At this point Glazer and Moynihan, in claiming that ethnicity
involves '*more* than interests' (1975: 19) (their emphasis), point to
Daniel Bell (1975: 169) who argues that 'Ethnicity has become more
salient (than class) because it can combine an interest with an affective
tie'. By 'affective tie' he is referring to 'a tangible set of common
identifications – in language, food, music, names . . .' (1975: 169),
identifications which would obviously include religion. While Bell
explicitly refers to ethnicity in terms of group membership, arguing
that 'identity' has psychological connotations (1975: 153), individual
and group identity are implicit in his viewing ethnic groups as both
symbolic-expressive and instrumental social units. The former refers to
affective ties providing the subjective or individual basis for emotional
support, the latter being that quality which binds a group through a
common set of material interests (1975: 165). Furthermore, one can
derive from Bell a relation between individual and group identities of
members of ethnic groups and a wider social identity. In addition to his
comment concerning the combination of affective ties and group

interests Bell notes that ethnicity can be regarded as a ' "strategic site", chosen by disadvantaged groups as a new mode of seeking political redress in the society' (1975: 169). In these situations ethnicity can be a reaction against the definition of the situation or stereotypes of ethnics held by the dominant group(s) in the wider society. In short, a reaction against an unfavourable social identity (cf. Horowitz, 1975: 131-32; see also Gordon, 1975: 92; Isaacs, 1975: 34; and Patterson, 1975: 305 ff.).

This discussion is a necessary preamble to understanding the precise relationship between religion, ethnic identity and interests. Given that religion is a significant aspect of many ethnic subcultures and an example of Bell's 'affective tie', it appears that, for Bell and Glazer and Moynihan, religion and ethnic identity are intervening variables between interests and ethnic group formation. Does religion merely act as a vehicle for legitimatizing ethnic group interests? Or can religion, together with other elements of an ethnic subculture, act back and influence interests? (see Figure 1). The answers to these questions bear directly on the role and importance of religious beliefs in the social world (cf. Weber, 1958: 27, 183). The two ethnic groups I now discuss will, I hope, illuminate the answers to these questions.

ITALIAN AND UKRAINIAN CATHOLICS IN AUSTRALIA

Italian and Ukrainian Catholics[1] are not necessarily representative of the experience of ethnic groups in Australia. Rather, they represent extremes in terms of the relative roles of cultural and situational factors in influencing ethnic group and identity formation and therefore serve a useful purpose for this chapter.

Italian Catholics

Of the near 272,000 Italian-born migrants in Australia (Pyne and Price, 1975: A20-21) – the figure is closer to 500,000 if Australian-born

FIGURE 1

Factors Influencing Ethnic Identity and Group Formation among Italian and Ukrainian Catholics in Australia.

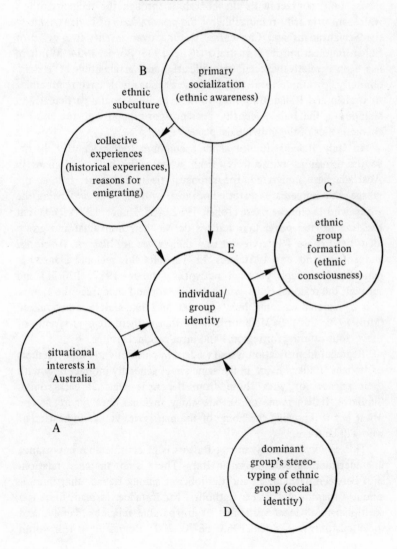

children and other descendants of Italians are included (Price and Pyne, 1976) — approximately 94 percent claim to be (Roman) Catholic (*Census*, 1971). The bulk of those who practise their religion worship in their local territorial parish. This is despite the significant number whose only contact with the church is through the religious orders which are primarily responsible for the pastoral care of Italians, namely the Scalabrinians and Capuchins. Despite over seventy-five years of Italian immigration into Australia (Pyke, 1948; Borrie, 1954: 39) there has been a relatively recent crystallization and articulation of 'Italian' ethnicity, or ethnic identity,[2] in those parishes with large numbers of Australian and Italian Catholics. In these parishes, found particularly in Melbourne, the Italian identity does not correspond with the cultural characterstics of the individuals' places of origin.

In Italy Italians do not share a common Italian identity. In the southern regions particularly, from whence the bulk of Italians in Australia have emigrated, the strongest tie is the *paese*, that is, the village and immediate surrounding area, with the *paesano* being the group who live in the paese (Jones, 1962: 405; Huber, 1977: 2). It is at the level of the paese that Italians derive their individual and group identities. Those I interviewed saw themselves as *Calabresi, Abruzzesi* and so on, and not as Italians. In Australia this regional identity is maintained through personal networks (Huber, 1977: 170-71) and through the regional clubs, which provide for and encourage the expression of regional customs, habits, games, and 'like-seek-like motivation' (Mol, 1976: 262). In Melbourne, for instance, there are over seventy of these clubs catering for regional and intra-regional groups.

Regional identification is also evident in parishes with large numbers of Italians. Italians living in the same street generally interact only with their *paesani* or with those from the same regional background. Similarly, Italian home masses are along regional lines, where, as one priest put it, knowing the home of the mass gives you an indication of who will be there.

This regional identity among Italians is of considerable importance in understanding Catholicism in Italy. There is not the close relationship between nationalism and Catholicism among Italians that there is among Croatian and Polish Catholics, for instance. Instead, there is a multiplicity of local variations of inseparable religious, family, and social customs (see, Price, 1963: 68-70, 299). Bound up as it is within the particular regional subculture of the south, being a Catholic is an aspect of an individual's taken-for-granted regional identity, which is heavily reinforced by local religion. The ritualistic use of statues of regional saints and village madonnas in religious services and processions evokes emotion and nostalgia and thereby elevates, from the geographical to the transcendental, the significance of regional identity. In those areas with a strong religious tradition regional identity is further reinforced by the measure of social control which local religion obtains. Church attendance, for example, takes on a normative character in some areas. As one southern Italian expressed it, 'you have to go to church . . . everyone (in the village) would know if you didn't'. A similar normative aura surrounds other religious observances. A woman from Friule, for instance, remarked that it was 'unthinkable' for a woman from her village who had given birth to a child not to seek religious purification from the priest.

Diversity along regional lines is sufficiently strong among Italians in Australia to present problems to Italian priests who are responsible for Italians' pastoral care. One Scalabrinian claimed that because of the number of paesani in his parish he was not sure whether he was 'reaching many of his parishioners from the south (of Italy)'. In expressing his frustration at having to care for the needs 'of people from different cultures' he summed up his feelings by saying that 'Italy is not a nation as yet . . . it is a summary of different civilisations'.

This background material is necessary here as it stands in contrast to the relatively recent emergence of an Italian ethnic identity in Catholic parishes with large numbers of Italians. As already mentioned, although Italian Catholics continue to maintain regional identity by participating in home masses, it is in their interaction with Australian Catholics in the public, parish arena that one finds Italians organizing as 'Italians'. In this situation this convergence of regional backgrounds into an Italian identity is *primarily* a consequence of Italians recognizing their lack of power and participation in parish affairs and Australians refusing to accept Italians as anything other than conforming, potential Australians (cf. Breton, 1964: 199). Collective action is for Italians a viable means of attaining their goals. Their group identity – 'Italians' – is reinforced by Australian Catholics' lack of awareness of regional differences and their labelling all Italians as 'Italians'. The separation of Italian and Australian Catholics is further accentuated by Australians negatively stereotyping Italians as 'poor Catholics' who 'don't pull their weight' because they are 'poor givers to parish finances' (cf. Jehovah's Witnesses in Mol, 1978).

Considering the salience of Italians' regional subculture it is not surprising that many disregard Australian parish life because it is not a focal point for maintaining regional ties but, instead, is a source of tension between them and Australians (Lewins, 1976a: 221-26; 1976b: 128). While more could be said about other avenues of Italian religious life and their (and other migrants') increasing recognition of their social disadvantage (e.g. Storer, 1975; cf. Cox, 1975), this chapter is primarily concerned with the role of religion in the formation of Italian identity in the parish context.

To this point it has only been demonstrated that Italian identity is reinforced by relations with Australian Catholics as members of the same religious organization. Given that Italians can belong to a number of groups at any one time (cf. Horowitz, 1975: 118; Bell, 1975: 171), does being *Catholic* have any significance? That is, do Catholic beliefs influence Italian identity? (cf. Lenski, 1963: 323).

Returning to an earlier point, i.e. that Italian identity in the parish situation is primarily a consequence of Italians' recognition of their lack of power and participation, I want to argue that Italian identity is a complex phenomenon which is also influenced by Italians' religious beliefs. This can be demonstrated by returning to the background material above and tracing the consequences of Italians' beliefs. The origin of these beliefs is Italian regional Catholicism (see 'B', Figure 1), which explains why individual Italians identify themselves as Catholics and are attracted to Catholic parishes in Australia (see 'E'' Figure 1). Because these Italians are rejected by Australian Catholics for not fitting into parish life as Australians and are regarded as 'poor Catholics' they are not able to participate fully as *Catholics*. Their desire for greater participation in, and control of, parish life (see 'A', Figure 1) is primarily responsible for the crystallization of an Italian group identity (see 'E', Figure 1) which is facilitated by Australians lumping all Italians under the one category (see 'D', Figure 1). All this leads to the formation of organized Italian groups in Australian parishes (see 'C', Figure 1).

Like the Italian identity, of which they are a part, the overt expressions of Italian religious beliefs are something of a skeleton, consisting only of those elements which cut across regional lines. These are religious affiliation — Catholic — and nationality — Italian. Hence one finds few religious issues, that is, issues centred around beliefs and the practice of the sacraments, among *Italian* Catholics. One issue which has had some effect in shaping Italian interests is the right for Italians to have masses said in Italian. It must be remembered that this instance, of what is a deeply-felt issue (see below) influencing Italian interests, is in the face of a larger influence in the opposite direction — the Italian's desire for greater power and participation in parish life.

In Italians' demands for Italian language masses is an appeal for the right of all Italians to worship in the way they were brought up in the church. This appeal gives religious legitimation to an otherwise Italian preference by linking regional Catholicism with a skeleton-like *Italian* Catholicism and its impression of religious continuity. It is of interest to note that the commitment to the issue of Italian masses by Italian Catholics is separate from the commitment which Italian masses themselves engender. This distinction between the political and religious elements of this issue is important because attendance at these masses is not in accord with the enthusiasm associated with their implementation. While many Italian parishioners attend Italian language masses at their local parish church, a significant number of Italians attend English language masses. Some of these Italians cannot understand Italian as their native tongue is a regional dialect. Most, however, claim that Italian masses said by Italian-speaking Australian priests do not create the atmosphere they were used to in Italy. It is therefore not unusual to find that in those parishes where the parish is administered by Italian-born priests only one mass out of six or seven each Sunday is said in Italian.

As I have already indicated this account of Italian Catholics has concentrated on those aspects of their religion which relate to the overt expression of their ethnic identity in Australian parishes. I have not attempted to analyse religious practice along regional lines, which supplements the wider parish participation of Italians. It is in regional religious observance that one would no doubt find evidence of a sacralizing of regional ethnic identity (see Mol, 1976). However, it is not clear how regional religious practice reinforces an Italian ethnic identity, apart from the fact that it constantly affirms Italians' *Catholic* identity and thereby their desire to participate more fully in wider parish life.

While this account of Italian Catholics generally supports Glazer and Moynihan's perspective on the formation of ethnic groups and the nature of their identity, it is as I have indicated, one extreme in terms of the relative contribution of cultural (including religious) and situational factors in influencing ethnic identity. A different picture is obtained by examining Ukrainian Catholics in Australia.

Ukrainian Catholics

As far as can be ascertained Ukrainian Catholics in Australia number around 22,000. This is the Ukrainian Catholic Church's own estimate and includes Australian-born children of Ukrainian Catholics.[3] Most Ukrainians came to Australia as refugees in the early years following World War II. They have settled mainly in the capital cities, especially Melbourne, Sydney and Adelaide, where they have established their own Ukrainian churches. The Ukrainian Catholics, as members of an Eastern Catholic rite (Byzantine), are independent of the jurisdiction of the Australian Catholic Church. Since 1958 they have had their own bishop (hierarch), unlike most other Eastern rite Catholics who, without their own bishop in Australia, are subject to their local Australian (Latin rite) bishop. This legal independence of the Ukrainian Catholics is reinforced by the permanence and continuity of their rite. Ukrainian Catholics cannot change their rite, except through special authority from Rome, and their children are also Ukrainian Catholics. Marriage between Ukrainian Catholics is valid only if performed by a priest of the same rite.

The separate legal status of the Ukrainian Catholic Church casts a definite perimeter around their group identity, for to be a Ukrainian Catholic is to be a Ukrainian nationalist. The content of Ukrainian nationalism is a complex of political attitudes and a deep regard for the value of Ukrainian culture and history, regardless of whether one is Orthodox or Catholic. One cannot have prolonged contact with Ukrainian Catholics, particularly Ukrainian priests, without their mentioning the 'evils of communism', the denial of freedom in Ukraine through its 'Russification', and the need to preserve Ukrainian culture and history.

Historical circumstances have helped to shape such nationalism and

Ukrainian identity. As political refugees who fled from the advancing Russians at the close of World War II, Ukrainian Catholics view their present situation in Australia often in terms of past political and religious 'suffering'. Not only do they speak of their 'oppression' by the Russians and the 'tragedy' of their country's absorption into Russia, with the consequent disappearance of the Ukrainian Catholic Church, but also of the current growth of the Ukrainian Catholic Church in the 'free' world and their lack of 'recognition and freedom' from the authority of the Roman Curia. The latter concerns Rome's refusal to give Cardinal Slipyi, the leader of Ukrainian Catholics in exile, the status of patriarch (see, *The Advocate*, 1974; 17; *Ukraine – A Christian Nation*, 1973). The concern for 'freedom' is also evident in Ukrainian Catholic priests expressing their satisfaction over the Ukrainian Catholic Church in Australia gaining its autonomy in 1958. The insulated and inward-looking nature of this church is indicated by the comments of one of its prominent priests. In answering my query about whether he was creating his own form of Ukrainian nationalism by encouraging Ukrainians to marry Ukrainians, he replied that this was not nationalism but 'a necessary act. If Ukrainians do not marry Ukrainians then the Ukrainian value of the faith will be lost . . . for we as Ukrainians are always the losers'.

The link between Ukrainian nationalism and religion among Ukrainian Catholics is complex. As already noted, to be a Ukrainian Catholic is to be a nationalist, but at the same time Ukrainian Catholics confess to having little in common with Australian Catholics, holding that they have more in common with the Ukrainian Orthodox (cf. Zubrzycki, 1964: 181). This relationship of national and religious elements in Ukrainian ethnic identity has been described as the 'sanctification of ethnicity' and the 'ethnization of religion' (Nahirny and Fishman, 1966; see also Zubrzycki, 1964: 164 ff.; and Martin, 1972: 28).

The 'sanctification of ethnicity' is closely related to an attempt to institutionalize the Ukrainian Catholic way of life in Australia. There has been a conscious effort, especially by priests, to achieve a measure of community self-containment. Not only are priests involved in many aspects of Ukrainian Catholics' lives, such as organizing Saturday schools and acting as financial advisers and advocates in business, but both priests and laity participate cooperatively in activities beyond worship (see Marin, 1972: 28). The 7,000-strong Ukrainian Catholic community in Sydney, for example, while not having full 'institutional completeness' (Breton, 1964), intend building an old people's home in the church grounds for elderly Ukrainian Catholics. This, together with the weekend school and various recreational activities, makes this church, as the Ukrainian parish priest put it, 'more than just a center'. He added that

> there is a total community effort towards the preservation and education in the faith and what it means to be Ukrainian. Although it is difficult to keep the original national consciousness alive, there is a strong effort to keep the religion, history, culture, and language alive. This distinguishes us from the rest of the community and keeps us all together . . . being a minority group helps our solidarity.

At this point it is fruitful to ask whether Italian Catholics serve as a useful comparison alongside Ukrainian Catholics. Does religion again play an intervening role between situational interests and the formation of Ukrainian Catholic groups? What are the mechanisms involved if religion influences Ukrainian identity?

If Glazer and Moynihan are correct in their perspective on (all) ethnic groups then one would expect to find similar interest factors among Ukrainian Catholics as exist among Italian Catholics. Do such interests arise from Ukrainians' relations with Australian Catholics or other Australians? From my own research and from the observations of other scholars there is no evidence to support the saliency of political and material interests in Ukrainians' relations with non-Ukrainians. Ukrainian Catholics, like the rest of their countrymen, have little contact with Australians and are 'seldom in the news' (Zubrzycki, 1964: 67; Kunz, 1970: A54; Martin, 1972: 136; Cox, 1975: 93; and Lewins, 1976a). Their low participation in Australian institutional life gives them fewer opportunities than, say, Italians to interact with Australians and to experience conflict over their social disadvantage. Although most Ukrainian Catholics have not improved their occupational levels since arriving in Australia — the majority work in semi-skilled jobs (Cox, 1975: 93) — the formation and maintenance of ethnic group life is not, and has not been, associated with perceived disadvantage vis-à-vis Australians, or any other group. What then has influenced the organization of Ukrainian Catholic group life and the articulation of Ukrainian identity?

Research on the ethnic identity of other groups points to a number of factors which could influence Ukrainian identity and group maintenance. Bottomley, in her research on Greek migrants in Sydney, speaks of a number of factors influencing Greek ethnic identity. As she notes

> the relative strength of ethnic identities amongst my Greek subjects was clearly related to the nature of primary socialization, the presence or absence of a close-knit kin network and its generational layers, and the extent to which subsequent experiences challenged earlier identities. But it was also related to people's perception of themselves as satisfactorily coping with two cultural milieux and/or forming part of a strong and diverse ethnic community (1976: 124).

It is primary socialization, together with the collective experiences of Ukrainian Catholics before their arrival in Australia, which I regard as principal influences on Ukrainian Catholics' behavior and identity. It should be stressed, however, that I am not suggesting a model of cultural determinism, but rather the principal factors in determining Ukrainian Catholics' organization and their identity in Australia (see *B*, Figure 1). The absence of a clear social identity of Ukrainians (see *D*, Figure 1) and the fact that a cohesive Ukrainian group can reinforce Ukrainian identity but not cause itself to come into being (see *C*, Figure 1) leaves situational interests ('subsequent experiences') and primary socialization to be explored (see *A* and *B*, Figure 1).

The reason for linking primary socialization and the collective experiences of Ukrainian Catholics is that together they represent influences on Ukrainian behavior which are independent from the Australian situation. These include those factors already mentioned, such as viewing World War II experiences in terms of the history of Ukrainian suffering and lack of freedom; the flight from the advancing Russians at the close of World War II; the suppression of Ukrainian culture by the latter; and the current status of the Ukrainian Catholic Church vis-à-vis Rome, which, collectively form the Ukrainian Catholics' 'ethnic subculture' (see *B*, Figure 1). These prior factors are independent from the Australian situation only in terms of their historical location. They are not causally independent of certain Australian situational influences. While Ukrainian Catholics point to their past to explain their responses by saying, as one middle-aged man did, that 'it has a lot to do with the way you are brought up . . . with the Ukrainian spirit', they also emphasize that it is their location in Australia which has cut them off from the Ukraine — 'the source of our culture' — and given them the spur to 'preserve all that we have'. Cox (1975: 93) gives weight to this point of view by noting that, 'One need that is stressed by the Ukrainians is the perpetuation and fostering of their culture'. Viewed in terms of the high degree of institutional development in the Ukrainian Catholic community this 'need' can be regarded as an 'interest', using the term in the broadest sense to indicate priority of group concerns. This being the case it is possible to regard situational interests as being shaped by Ukrainian Catholics who have a consciousness of their identity and the salience of their background (see Figure 1).

While it is possible to demonstrate that Ukrainians' interests are heavily influenced by Ukrainian factors, what is the role of religion in influencing Ukrainian identity and interests? To borrow from Nahirny and Fishman (1966), how does being a Ukrainian *Catholic* lead to a 'sanctification of ethnicity'? This can be illuminated by regarding Ukrainian Catholicism in terms of the mechanisms involved in the sacralization of identity (Mol, 1976). The most apparent mechanism is the 'objectification' of Ukrainian identity through the legal separation and continuity of the Ukrainian Catholic rite. Even though Ukrainian Catholics become naturalized and will produce generations of Australian-born children, all remain within the religious realm as *Ukrainian* Catholics. This close link between religion and nationalism is related to another mechanism of sacralization — 'commitment'. Through this link emotion and nostalgia over Ukraine take on a religious significance. In his chapter in *Ukrainians in Australia*, Bishop Prashko, the Ukrainian Catholic bishop (exarch) of Australasia, notes that news received in Australia of the suffering of Ukrainian Catholics in the Ukraine is closely followed by a religious revival among Ukrainian Catholics in Australia (Prashko, 1966). This empathetic response is primarily because the religious life of Ukrainian Catholics is consciously linked to a love of country. On the basis of accounts of several Ukrainian priests and older laity the importance of constructing a Ukrainian way of life in Australia rests on what is only a hope; that some day Ukrainians can return to Ukraine. As if recognizing the unrealistic nature of this goal one priest expressed his hope that 'some day we may be able to go back if the regime changes', but qualified this by adding that 'we know that we will be here permanently'. This is not an isolated comment for Bishop Prashko notes in his closing summary in *Ukrainians in Australia* that

> we hope to raise our children to be religious and to preserve our rite. We hope to have priests ordained here who may someday return to our native land and serve the faithful there. . . .

The reinforcement of Ukrainian identity is also achieved by 'ritual' which, for Ukrainians, is a constant reminder of their origins. Consisting of the Ukrainian language mass, vestments, and the use of national symbols (e.g. decorated eggs at Easter) religious ritual practised in the Byzantine-style churches and guided by the Julian calendar reinforces the isolation of Ukrainian Catholics from other Catholics and confirms their Ukrainian identity.

Generally, the importance of a Ukrainian identity is most evident among the original, middle-aged Ukrainian Catholics who fled Ukraine following World War II. This group, who comprise 70 percent of the faithful and described by Bishop Prashko as 'the backbone of the Church' (Prashko, 1966), has provided the means to build or acquire around ten churches, plus church halls, buildings for weekend schools for language and history instruction, presbyteries, and the use of several dozen mass centers.

CONCLUSION

The data presented illustrate the variety and interaction of factors which impinge on Italian and Ukrainian Catholic group organization and identity. Furthermore, they indicate the varying relationship between ethnic identity and religion. Although representative of extreme positions in terms of the relative contribution of cultural factors (primary socialization − ethnic subculture and experience) and situational interests, these groups demonstrate the inadequacy of viewing *all* ethnic groups and their ethnic identity solely in terms of Glazer and Moynihan's perspective. Whether most ethnic groups can be better understood through this perspective is not the point here. What is important is the mistake of generalizing all ethnic groups from those which fit the Glazer and Moynihan picture.

These data, especially the Ukrainian Catholic data, also stress the need to view situational interests in the broad sense. Rather than seeing interests in terms of goals centered around correcting the mal-distribution of power and material wealth, which are essentially nega-tive interests, interests can include positive elements such as goals derived from significant cultural values and religious beliefs. By widening the scope of interests it is possible to illuminate group formation, ethnic identity and the role of religion among Italian and Ukrainian Catholics in terms of the model depicted in Figure 1. Whether this model can be applied to other ethnic groups will depend on future research.

Concerning the influence of religion both groups demonstrate that a common faith — Catholic — does not imply a common experience in terms of its influence on ethnic identity and interests. Italian Catholics demonstrate religion's circuitous path of influence and intervening role between Italian interests and Italian group formation. Ukrainian Catholics, by contrast, illustrate a direct influence of religious beliefs on ethnic identity and group interests. This variation corresponds to the differing degrees to which Italian and Ukrainian Catholic beliefs sacra-lize ethnic identity.

Finally, it should be stressed that this analysis of the relation between religion and ethnic identity is based on two ethnic groups who, as migrants in Australia, are ex patria. As Figure 1 illustrates, their respective ethnic identities are the result of a number of interacting factors and apply only to the Australian situation. As the Italians clearly indicate, ethnic identity in Australia is not a continuation of ethnic identity in Italy. This qualification, however, goes further than the content of ethnic identity. It also applies to the extent to which an ethnic group's boundary and other ethnic groups figure in the 'new' ethnic identity in Australia. The force of this point can be illustrated by drawing on the distinction Giddens (1973: 111) makes between 'class awareness' and 'class consciousness'. Where 'class' involves the tendency of its members to share an 'awareness and acceptance of similar atti-tudes and beliefs, linked to a common style of life . . ., "class awareness" . . . does *not* involve a recognition that these attitudes and beliefs signify a particular class affiliation, or the recognition that there exist other classes . . .; "class consciousness" . . . does imply both of these' (his emphasis). Substituting 'ethnic' for 'class', ethnic awareness can be used to characterize the identity Italian Catholics acquire in Italy at the regional level as a result of their primary socialization. In this situation individual Italians could answer the question 'who, what am I?' (see Gordon, 1964: 29) by drawing on a pool of common beliefs, attitudes and behavior. But this identity is not crystallized or articulated because of a heightened and lingering sense of ethnic group isolation vis-à-vis other groups. It is not until Italians confront the dominant *Australian* Catholics at the parish level (and other Australians) that they become 'Italians' and acquire an ethnic consciousness. It is difficult to apply this distinction between ethnic awareness and ethnic consciousness to Ukrainian Catholics, as the primary socialization of Ukrainians in Ukraine has been punctuated by historical accounts of the suffering of Ukrainians at the hands of other groups, such as the Turks and Russians. In short, it is difficult to say when Ukrainian Catholics ever had anything other than an ethnic consciousness, an important point in understanding their group behavior and identity in Australia. However, despite the different experiences encountered by Italians and Ukrainians conflict in inter-action between Ukrainians and their historical antagonists, on the one hand, and Italians and Australians, on the other, has had, along with the varying role of religion, a reinforcing effect on ethnic identity (see Coser, 1968: 31, 38).

NOTES

1. The data for this account of Italian and Ukrainian Catholics are drawn from my wider research into the relationship between the Australian Catholic Church and Catholic migrants; see Lewins (1976a). Sources include a case study of a northern suburban parish in Melbourne with a high concentration of Italians; interviews with Australian, Italian and Ukrainian clergy and laity in Sydney, Melbourne and Adelaide; ethnic literature and migration documents; Jean

Martin's private files; and a survey of the Australian Catholic press in the above cities.

2. In this chapter I use 'ethnicity' and 'ethnic identity' synonymously. Where I use these concepts I am referring to an individual's or group's 'consciousness of kind' or 'sense of peoplehood'; see Gordon (1964: 24-30); Bell (1975: 171); Isaacs (1975: 34); and Bottomley (1976: 119). 'Ethnicity' and 'ethnic identity' should not be confused with 'ethnic group'; cf. Gordon (1964: 28). The material on Italian Catholics is drawn mainly from two earlier papers; see Lewins (1975; 1976b).

3. *The Official Directory of the Catholic Church in Australia, Papua-New Guinea, New Zealand and the Pacific Islands* (1973; 219). Cf. Cox (1975: 91) and Australian Government Census 1971 for numbers of USSR Ukraine-born (Roman) Catholics.

REFERENCES

ABRAMSON, Harold J. (1971) 'Ethnic Diversity within Catholicism: a Comparative Analysis of Contemporary and Historical Religion', *Journal of Social History*, 4: 359-88.

Australian Government *Census* (1971).

BEALS, Ralph (1978) 'The Levels of Identity', in a later volume.

BELL, Daniel (1975) 'Ethnicity and Social Change', in Nathan GLAZER and Daniel P. MOYNIHAN (eds.), *Ethnicity: Theory and Experience*. Cambridge, Mass.: Harvard University Press, pp. 141-74.

BORRIE, W. (1954) *Italians and Germans in Australia*. Melbourne: Cheshire.

BOTTOMLEY, Gill (1976) 'Ethnicity and Identity among Greek Australians', *The Australian and New Zealand Journal of Sociology*, 12 (2): 118-25.

BRETON, R. (1964) 'Institutional Completeness of Ethnic Communities and Personal Relations of Immigrants', *American Journal of Sociology*, 70 (2): 193-205.

COSER, L. A. (1968) *The Function of Social Conflict*. London: Routledge & Kegan Paul.

COX, David (1975) 'The Role of Ethnic Groups in Migrant Welfare', in *Welfare of Migrants*. Australian Government Commission of Inquiry into Poverty. Canberra: Australian Government Publishing Service, pp. 3-149.

GIDDENS, Anthony (1973) *The Class Structure of the Advanced Societies*. London: Hutchinson.

GLAZER, Nathan and Daniel P. MOYNIHAN (1975) *Ethnicity: Theory and Experience*. Cambridge, Mass.: Harvard University Press.

GORDON, Milton (1964) *Assimilation in American Life: The Role of Race, Religion, and National Origin.* New York: Oxford University Press.

GORDON, Milton (1975) 'Toward a General Theory of Racial and Ethnic Group Relations' in Nathan GLAZER and Daniel P. MOYNIHAN (eds.), *Ethnicity: Theory and Experience.* Cambridge, Mass.: Harvard University Press, pp. 84-110.

HOROWITZ, Donald L. (1975) 'Ethnic Identity', in Nathan GLAZER and Daniel P. MOYNIHAN (eds.), *Ethnicity: Theory and Experience.* Cambridge, Mass.: Harvard University Press, pp. 111-40.

HUBER, Rina (1977) *From Pasta to Pavlova: A Comparative Study of Italian Settlers in Sydney and Griffith* (The University of Queensland Press).

ISAACS, Harold R. (1975) 'Basic Group Identity', in Nathan GLAZER and Daniel P. MOYNIHAN (eds.), *Ethnicity: Theory and Experience.* Cambridge, Mass.: Harvard University Press, pp. 29-52.

JONES, F. L. (1962) 'The Italian Population of Carlton: a Demographic and Sociological Study', Ph.D. thesis. Canberra: Australian National University.

KUNZ, E. F. (1970) 'Refugees and Eastern Europeans in Australia', in C. A. PRICE (ed.), *Australian Immigration: A Bibliography and Digest*, (2). Canberra: Department of Demography, Australian National University, pp. A46-A61.

LENSKI, Gerhard (1963) *The Religious Factor.* New York: Anchor Books.

LEWINS, Frank (1975) 'Ethnicity as Process: Some Considerations of Italian Catholics', *The Australian and New Zealand Journal of Sociology*, 11 (3): 15-17.

LEWINS, Frank (1976a) 'The Australian Catholic Church and the Migrant', Ph.D. thesis. Bundoora: La Trobe University.

LEWINS, Frank (1976b) 'Ethnic Diversity within Australian Catholicism: A Comparative and Theoretical Analysis', *The Australian and New Zealand Journal of Sociology*, 12 (2): 126-35.

MARTIN, Jean I. (1972) *Community and Identity: Refugee Groups in Adelaide.* Canberra: Australian National University Press.

MOL, Hans (1976) *Identity and the Sacred.* Agincourt: The Book Society of Canada Ltd.

MOL, Hans (1978) 'Introduction', in this volume.

NAHIRNY, Vladimir and Joshua A. FISHMAN (1966) 'Ukrainian Language Maintenance in the United States', in Joshua A. FISHMAN et al. (eds.), *Language Loyalty in the United States.* The Hague: Mouton.

PATTERSON, Orlando (1975) 'Context and Choice in Ethnic Allegiance: A Theoretical Framework and Caribbean Case Study', in Nathan GLAZER and Daniel P. MOYNIHAN (eds.), *Ethnicity: Theory and Experience.* Cambridge, Mass.: Harvard University Press, pp. 305-49.

PRASHKO, Ivan (1966) 'The Ukrainian Catholic Church in Australia', in *Ukrainians in Australia.* Melbourne: Federation of Ukrainian Organizations in Australia. Translation from the original Ukrainian from private files of Jean I. Martin.

PRICE, C. A. and P. PYNE (1976) Unpublished data on Italian population.

PRICE, C. A. (1963) *Southern Europeans in Australia*. Melbourne: Oxford University Press.

PYKE, N. (1948) 'An Outline of Italian Immigration into Australia', *The Australian Quarterly*, (3): 99-109.

PYNE, P. and C. A. PRICE (1975) 'Selected Tables on Australian Immigration 1947-74', in C. A. PRICE and Jean I. MARTIN (eds.), *Australian Immigration*, (3) Part 1. Canberra: Department of Demography, Australian National University, pp. A15-A56.

STORER, Des (1975) *Ethnic Rights, Power and Participation: Toward a Multi Cultural Australia*. Melbourne: Clearing House on Migration Issues, Ecumenical Migration Centre and Centre for Urban Research and Action.

The Advocate (1974) 15 August. Weekly of the Melbourne Archdiocese.

The Official Directory of the Catholic Church in Australia and Papua-New Guinea, New Zealand the the Pacific Islands (1973).

Ukraine — A Christian Nation (1973) Booklet published for the 40th International Eucharistic Conference, Melbourne.

WEBER, Max (1958) *The Protestant Ethic and the Spirit of Capitalism*, translated by Talcott PARSONS. New York: Charles Scribner's Sons.

ZUBRZYCKI, J. (1964) *Settlers of the La Trobe Valley*. Canberra: Australian National University Press.

2

WITNESSING AS IDENTITY CONSOLIDATION:

The Case of the Lubavitcher Chassidim

William Shaffir
McMaster University, Canada

Bill Shaffir's chapter has a single, clearly-stated theme: at first sight witnessing or proselytizing increases the members' exposure to outsiders and appears to threaten their well-defined identity, but in actual fact it consolidates the latter.

The example he takes is from the Lubavitch community in Montreal, a group of chassidic Jews who embarked on an extensive and successful Tefillin *campaign: the promotion of the orthodox practice of wearing phylacteries, small leather cubes containing a piece of parchment inscribed with specific Biblical verses.*

The author suggests that this kind of successful witnessing and buttressing of identity can only be accomplished by controlling the context of discussion in which the proselytizing occurs.

The chapter is primarily descriptive but the observations fit rather well in the frame of reference of the introduction. Lubavitcher identity is consolidated by witnessing as a ritual of commitment to a practice and a faith. Witnessing has the simultaneous effect of learning to articulate, and thereby thoroughly appropriate, a basic set of beliefs. And all these (beliefs, rituals and commitments) are important means of sacralization.

Author's Note: I wish to thank Richard Brymer for valuable comments on an earlier draft of this chapter.

INTRODUCTION

All groups wishing to separate themselves from the larger society must take into account the problem of how they will maintain and consolidate themselves as a group. The way groups tackle this problem is clearest among those organized to resist the assimilative influences of the larger society. As the literature about such groups suggests, they have adopted a variety of mechanisms to strengthen their commitment to their own distinctive way of life (Gutwirth, 1970; Peters, 1971; Kanter, 1972). One of the most important tasks in consolidating a separate identity is to establish social and cultural boundaries to set the group clearly apart from outsiders.

A common feature of these groups is their efforts to insulate themselves. Since it is believed that if the group does not effectively insulate itself from the surrounding society it will disintegrate, efforts to keep itself separate are given a high priority. At the same time, however, some of the same groups are involved in the apparently incongruous activity of witnessing; an activity that increases the members' exposure to outsiders and would appear to threaten their well-defined identity. The argument of this chapter is that witnessing, far from eroding a group's distinctive identity, in fact helps to *consolidate* it. I will attempt to show that this happens precisely because those engaged in witnessing make sure that their interaction with outsiders has a specific rather than a general basis.

The argument presented in this chapter can apply to any group with an alternative world view. All such group's world views can be buttressed by witnessing. While most of the literature on this topic deals with religious groups, my argument can apply equally well to political or even cultural groups. In this chapter my general focus is on religious groups and, within such groups, on the witnessing activity of an orthodox community of chassidic Jews — the Lubavitcher.[1]

OUTSIDERS AND IDENTITY MAINTENANCE

A feature common to groups that perceive the outside world as a threat is the belief that they must resist the assimilative influence of the larger society. These influences are thought to undermine the group's efforts to inculcate and maintain a distinctive identity among its members (Shaffir, 1976). The groups have various ways of channelling their members' lives so that they conform to specific group standards. Some of the mechanisms these groups have used to make their members feel they belong to a distinct group have included geographical isolation (O'Dea, 1957), specific dress (Poll, 1962; Redekop, 1969; Isichei, 1970), keeping up their own language (Hostetler, 1968), and cultural and social insulation (Kranzler, 1961; Rubin, 1972: Shaffir, 1974). These identifying features are intended to strengthen the members' commitment to the group and distract them from those aspects of the larger society that conflict with the group's ideology and way of life.

These groups work to create a set of boundaries marking off the group and those within from the outside world. Such strong and distinct boundaries − physical, social and behavioural − help to define the group and give it a sharp focus. They also differentiate sharply what is permissible within the group from what occurs on the outside. In addition, clear boundaries indicate to everyone the distinction between those who belong to the group and those who do not. It is not surprising, therefore, that an important way such groups try to maintain their distinctive identity is through strict criteria distinguishing those on the inside from those on the outside. As Kanter has noted, the group's efforts to create and maintain distinctive boundaries help it distinguish itself from its environment 'so that members create for themselves psychic boundaries that encompass the community' (Kanter, 1972: 170). This in turn helps group members to feel more committed and increases their awareness of their separate identity.

Such affirmative boundaries restrict group members' contacts to 'acceptable' others. It is precisely the group's ability to limit and control its members' interactions and associations with outsiders that helps safeguard its tenability. The outside world is seen as a dangerous place and contact with individuals whose behaviour and ideas are contrary to the group's is to be avoided. The very nature of such contacts could, it is believed, make members doubt their way of life and open the way for disaffection with the group's organization and purpose. Such groups must meet the need for isolation and insulation from potential sources of ideological contamination to safeguard their distinctive identity. It is not surprising, therefore, that religious communities and cults are careful to screen and organize members' social relations with outsiders and with ideas foreign to the group.

If, as I have suggested, contacts across the group's boundaries are carefully checked and are avoided if unnecessary, then it is surely a curious phenomenon that some groups, although organized to ensure separation from the outside world, also have a missionary zeal and see themselves as serving society. Because of their belief that they possess a special knowledge and understanding of how man ought to conduct his everyday life they have developed a series of proselytizing activities, such as witnessing, to impress their views on others. The obligation to engage in witnessing means that group members have to meet people of widely differing outlooks who are likely to challenge the group's views and even ridicule the members' beliefs. Such activities, then, increase the risk that members' outlooks will be compromised or completely changed (Beckford, 1975: 89).

The rejection and derision encountered by those engaged in witnessing activities has been documented in various reports. In his study of a religious cult Lofland (1966: 210) mentions that the cult met with opposition during its witnessing activities: 'On one occasion a minister publicly denounced Lester . . . (a cult member) to his fae as a neurotic in need of a psychiatrist'. Sterling (1975: viii), in an apology for the Jehovah's Witnesses, says that 'they are also always ready to brave the scorn, contempt, and abuse of hostile and unsympathetic people who look down upon them as "religious nuts" '. In a more sociological analysis of the Jehovah's Witnesses, Lottes (1972: 85) asserts that 'the Society implants in the newcomer the notion that he will be persecuted for his beliefs'. In her discussion of communes with messianic causes, Kanter (1972: 192) notes that outsiders may refuse to accept their message and sometimes even persecute the helpers. My cursory observations of Hare Krishna's witnessing activities clearly indicate that the members often meet with scorn and abuse. Finally, outsiders quite often react to the Lubavitcher chassidim's witnessing by challenging the group's religious beliefs and refusing to cooperate in any way.

The available evidence suggests that the intensive interaction necessary during witnessing apparently weakens the boundaries of the group, and challenges the members' distinctive identity. If such activities do, in fact, weaken the group's efforts clearly to demarcate the boundaries between insiders and outsiders, why are they pursued so tenaciously? In attempting to account for this apparently incongruous behaviour I will rely primarily on data gathered through participant observation of a community of chassidic Jews – the Lubavitcher.[2] After giving some background information on this religious group I will then examine the religious basis for their witnessing and describe, in some detail, one example. Next, I will look at which members of the group are most actively engaged in witnessing and conclude that while witnessing may appear to endanger the community's ability to maintain its identity, it in fact helps to strengthen it.

THE LUBAVITCHER CHASSIDIM

The Lubavitcher chassidim are a group of orthodox Jews who, together with other groups within the chassidic movement, have attempted to insulate themselves socially and culturally from the larger community to maintain their distinctive way of life. The religious headquarters of this group are in Crown Heights, Brooklyn, and it is from there that the group's religious leader, the *Rebbe*, directs the affairs of the movement, which maintains followers throughout the world. Unlike other chassidic groups, in which the followers are strongly discouraged from any unnecessary interaction with outsiders whether or not they are Jewish, the Lubavitcher chassidim try to impress on Jews of all degrees of religious observance the importance of adopting orthodox Jewish principles as a guide to everyday life. Lubavitcher are set apart, and set themselves apart, from other chassidic groups by their efforts to establish contact with non-observant Jews and interest them in orthodox Judaism. To this end they have organized a series of activities to involve the larger Jewish community and infuse it with a feeling for this kind of Jewish life.

The Lubavitch community's relationship with other Jews is best understood by describing their attitude and feelings towards non-Lubavitcher. This attitude is part of the history of Lubavitch and today is the chief social characteristic distinguishing it from other chassidic groups.

The essence of the Lubavitch movement's teaching is *Ahavas Yisroel* — love for one's fellow Jew. The founder of the Lubavitch movement once said:

> *Ahavas Yisroel* means to love Jew. . . . The manner of love in *Ahavas Yisroel* should be a brotherly one. Brotherly love, i.e., love for a brother does not cease or change, because it is natural. One cannot divorce himself from a brother, since he and his brother are the same flesh and blood (*Di Yiddishe Heim*, 4, 1967: 18).

This interpretation of *Ahavas Yisroel* has become the foundation of Lubavitcher's conduct. All the Lubavitch leaders have reflected this basic philosophy in their devotion to, and interest in, Jews regardless of their degree of religious observance. They have all insisted that one is to love a Jew not because of his future, that is whether he can be attracted to the Torah, but because of what he is now.

An equally important philosophical foundation of the movement, and one that has served as a motivating force for its missionary zeal, has been its teaching that no Jew is ever lost to God. Within every Jew, so the teaching goes, there is a point of authentic religious faith, *dos pintelle Yid*. As Weiner, writing about the Lubavitch movement, has observed:

> One had to remember that 'the soul itself was so much deeper than what appeared to the eye', and hence surface appearances ought never to discourage one from attempting to tap a man's inner capacity for faith in and love for Judaism. It was this principle that gave the movement its missionary spirit (1969: 145).

The Lubavitcher chassidim have actively tried to establish channels of communication with less orthodox Jews. Although they realize that their commitment to orthodox Judaism means that they are a minority among Jews today, they are none the less convinced that even their small numbers can make an impact on their fellow Jews. To help achieve their goal and preserve orthodox precepts while simultaneously drawing less religious Jews into the orthodox fold, the Lubavitcher Rebbe sends his followers to Jewish communities throughout the world to serve as his emissaries.

THE TEFILLIN CAMPAIGN

A primary prerequisite for the Lubavitcher chassidim's aim of drawing Jews closer to orthodox Judaism is establishing contact with non-observant Jews whenever and wherever possible. To this end Lubavitcher have organized as series of proselytizing activities aimed at all levels in the larger Jewish community and intended to strengthen their ties to their religious heritage.[3]

One way of achieving this is through the observance of religious precepts, or *mitzvess* (singular, *mitzveh*), which are religious obligations incumbent on all Jewish adults. These precepts cover all the circumstances an orthodox Jew may meet in his daily life, including prescriptions and proscriptions concerning marriage, charity, care of the sick, business practices, sexual relations, property law, and a number of other subjects. An orthodox Jew believes that God has decreed these precepts and that they, therefore, represent the complete code for the Jew's moral conduct. As the Lubavitcher Rebbe once said, 'The Jew must observe the *Mitzvoth* whether or not he understands their deeper significance; his experience of the *Mitzvoth* eventually will develop the faculties of his understanding, and in this he has Divine Providence' (*Di Yiddishe Heim*, 10, 1968: 1). As the observance of these religious precepts is a central feature of the Lubavitch community, the chassidim attempt to impress on others how important they are.

One such precept, the observance of *Tefillin*, is incumbent on all Jewish males who have reached the age of thirteen. The Tefillin, or phylacteries, consist of two small leather cubes, each containing a piece of parchment inscribed with specific Biblical verses. They are worn by men during the morning religious services on days other than the Sabbath and holy days, one strapped to the left arm, the other to the forehead. To popularize the observance of Tefillin, Lubavitcher organized a Tefillin campaign which was their single most important and best-known activity and eventually became identified with them.

The Tefillin campaign was initiated by the Lubavitcher Rebbe and, while endorsed by much of the larger orthodox Jewish community, became associated with Lubavitch. It started shortly before the outbreak of the Six Day War in the Middle East in 1967 when the Rebbe urged his followers throughout the world to ensure that as may Jews as possible observed this precept. Its observance, claimed the Rebbe, would inevitably aid the Jews in Israel, especially those in the army, in their war with the enemy. Pamphlets and newspaper advertisements in the English and Yiddish press extended invitations to people to perform or observe this precept at the Lubavitch synagogue and community centre, or other synagogues in the city. For instance, one newspaper advertisement read:

> . . . a *Tefillin* campaign is being proclaimed by the undersigned religious leaders of our community. . . . We call upon our Jewish brethren, from teenagers to senior citizens, who have until now not observed this *Mitzvah* regularly to commence to do so this Sunday morning, preferably at Services held in their synagogue. Anyone in need of guidance and assitance is invited to call one of the undersigned of the *Tefillin* campaign headquarters.

A pamphlet added:

> There will be a strengthened effort to make the Jewish populace aware of the importance of this *Mitzvah*. Lectures and newspaper articles are being devoted to this subject. Hospitals and organizations, offices and homes are some of the places where visitations have accomplished undreamed of results. Many, inspired by this have decided to continue putting on *Tefillin* daily; thousands are responding to this call as the campaign steadily expands.

Lubavitcher carefully co-ordinated a witnessing drive to reach as many Jews as possible. In addition to approaching Jews at Jewish cultural and political gatherings, Tefillin booths were set up and regularly manned at strategic Jewish locations, such as shopping centres and plazas that attracted a mainly Jewish clientele. Several trucks, decorated with slogans like 'Join millions of Jews the world over who have begun to put on Tefillin', were aptly called by Lubavitcher the 'Tefillin mobiles' or 'Tefillin tanks'. They were extremely conspicuous as they drove through Jewish residential and business sections of the city. As the Tefillin campaign continued, the Lubavitchers' excitement and its success mounted. Two older students described their part in the campaign:

> We would ask people to put on *Tefillin* for Israel. Sometimes we would go to the person's house in the morning, or sometimes we would even go to factories or stores. It's really fantastic how many people we got. Have you ever heard of [name of a restaurant]? We even got him to put on *Tefillin*. There are so many stories about the number of new people that we got to put on *Tefillin*.

When we started it was really an all-out effort. We still learned, but everyone was really involved. The stories from the campaign are really something. We used to go down to the St. Lawrence to the Israeli ships. This was once every two weeks or once a month. And, after a while, we really got to know the people there. And so we would come on the ship and we would say: 'Oh, he's a good guy, let's get him'. . . . Another time we were on our way to New York and the bus broke down. . . . It was near a college town. So we got off the bus and we *davned* (prayed) and then we went looking for people. It's something which has gotten into everyone's veins, it really has.

One way the Lubavitcher made sure both that they covered the greatest possible area and involved as many of their members as possible was by organizing Tefillin routes. A Tefillin route was a specified area that two or three Lubavitcher were responsible for establishing. They then had to maintain contact with the Jews in that area and teach, encourage, and remind them to observe Tefillin and, depending on the individual, other precepts. Some Lubavitcher became skilled at setting up Tefillin routes and would then hand these over to other Lubavitcher who would devote their energies to maintaining a relationship with the people already contacted. Others, who perhaps felt bashful or were unwilling to approach strangers, assisted by driving other Lubavitcher to their Tefillin route, helped distribute the literature on the campaign, or contributed financially towards the campaign's expenses.

Lubavitcher discovered, while initiating and maintaining a Tefillin route, that it was not unusual for those approached to disclaim interest in the campaign, to insist that they be left alone, and even to claim that Lubavitcher's witnessing and proselytizing efforts were a disgrace to the larger Jewish community. Such reactions did not diminish the intensity of the campaign. Unfavourable reactions were interpreted to suggest that even more time, energy, and commitment should be devoted to raising the level of orthodox Jewish consciousness in the larger Jewish community. A young Lubavitcher remarked:

It's easy to be discouraged but we must never think that our work is not worthwhile. If someone turns us down then we have to work even harder, with more energy. You see, if I'm planting a tree and putting in the seed today, when it's going to start to grow depends on many things. But you know one thing – it's going to grow. We have . . . one thing that we are guaranteed – that any work, any investment that a person makes into any human being . . . will not return empty-handed. In other words, some result is going to hit.

In spite of criticism of their work Lubavitcher were certain that their efforts would ultimately have some impact on the people they encountered:

> You know, I've met a number of Jews who say that they don't really care about being Jewish. . . . But one day a Lubavitcher is going to bring these people back because no matter how hard they try to lose their Jewishness, *dos pintelle Yid* [the point of authentic Jewish faith] is still going to remain and once you reach that point in a person, and you'll reach it eventually, you're going to make an impression on him.

A lack of interest and enthusiasm is usually equated with a lack of an orthodox Jewish upbringing and/or misinformation about the place of orthodox Judaism in modern society. Lubavitcher consider that an accurate analysis of the meaning of orthodox Judaism can often overcome this. As a Lubavitcher observed:

> You see, I think that many people have to be given the facts; they have to be educated. Like for some, their family background is so far away from *Yiddishkayt* [orthodox Judaism] that they just don't know what it offers. Then there are those who think they know, who think they understand, who really don't. If we can get to these people, eventually we'll win them over.

To impress those approached favourably Lubavitcher developed a variety of convincing arguments to persuade people to observe the precept of Tefillin. An older Lubavitch student discussed some of the techniques he used:

> Each person has his own set [speech]. What I mean is that you can't come in to somebody and say: 'I'm here to put on *Tefillin*. Roll up your left sleeve'. . . . I'd walk in, I would say: 'Good morning, are you Jewish?' And some people say: 'No, I'm sorry'. I'd say: 'It's O.K.'. Some people will say: 'Yes, can I help you?' You see, when we're trying to put *Tefillin* on somebody, we're going to use the best approach. If it's around a holiday, like if it's around *Chanekkeh* [Feast of Lights], we're going to tell them: 'Listen, *Chanekkeh* is approaching. Being as it's a Jewish holiday, we've got to show our solidarity to Judaism. Why don't you put on *Tefillin*?' If something happened in Israel last week, I'll say: 'Listen, our brothers are having a tough time in Israel and the Lubavitcher *Rebbe*, he's a very great leader among the Jews, said that putting on *Tefillin* helps our soldiers fight in Israel. Would you like to help us out and put on *Tefillin*?' 'Or I might say: 'How about doing a *mitzveh* [a good deed, religious precept]? When was the last time you put on *Tefillin*?' You have to warm up to a person.

The ultimate objective of the Tefillin campaign was more than simply convincing others to observe this religious precept. Lubavitcher hoped that once a person had begun to observe this precept regularly, the practice of additional ones would follow naturally. Tefillin observance was regarded as a critical step in a process in which a person was urged to become more observant. The following comments illustrate this:

> You want to remain in contact with him because eventually it would be great if these people would, of course, not only just put on *Tefillin* but would observe *kashress* [Kashruth] and become *baalei tshuvess* [orthodox Jews] and *shoimrai Shabbess* [Sabbath observers] and everything. But that's a very long-range goal. But the beginning, the first part, is to get him to put on *Tefillin*.

> And we sit with them and we explain our view and they become quite receptive after a time and afterwards they'll start putting on *Tefillin* on their own. That's generally the goal. The eventual goal, of course, is that that can lead to other things.

WHO DOES THE WITNESSING?

The collective identity of many groups and communities has been considerably weakened either because outsiders have been accepted into the community or because of members' contacts with the larger society. Kanter (1972: 170), for example, has attributed the problems of some unsuccessful communes and utopias to boundary issues; to the fact that there was little selectivity in admitting newcomers. Other such communities have been weakened by educating their children in the larger society's schools and by adopting the social changes of the outside community. Along similar lines, the size and strength of ethnic communities has declined as they have been unable to offset the assimilative influences of the surrounding society on their young members (Wirth, 1927; Young, 1932; Gottlieb and Ramsey, 1964; and Shibutani and Kwan, 1965). When not controlled, exposure to the surrounding culture has frequently led to culture conflict between parents and children as the two have not shared a similar perspective on how to organize their lives. As a result, the younger generation has drifted away from the ideas and ideals important to its parents and grandparents. This weakens and alters the organization, tenability, and collective identity of the ethnic community.

Since religious communities are organized to shield themselves from the surrounding society it would be expected that they would be especially concerned about their adolescents' undue exposure to the more attractive features of that society. Young people are believed to be highly impressionable and susceptible to outsiders' influences and behaviour that might challenge or contradict their understanding of the world. It might, therefore, be expected that the group members engaged in witnessing would not include the young, who might appear to be the least committed to the group's way of life. Witnessing would be reserved for those most committed to the group's lifestyle – the adults. In fact, however, the data do not confirm this expectation.

In the community under study, witnessing is not officially delegated to a specific age group. All Lubavitcher are expected both to take an active interest in such activities and to participate. Practically speaking, however, the community's formally-organized activities are developed and administerd mainly by the Rabbinical students who range in age from fifteen to twenty-one. Although the Lubavitcher were convinced that the Tefillin campaign was important and proudly boasted of its successes, the Rabbinical students were mainly responsible for organizing the Tefillin routes, manning the Tefillin booths, and regularly visiting college campuses and high schools to contact Jewish youth and adults. In addition, they played prominent roles in many of the Lubavitchers' other proselytizing efforts. For example, it was the Rabbinical students who called on the orthodox synagogues in the city on Saturday afternoons to relate their Rebbe's discourses and acquaint Jews with his work on behalf of all Jews. They also served as the counsellors in the Lubavitch boys' camp, where most of the boys came from non-Lubavitch families, and organized religious and social programmes for Jewish youth and college students in the city. Similarly, Stevenson (1967) claims that among the Jehovah's Witnesses the call to pioneer or witness is mainly dirted at the teenagers about to leave school. The Society frowns on university education and discourages advanced secular learning in favour of the pioneer work.

Just as young people are encouraged to witness, so recent recruits to the movement are encouraged to proselytize. The recent convert is sent out to speak with outsiders to demonstrate to them that they too can find fulfilment and purpose by altering their ways. Among the Jehovah's Witnesses, about one hour after baptism, the witnessing starts with the newly created 'publishers' leading the way. This is the first time these new publishers actually take responsibility for their witnessing. In the same way, newcomers to Lubavitch often attend activities organized for the less observant and informally witness about the religious lifestyle of the Lubavitcher chassidim.

Particularly for young people and newcomers to the group, witnessing often entails going into settings that might expose them to ideas and arguments contradictory to their way of life. Lubavitcher, for instance, regularly expected that their witnessing would meet with doubtful and often negative reactions from the larger Jewish community. It was partly in response to the expected outcome of encounters with non-observant Jews that followers of other chassidic groups in the city strongly discouraged and, at times, forbade their children to converse with outsiders, whether Jewish or Gentile.

Lubavitch's witnessing efforts resulted in contacts with less observant Jews that were initiated and maintained outside the community's institutions. In addition, the Lubavitcher invited these less observant Jews to the community's celebrations and encouraged them to attend the organizations and institutions available to Lubavitcher themselves. It is reasonable to suggest that the presence of outsiders within the community boundaries could obscure the distinction between insiders and outsiders, a distinction so crucial to the very existence of any community.

It appears that Lubavitcher's witnessing in the larger Jewish community could threaten the preservation of their distinctive identity by blurring the group's boundaries. This threat does not, however, decrease the Lubavitcher's witnessing zeal, nor in fact does it weaken the community boundaries. In fact, far from threatening the community's efforts to maintain and consolidate their identity by eroding the boundaries, witnessing served to reinforce Lubavitcher's distinctive identity both at the individual and community levels. As Mol (1976: 238) has written, 'Every act of witnessing anchors the belief system deeply in the emotions of the believer, since faith has to be proclaimed against the non-believer. The boundaries around the belief system are thus firmly drawn'. The literature suggests there is a connection between witnessing and identity consolidation and, in the case of the

Lubavitcher, witnessing certainly appears to strengthen and reinforce their feelings of identity.

WITNESSING AND
IDENTITY REINFORCEMENT

It is commonly believed that witnessing, especially among those who challenge a group member's set of beliefs, is a threat to the group's identity. Confronted by sceptics, and disinterested, and non-believers, the individual may come to question and eventually doubt the set of principles around which he has organized his identity. It is for this very reason that certain groups and communities trying to cultivate and maintain a distinctive identity have intentionally segregated themselves from the larger society by minimizing their members' contact with outside influences.

While one effect of witnessing is its immediate threat to the group member, a less obvious result is that, in fact, it strengthens the very self-concept that it is believed to weaken. That witnessing reinforces the person's identity has been documented by various observers and, though few have analysed the process by which this occurs, it is useful to note some of the observations. In his analysis of how the Bolshevik Party turned its members into dedicated and highly committed people, Selznick (1960) suggests that such total commitment was achieved because of the sheer volume of the members' activity for the Party.[4] Lofland (1966), in his study of a religious cult, maintains that the Divine Precept's (DP's) proselytizing efforts had a salutary effect and that criticism, in fact, solidified the group's system of beliefs. The DP's maintained that 'witnessing and rejection were absolutely necessary in order to have a favorable position in the New Age' (Lofland, 1966: 210). Lottes (1972: 91), writing about the Jehovah's Witnesses, suggests that 'proselytization will strengthen rather than weaken the newcomer'. The effect of proselytizing for the Jehovah's Witnesses is spelled out more clearly by Zygmunt:

> While it [proselytizing] is often explitly concerned with recruiting new group members, not to be overlooked are the opportunities implicit in proselytizing

endeavor along the lines of expressing and affirming the group's identity through public activity. To preach the group's message publicly is . . . the ultimate act of commitment to its faith, an overt demonstration of it. . . . The identity expressing and affirming functions of evangelization appear to have been as important as a direct interest in the organizational expansion per see (1967: 729-30).

Festinger et al., in their study of a religious cult, the Seekers, suggest that if the group's central beliefs are either questioned or not believed by others, proselytizing is an effective means of reaffirming the member's identity with the group. As the writers state: 'If more and more people can be persuaded that the system of belief is correct, then clearly it must, after all, be correct' (Festinger et al., 1956: 28). Mol, writing about the general process of conversion, claims that 'the convert feels that he has obtained a new identity, and very often he strengthens his new assumptive world by repeating over and over again how evil, or disconsolate, or inadequate he was before the conversion took place' (Mol, 1976: 50-51).

While the relationship between witnessing and maintaining and consolidating an identity has been noted, in many accounts one pre-requisite has been referred to only indirectly. For instance, Glick, in describing the Hebrew Christians' proselytizing, claims that 'the religious aspect of the programme was of greater importance than the more obvious content' (Glick, 1958: 417). Stevenson's analysis of the Jehovah's Witnesses' technique for organizing their witnessing includes the following:

> The Witness is too well trained to allow such a free-ranging discussion to continue for very long. He will point out to you that religion is a very big subject, and that you and he could go on discussing it for hours, flitting from one subject to another without settling once and for all any point at issue (Stevenson, 1967: 33).

Writing about the Jehovah's Witnesses' first contact with a prospective member, Lottes (1972: 130) claims that 'the subject of religion is introduced rather quickly'.

What these analyses of witnessing suggest, but do not directly state, is that, while these groups do not isolate themselves, they are expected to control the contexts in which they meet with outsiders. The context of witnessing is always expected to have a specific basis. For religious groups this is a religious basis which emphasizes the group's distinctive differences and makes these differences an explicit focus of attention or behaviour. Such contacts, while apparently threatening the individual's identity, in fact reinforce it. The kinds of contact situations that may threaten both the individual and the group would be those in which the distinctive differences separating the group members from outsiders are not the focus of concern; that is, where the context does not impose the differences as the reasons for contact.

We can now understand better how witnessing consolidates the Lubavitcher chassidim's identity. It is precisely the act of witnessing in the larger Jewish community that reinforces the members' beliefs and enables the Lubavitch community to retain its specific boundaries. When a Lubavitcher attempts to influence and convince a non-observant Jew of the relevance of orthodox Judaism and the Lubavitcher Rebbe's role as an important Jewish leader, he is, in fact, influencing and convincing himself. As Mead (1934: 199-246) observed, this is because a person can act socially towards himself just as he acts towards others and can thus become the object of his own actions. An important result of Lubavitcher's witnessing is that by discussing and arguing with non-observant Jews about orthodox Judaism, the Lubavitcher Rebbe's accomplishments, or the everlasting significance of Torah observance, they have to think about the facts and information themselves, which further reinforces their identity as Lubavitcher chassidim.

In the light of this argument the involvement of the Rabbinical students in witnessing is now understandable. These students, ranging in age from fifteen to twenty-one, are the very people whose beliefs require strengthening. Their commitment to the Lubavitch way of life is less intense than that of the adults who have raised families and organized their lives around the chassidic group. Involving these students in witnessing is no doubt an important way of building their belief systems. By teaching and becoming witness to their beliefs, and by urging them on others, they learn to think of themselves as Lubavitcher chassidim.

CONCLUSION

While I have contended that witnessing serves to maintain and strengthen the group's distinctive self-concept, I have not meant to imply that such activities are sufficient to preserve the group's boundaries against outside influences. As various studies have shown, groups attempting to isolate and insulate themselves from such influences use a variety of mechanisms. Witnessing, however, while apparently endangering the group's and the individual's separate identity, in fact helps to buttress that very identity. I have suggested that this is only done by controlling the context of the discussion in which the witnessing occurs.

Studies of groups seeking to protect their individual lifestyles usually concentrate on the methods members use to organize their identity. Such studies have usually failed to distinguish between *creating* or *defining* a separate identity and *maintaining* and *consolidating* it.[5] I have argued that witnessing helps to maintain and consolidate an identity and have attempted to show how this applies to a religious community of chassidic Jews.

NOTES

1. The chassidim are a religious movement within the framework of Jewish laws and practices, but with their own unique customs and traditions. Their everyday way of life is circumscribed by religious ideas and principles that differentiate them from other Jewish minority groups, both orthodox and non-orthodox. The commonly-referred-to 'chassidic community' (Poll, 1962) in fact consists of a number of different chassidic groups, each with a loyalty and devotion to its own leader, or Rebbe. The Lubavitcher chassidim is one group in the chassidic community.

2. The data on the Lubavitcher for this paper were gathered by participant observation in the Lubavitch community in Montreal, Canada, for approximately two and a half years. During this period I spent a considerable amount of time with the Lubavitcher, taking part in a wide range of their activities. I had many opportunities to observe them witnessing and accompanied them on their

proselytizing work. In addition to discussing their witnessing with Lubavitcher, I also attended the various activities they organized.

3. The Tefillin campaign is only one effort at proselytizing in the larger Jewish community. In fact, Lubavitcher have organized a series of activities intended to appeal to various age groups. A common feature of these activities is the intention to bridge and eventually to close the gap between orthodox and non-observant Jews. Lubavitcher have, in recent years, organized a Mitzveh campaign which is intended to ensure that 'everyone set aside time every day for Torah study, that men and boys over thirteen put on Tefillin every weekday, that a *Mezuzah* be properly affixed to every right doorpost, that every home have a charity box to facilitate frequent charitable contributions, and that every home have sacred books, at least a Bible, Prayer Book and Book of Psalms' (*Lubavitch News Service*, March, 1976).

4. In his analysis of the organization of radical movements Bittner claims that such 'action groups must have some way to reduce the horizon of possible encounters and cause the remaining contingencies of potential embarrassment to be seen as either not pertaining or, when "correctly" seen, further boosting the doctrine' (1963: 934). Bittner fails to consider the possibility that witnessing may help such groups achieve their end. Further on he adds that 'all groups must develop symbolic expressions to emphasize their distinctiveness and to celebrate their cause' (1963: 939). As I suggest, witnessing may be used for precisely this purpose.

5. For an interesting analysis of how the Jesus movement serves to consolidate the member's identity, see Gordon (1974).

REFERENCES

BECKFORD, James A. (1975) *The Trumpet of Prophecy: A Sociological Study of Jehovah's Witnesses*. Oxford: Basic Blackwell.

BITTNER, Egan (1963) 'Radicalism and the Organization of Radical Movements', *American Sociological Review*, 28: 928-40.

Di Yiddishe Heim. New York: Council Neshai Ub'Nos Chabad.

FESTINGER, L., H. W. RIECKEN and S. SCHACHTER (1956) *When Prophecy Fails*. New York: Harper & Row.

GLICK, Ira O. (1958) 'The Hebrew Christians: A Marginal Religious Group', in Marshall SKLARE (ed.), *The Jews: Social Patterns of an American Group*. New York: The Free Press, pp. 415-31.

GORDON, David F. (1974) 'The Jesus People: An Identity Synthesis', *Urban Life and Culture*, 3: 159-78.

GOTTLIEB, D. and C. E. RAMSEY (eds.) (1964) *The American Adolescent*. Homewood: The Dorsey Press.

GUTWIRTH, Jacques (1970) *Vie Juive Traditionnelle: Ethnologie D'Une Communauté Hassidique.* Paris: Les Editions de Minuit.

HOSTETLER, John A. (1968) *Amish Society.* Baltimore: The John Hopkins Press.

ISICHEI, Elizabeth (1970) *Victorian Quakers.* London: Oxford University Press.

KANTER, Rosabeth M. (1972) *Commitment and Community: Communes and Utopias in Sociological Perspective.* Cambridge, Mass.: Harvard University Press.

KRANZLER, Gershon (1961) *Williamsburg: A Jewish Community in Transition.* New York: Philip Feldheim.

LOFLAND, John (1966) *Doomsday Cult: A Study of Conversion, Proselytization, and Maintenance of Faith.* Englewood Cliffs, N.J.: Prentice-Hall.

LOTTES, Klaus V. (1972) 'Jehovah's Witnesses: A Contemporary Sectarian Community'. Unpublished Master's thesis, McMaster University.

MEAD, George H. (1934) *Mind, Self and Society.* Chicago: University of Chicago Press.

MOL, Hans (1976) *Identity and the Sacred: A Sketch for a New Social-Scientific Theory of Religion.* Agincourt: The Book Society of Canada Ltd.

O'DEA, Thomas F. (1957) *The Mormons.* Chicago: University of Chicago Press.

PETERS, Victor (1971) *All Things Common: The Hutterian Way of Life.* New York: Harper & Row.

POLL, Solomon (1962) *The Hasidic Community of Williamsburg.* New York: Free Press of Glencoe.

REDEKOP, Calvin W. (1969) *The Old Colony Mennonites: Dilemmas of Ethnic Minority Life.* Baltimore: The John Hopkins Press.

RUBIN, Israel (1972) *Satmar: An Island in the City.* Chicago: Quadrangle Books.

SELZNICK, Philip (1960) *The Organizational Weapon. A Study of Bolshevik Strategy and Tactics.* Illinois: The Free Press of Glencoe.

SHAFFIR, William (1974) *Life in a Religious Community: The Lubavitcher Chassidim in Montreal.* Toronto: Holt, Rinehart & Winston of Canada, Ltd.

––, (1976) 'The Organization of Secular Education in a Chassidic Jewish Community', *Canadian Ethnic Studies*, 8: 38-51.

SHIBUTANI, Tamotsu and K. M. KWAN (1965) *Ethnic Stratification: A Comparative Approach.* New York: Macmillan.

STERLING, Chandler W. (1975) *The Witnesses: One God, One Victory.* Chicago: Henry Regnery.

STEVENSON, E. C. (1967) *The Inside Story of Jehovah's Witnesses.* New York: Hart Publishing Company Inc.

WEINER, Herbert (1969) *9 1/2 Mystics: The Kabbala Today.* New York: Holt, Rineheart & Winston.

WIRTH, Louis (1928) *The Ghetto.* Chicago: University of Chicago Press.

YOUNG, P. V. (1932) *The Pilgrims of Russian-Town.* Chicago: University of Chicago Press.

ZYGMUNT, Joseph F. (1967) 'Jehovah's Witnesses: A Study of Symbolic and Structural Elements in the Development and Institutionalization of a Sectarian Movement.' Doctoral Dissertation, University of Chicago.

3

PARADIGM SHIFTS AND IDENTITY THEORY:

Alternation as a Form of Identity Management

R. Kenneth Jones
Ulster College, Northern Ireland

Kenneth Jones's chapter revolves around the relation between identity and conversion, or 'alternation' as the author prefers to call it. Religion as such does not figure largely, as Jones adopts the social interactionist's viewpoint and consequently thinks about identity as negotiable and exchangeable; an orderly arrangement of roles. It is not 'wholeness' or 'sameness' bolstered or sacralized in order to keep it from changing. Therefore religion is peripheral by definition.

The author correctly treats the Kuhnian paradigm shift as basically similar to orientation change of new recruits to Alcoholics Anonymous, the Socialist Party of Great Britain, or pacifism.

The values of Jones's chapter lies particularly in its bibliographical comprehension. The unresolved problem lies in the place of commitment in the social interactionist frame of reference. A shallow commitment fits best because transition is by definition relatively facile. Yet a deep commitment and a traumatic conversion experience jar with this viewpoint because, again by definition, human beings are implied to be like chameleons, adjustable to circumstance. If people tend to have a strong emotional stake in the sameness and predictability of order then they need a model highlighting the traumatic stripping of an old identity and the painful welding of a new one.

> *'Identity is the answer to everything. There is nothing that cannot be seen in terms of identity. We are not going to pretend that there is the slightest argument about* that.*' (Nigel Dennis:* Cards of Identity, *London: Weidenfeld & Nicholson, 1955.)*

> *'Outside these walls, in the open air, many of you may feel a certain sense of* exposure. *The best answer to that is pipes, cigars, and cigarettes, which leave a familiar mark upon the void. The wearing*

of a hat is also helpful: I do not have to remind you of the late Dr.
Black Planorbis's superb paper on the relation between modern
hatlessness and loss of identity.' (Nigel Dennis: Cards of Identity,
London: Weidenfield & Nicholson, 1955.)

A great deal of work has been done on what constitutes 'disentangle-
ment' from one particular pattern of identity and the processes involved in the adoption of another, very often entirely different and
contrasted.[1] A number of descriptive terms have been used to describe
such a process: 'brainwashing', 'conversion', or 'alternation'.[2] This
section will deal with the management of identity in cosmological
settings, such settings not being confined to religious transformation
systems, and consequently the term alternation and its concomitant
dramaturgy will be used to denote a process of transformation from
one world view to another and to embrace both secular and transcendental areas of activity.

By the 'management of identity' is meant the manner in which
identity is controlled in a way which is in keeping with some overall
formulation or set of precepts.[3] Basically, the social interactionist
perspective views an individual's identity as being the result of various
social experiences 'intrinsically associated with all the joinings and
departures of social life' (Stone, 1970), and such identities are social
because they emerge and are sustained by a process of negotiation
through interacting with others. Thus, one means by identity, according
to this version or perspective, that one is *situated* within a series of
social relations and *placed* as a social object. In opposition to this view
is the one that traditionally regards identity as something unaltered and
fixed, a kind of given potential.

The sustaining and modification of identity, established by social
relationships and processes, is to a large extent a determinant of the
social structure but, as Berger has said, this is a dialectical process in the
sense that such identity does itself act upon the social structure.
Goffman talks of 'identity kits', which can be viewed as accessories to
the presentation of the self, and identity can be changed or managed by
covert and overt manipulation of such kits to the extent that the
personal front is altered in some way. Thus, the initiatory procedures in
Synanon and Daytop (Sugarman, 1967, 1968), the 'stripping down' of
the old identity in Alcoholics Anonymous (Jones, 1970) and certain

T-groups (Slater, 1968), are all means which attempt the creation of new identities for the joiners. This is particularly stark in total institutions such as prisons when social and individual identity is drastically broken down in an attempt at remodelling.

Identity is not simply, either, something which hides behind one of Goffman's many masks which are worn for the purposes of impression management, for we are not in a position to talk in terms of core-performances of identity, as we shall argue shortly. We are what we socially are, which in turn we reveal through our social performances. Berger talks of the manner in which our identity can become transformed through the process of alternation, a process which requires appropriate social and conceptual conditions, in particular the availability of relevant 'plausibility structures'. In itself alternation or conversion experience is 'nothing much. The real thing is to keep on taking it seriously . . .' (Berger, 1966). The groups we will be mentioning manage the identity of adherents by providing plausibility structures which sustain and reinforce the initial alternation of the individual identity. A legitimating apparatus is consequently brought to bear on the adherent, an example of which is pre-alternation biography which is 'typically nihilated *in toto* by subsuming it under a negative category occupying a strategic position . . .'. Examples might be found in such statements as, 'When I was living the life of a wretched sinner', or 'When I had sunk rock bottom'.

To Goffman (1961) identity is intrinsically bound up with the mortification of the self. He deals at length with the stripping of civilian identity layer by layer on entry to a total institution. Garfinkel (1956) is anxious to link 'status degradation' with identity. Brim and Wheeler (1966: 14) describe identity as the 'core-periphery', in fact 'components of the personality — certain groupings of self-other relationships — that are highly determining of the individual's behaviour . . . these would be primarily of the "I-me" type, in which the perception of one's self in relation to others has been laid down early and frequently, both from powerful figures such as parents and also from a broad and diverse group of human beings, so that these come to constitute his sense of identity'. Wheeler (1966: 65) cites

> Those modes of socialisation or resocialisation that we think of as most extreme and that have as their goal not a mere change in the skill level or the attitude of the person being socialised but *rather a thorough reconstruction of*

his personality typically involving an individual and disjunctive pattern. A prime example is psychoanalysis. In some cases other recruits may be present but are used to destroy prior patterns rather than sustain them, to build mutual mistrust rather than action in concert. Examples are brainwashing and thought-reform programs. Indeed, in a recent analysis of radical individual change, McHugh argues that such destructive conditions are necessary before new patterns can be established (McHugh, 1964) (italics added).

In Garfinkel's (1956) analysis of the process by which an individual's total identity is transformed into an identity which is lower in the group's scheme of social typing or types, which he calls a 'status degradation ceremony', he gives some indication of what he means by the term. The identities must be 'total'. 'That is, these identities must refer to persons as "motivational" types rather than as "behavioural" types (Schutz, 1953), not to what a person may be expected to have done or to do (in Parsons' term [Parsons and Shils, 1951]; to his "performances") but to what the group holds to be the ultimate "grounds" or "reasons" for his performance.' Thus, Garfinkel means by 'identity', 'the grounds, as well as the behaviour that the grounds make explicable as the other person's conduct'. By reference to a framework of normative standards the 'preferences' of individuals constitute a pattern of socially categorized and socially understood behaviour resulting in a 'total' identification. To Garfinkel

> The transformation of identities is the destruction of one social object and the constitution of another. The transformation does not involve the substitution of one identity for another, with the terms of the old one loitering about like the overlooked parts of a fresh assembly, any more than the woman we see in the department-store window that turns out to be a dummy carries with it the possibilities of a woman. It is not that the old object has been overhauled; rather it is replaced by another. One declares '*How*, it was otherwise in the first place' (1956: 485).

Although concerned with the *denouncing* of individuals and the *lowering* of status, Garfinkel nevertheless makes several important points. There is a reconstitution rather than a change; a creation of a new person. 'The former identity, at best, receives the accent of mere appearance.' The transformation of essence is effected by public denunciation, which substitutes 'another socially validated motivational scheme for that previously used to name and order the performances of the denounced'. (1956: 485).

Davis (1966) discusses professional socialization as a subjective experience, a status passage in which the student nurse passes from a 'lay' to a 'professional' culture. It is a process of what Davis terms 'doctrinal conversion'. As Hughes (1958) describes it, 'a passing through the mirror so that one looks out on the world from behind it, and sees things as in mirror writing'. To Davis the doctrinal conversion of student nurses is a subjective, interactive experience, a 'social psychological process whereby students come to exchange their own lay views and imagery of the profession for those the profession ascribes to itself'. Such an experience consists of six successive stages. The first stage is initial innocence, 'one which abounds in feelings of worry, disappointment, frustration, and heightened self-concern . . .'. Stage two is the 'labelled recognition of incongruity' between their initial expectations 'and those which faculty directs at them'. The third stage is that of 'psyching out' or presenting to instructors what is expected of them. 'It is here that the cognitive framework for the students' later internalisation of school-approved perspectives assumes a certain rudimentary shape.' Following on from this, and barely distinguishable from it, is the process of role simulation. The fifth stage is provisional internationalization followed by a stable internalization.[4]

Identity as a concept must be empirically grounded in social interaction. It is manifested in overt behaviour within a social framework. Such social psychological perspectives on the nature of identity often maximize|the potential and actual conflict between personal and social identity, rather than the opposite (Mol, 1976). Identity, to be at all meaningful as a descriptive term, must be manifested in action and recognized by external performance, rather than being reflective in nature. Thus, Goffman constantly talks of identity as exchangeable, bargained for, and negotiated (1959, 1960). Is there just *one* identity or are there in fact many identities which are presented in particular contexts? We might answer in the affirmative without giving credence to Goffman's insistence that identities are masks donned at will in order to survive in the human scene of cynicism and pretence. 'Identities then are not worn on one's sleeve. They do tend to relate to critical life experiences. Masks, on the other hand, are forms of identities which are employed to maximise the benefits or minimise the losses accruing from social contexts' (Brittan, 1973: 153). To Brittan alternation from one identity to another not only does not imply that the individual or

person has changed *in himself* but that alternation as a process does not
have to imply commitment (1973: 155). Stone sees identity as

> established as a consequence of two processes, apposition and opposition, a
> bringing together and setting apart. To situate the person as a social object is
> to bring him together with other objects so situated, and at the same time to
> set him apart from still other objects. Identity is intrinsically associated with
> all the joinings and departures of social life. To have an identity is to join with
> some and depart from others, to enter and leave social relations at once
> (Stone, 1970).

Intrinsic to such an approach is the notion of boundary and delineation, which Stone does not discuss.[5] What he does analyse, and this is
discussed by Brittan (1973: 156-57), is the 'notion of identity not just
as a labelling process, but also . . . as an *announcement* on the part of
the individual about his interpersonal and structural location, his situation'. Thus, terms which are referrents for universality, names and
nicknames, titles and relational categories, are means of announcement
which, together with the notion of identity as role-taking, contribute to
the total process of identity.

   The manifestation of identity in action, in overt behaviour within a
social framework, introduces the notion of role-identity which McCall
and Simmons (1966: 67) define as 'the character and role that an
individual devises for himself as an occupant of a particular social
position. More intuitively such a role identity is his imaginative view of
himself as he likes to think of himself being and acting as an occupant
of that position.' There appears to be a need to legitimize our identities
if threatened by a loss of role support from an important audience,
which often results in a shift to a more successful role-identity. Parsons
sees it as imperative that there is an integration in the different
components of role involvement, such as expectations, rewards, and
obligations. He says that 'it seems useful and correct to use the term
identity in a technical sense to designate the core system of meanings of
an individual personality in the mode of object in the interaction
systems of which he is part' (1968: 14). Such integration is essential in
order to achieve the accommodation of different identities distributed
over different areas of life.

   The subjective reality of our individual consciousness is most
probably socially constructed. Berger (1973: 274) uses as items of

analysis *objective reality*, or 'knowledge about the world, as objectivated and taken for granted in society' and the *objective correlate*, 'that
is, the modes in which this objectivated world is subjectively plausible
or "real" to the individual'. The 'I' and 'me' dialectic of Mead expresses
the interaction between 'self' and 'society'. Thus, to Berger

> Every society contains a repertoire of identities that is part of the objective
> knowledge of its members . . . As the individual is socialised, these identities
> are internalised. They are then not only taken for granted as constituents of an
> objective reality 'out there' but as inevitable structures of the individual's own
> consciousness. The objective reality, as defined by society, is subjectively
> appropriated. In other words, socialisation brings about symmetry between
> objective and subjective reality, objective and subjective identity (1973: 275).

Such social constructions of reality and processes of socialization are
the product of language. To Berger

> Identity, with its appropriate attachments of psychological reality, is always
> identity with a specific, socially constructed world . . . One identifies oneself,
> as one is identified by others, by being located in a common world (1973:
> 277).

Such locating is carried out principally by *naming*, for we appropriate
the world in which we are located at the same time as appropriating our
identity.

We have so far argued that the dimension of identity is not attain-
able per se. Different definitions slice up reality, what is in fact the
case, and impose a metaphysical perspective on an otherwise overt
empirical phenomenon which is manifested in observed and sometimes
imputed actions. Consequently, identity becomes the articulated and
ordered arrangement of major constituents or roles.

THE KUHNIAN PARADIGMATIC THESIS

Long before Kuhn (1962, 1963, 1970) and Lakatos (1968; Lakatos and
Musgrave, 1970) argued that science was displaying many of the
characteristics of irrationality that religious conversion might show,

Fort (1923, 1974) was making a rather idiosyncratic stand against what he termed 'the blind dogmas of science'. The relative and unprovable realm of human knowledge makes us realize 'that the whole classical structure of intellectual values falls in ruins and has to be replaced' (Lakatos, 1968).

To put Kuhn's theory of paradigmatic change into perspective we must look to the empiricists of the 1950s and their claims for the *objectivity* of science on the grounds that data can be neutrally described and theories verified or falsified by comparison with these data, resulting in an objective and rational choice between rival theories. Profound disagreement was expressed in the late 1950s and early 1960s when it was felt that there could be no neutral description of data, conflicting data were categorized as 'one off', and there was no such thing as objective and rational choice. Kuhn further elaborated a view that the growth of scientific knowledge abounds in inconsistencies and contradictions leaving no room for the possibility of a solely rational approach. He regarded the work of scientific communities as controlled by *paradigms*, which he described as 'standard examples of scientific work which embody a set of conceptual, methodological and metaphysical assumptions'.[6] Scientific knowledge is *revolutionary* in the way that accepted frameworks of knowledge become overthrown and replaced by others. Kuhn regards normal science as dominated by paradigms which provide 'standard examples' of what questions to ask and how to set about answering them. Scientific revolutions are so significant to Kuhn as to be described as massive paradigm shifts. The paradigm which is overthrown is in fact at the beginning a socially constructed way of looking at the world, offering a perspective and structure to particular problems of meaning and explanation. Kuhn writes (1962: 147, 149):

> Though each may hope to convert the other to his way of seeing his science and its problems, neither may hope to prove his case. The competition between paradigms is not the sort of battle that can be resolved by proofs . . . Before they can hope to communicate fully, one group or the other must experience the conversion we have been calling a paradigm shift. Just because it is a transition between incommensurables, the transition between competing paradigms cannot be made a step at a time, forced by logic and neutral experience. Like a gestalt switch it must occur all at once or not at all.

He writes:

> Scientists then often speak of the 'scales falling from the eyes' or of the 'lightening flash' that 'inundates' a previously obscure puzzle, enabling its components to be seen in a new way that for the first time permits its solution (1962: 122-23).

He does, however, present a word of caution:

> To translate a theory or worldview into one's own language is not to make it one's own. For that one must go native, discover that one is thinking and working in, not simply translating out of, a language that was previously foreign.

Thus

> Translation may, in addition, provide points of entry for the neural reprogramming that . . . must underlie conversion (1962: 204).

Kuhn, in agreement with Feyerabend (1962, 1965) and Hanson (1958), denies the possibility of a language of neutral observation. Continuing his analogy with the gestalt switch Kuhn maintains that the same data can be viewed in differing ways. However, the choice between conflicting paradigms is itself subject to, or a product of, paradigms, and there appear to be few grounds, either actual or possible, as to the reasons why one paradigm could be considered superior to a rival. Thus, he describes the process as 'a transformation of the world' (1962: 6). Later critics of Kuhn have attacked his thesis on a number of grounds, such as his ambiguity in the use of the term 'paradigm' (Masterman, 1970), his ostensibly exaggerated contrast between normal and revolutionary science (Toulmin, 1970), and his criteria of paradigm-dependence (Lakatos and Musgrave, 1970). Lakatos writes of Kuhn's description of scientific change as a description of 'mystical conversion', a 'kind of religious change', bringing a 'totally new rationality' (Lakatos and Musgrave, 1970: 93, 178), while Watkins writes: 'My suggestion is, then, that Kuhn sees the scientific community on the analogy of a religious community and sees science as the scientist's religion' (Watkins, 1970: 33).

'Alternation', whether it is gradual or sudden, secular or supernatural, often utilizes a special language of description to describe the transformation of identity, such as 'seeing things in a new light', 'scales falling from the eyes' and so forth. To adapt an 'alternative conceptual system' (Warnock, 1958: 144) focuses our attention on the *relative* nature of 'ways of seeing'. So 'The occurrence of a paradigm shift brings with it a macro-transformation of an individual's cosmological stance, and he begins to manage his identity according to the mechanisms of transformation produced by the new paradigm' (Jones, 1977). The social-psychological importance of preparadigmatic choice, of the conditions which precede a commitment to a paradigm, is in essence akin to a choice between scientific paradigms and the choice between competing metaphysical systems. Mitchell's (1973: 75-95) admirable discussion of the process of choice between competing meaning systems or Weltanschaungen points to the fact that logical procedures become irrelevant, such choice being decided upon only by 'examining the nature of the group, discovering what it values, what it tolerates, and what it disdains'. Sociological and not logical accounts become the order of the day.

THE PROCESS OF ALTERNATION

Not only Kuhn but also Wittgenstein (1953) has drawn attention to the process of being able to see both social and natural phenomena differently from the way they may previously have been viewed. Kuhn gives as an example the change in the scientific community from Aristotle's to Galileo's theory of the motion of bodies. Wittgenstein uses Jarrow's duck-rabbit as an example, and differentiates between the 'dawning' of an aspect and the 'continuous seeing' of one. The *contextual* implications of viewing the duck-rabbit among other rabbit pictures may have the result of seeing it as a rabbit much more often than as a duck. 'But what is different: my impression? my point of view? − Can I say? I *describe* the alternation like a perception; quite as if the object had altered before my eyes.' Something has become reorganized; a new organization has emerged; 'My visual impression has changed.' Situations and objects are *interpreted*, but there is no 'inner picture' but 'a chimera; a queerly shifting construction' (Wittgenstein, 1953).[7]

Not only is there no 'inner picture' but alternation is not an 'inner experience' (Ryle, 1949). 'Mental', to Ryle, does not 'denote a status' and 'to talk of a person's mind is not to talk of a repository which is permitted to house objects that something called the "physical world" is forbidden to house; it is to talk of the person's abilities, liabilities and inclinations to do and undergo certain sorts of things'.[8] Alternation or conversion experience 'is not simply (or even need be at all) some specific "internal" experience, but a reorganisation of the "world" in a transformative manner with a concomitant plausibility structure to maintain the new reality' (Jones, 1977) and the new identity.

The biological basis of alternation exists in the sense that a different patterning is observed, although only in very unusual transformation cases would there be a physiological or chemical change which could be measured. Evidence suggests that the behaviour of the cortex is heightened following operant or instrumental conditioning. Neurological data recorded by changes in the electroencephalogram following alteration in tone signals certainly suggests physiological data in the sense of actual chemical change. Some have suggested that physiological mechanisms are utilized during both brainwashing and conversion behaviour (Sargant, 1957).

IDENTITY MANAGEMENT

Through the process of desacralization or emotional stripping of the old identity is born the sacralization or emotional welding of a new one (Mol, 1976). Such a process can be sudden and dramatic or slow and gradual, directed towards the social group or the individual, and located in either the transcendental or secular. Furthermore, homogenized settings function to reduce the impact of prior experience on the new identity while differentiated settings encourage the utilization of prior experience (Brim and Wheeler, 1966: 78). People-processing organizations that manage individual identity may vary substantially in the balance they strike between role socialization and status socialization (Bidwell, 1962); the felt conflict between the needs of the recruits and the external community; the emergence of separate organizational hierarchies to express such differences; and the extent of participation allowed to the recruit to establish goals which may or may not be meshed with those of the organization (Brim and Wheeler, 1966: 72). The settings for the management of identity take the form of groups and institutionalized arrangements which are lodged within the social process, and it is to some of these we shall now turn.

The Socialist Party of Great Britain is a fundamentalist, secular sect, and members describe their affiliation as follows:

> Life didn't mean very much before, you know. I had played around with the Labour party but when I received the SPGB literature it was fantastic. Everything I ever wanted was there. I've never looked back.

Conversion to the sect is described as 'seeing the light' or as being 'the only way' (Jones, 1977).

Settings for the treatment of drug addicts as described by Sugarman (1968, 1967, 1975), Shelly (1965) Volkman and Cressey (1963), and mental therapy groups (Jones, 1975) practice a process of 'devastation' aimed at reaching 'gut level' whereby addicts express willingness, positive attitudes, stripping, degradation, indoctrination, group cohesion and status ascription (Jones, 1977). Mental therapy group recruits express the situation thus:

> I like to think of myself as a lost soul. I feel I am irretrievable.
>
> I am disgusted with myself. I can't control my temper. The other day it was so bad that I cried out 'I am sick and tired of living'. Of course they were alarmed. I knew they would be (Jones, 1975).

Less obvious settings can also provide solutions to problems of identity, for example those that confront homosexuals, as described by Gagnon and Simon (1967), Humphreys (1970) and Warren (1973):

> For years I was just trade, wouldn't put one of those dirty things in my mouth. Look what I was missing.
>
> When I finally did kiss a guy romantically I realised I was a homosexual.
>
> The gay world *is* the world as far as I'm concerned.
>
> One time out of curiosity I went to a gay bar to see what these freaks really looked like. It really hit me. They looked just like me . . . One of the guys picked me up and we went home together.

The stress in Alcoholics Anonymous meetings is to both experience and describe a 'conversion' (Jones, 1970).

> Nearly every A.A. has a spiritual experience that quite transforms his outlook and attitudes. Ordinarily, such occurrences are gradual and may take place over periods of months or even years. A considerable number ... who have the sudden variety of spiritual experience see no great difference as far as the practical result is concerned between their quick illumination and the slower, more typical kinds of spiritual awakening.

The conversion and surrender process is common to both A.A. and religious sectarianism and shares a therapeutic process well documented by Tiebout (1949, 1961):

> When I got there something happened – I don't know to this day ... what it was, but when I took a look at the men and women there ... I knew they had something I needed (Tiebout, 1961).

CONCLUSIONS

The process of identity management, of controlling and changing individual identity, takes place in settings which are not only plausibility structures but which also supply a cosmological or total world explanation, which can be either secular or transcendental in nature and exhibit similarities of organization and structure.[9] Hobsbawn (1959: 68, 87-88, 140-41), for example, synthesizes both political and religious descriptions of conversion from the conversion in 1868 of Davide Lazzaretti, the frenzy of the spread of endemic anarchism in Andalusia at the end of the nineteenth century, to the similarities between the Labour sect and Labour movement in the process of conversion: 'Conversion of some kind is, of course, a commonplace in labour movements. British ones, however, are peculiarly archaic insofar as the conversion was normally a traditionally religious one, or a political one which took religious form' (1959: 141). Koestler's description of his conversion to communism (1951) describes how 'the whole universe [fell] into pattern like the stray pieces of a jigsaw assembled by magic at one stroke'. Later (1954) he analysed the conversion experience selecting what he calls the 'transference situation' in which a *guru* utilizes emotional investment in his role as proselytizer, a pattern Koestler finds common in both secular and religious conversion activity. Similarly, Ruitenbeek (1970) claims substantial elements in common in human experience of both revival meetings and marathon group therapy.

The conversion process in which individual identity is changed, whether in religious or secular settings, follows the same outline. Smelser's collective behaviour model posits a *negative* and a *re-generative* stage (1962) akin to Lofland and Stark's *predisposing* and *situational contingencies* (1965). Both approaches emphasize stress or strain which leads to seeking encounter with the agent or agency of change, resulting in a transformational pattern of behaviour with the convert now in the role of converter. However, if alternation or con- version is to be manifested it becomes so as the articulated and ordered arrangement of major constituents or roles in an interactional setting. To change an identity is to change the manner in which one sees oneself, one's reference group, and role-set. The 'facts' in the cultural milieu — mores, folkways, status-systems, sanction mechanisms — also change (Lewin and Grabbe, 1948). Whereas some (Brittan, 1973: 155) view commitment as an unnecessary concomitant of alternation others (Becker, 1960) see the two as closely connected although not neces- sarily by conscious decision. Affiliation, for Matza (1969), implies conscious commitment through choice: it is novel behaviour for the subject although already established for a number of others; what Brim and Wheeler term a serial process (1966: 60-61).

> The being who is converted is a subject. He engages his milieu and others in it, grapples with them, considers their beliefs, tries their style, anticipates or imagines the place he will have among them, and worries about whether choosing them will preclude others. Once engaged, he continues as subject, either building his commitment . . . or creating a distance between himself and the social role he occupies (Matza, 1969: 106).

To be in a state which some might describe as 'seeing the light' might be erroneously regarded as a choice between two possibilities. The first

> exploits the idea of *essence*: whatever it is that is becoming high is being altered *in itself*. The second possibility exploits the idea of *relation*: whatever is becoming high is being altered in context, in the place or standing occupied in a configuration; more simply, its alteration is *in something else* [Such a

choice is erroneous as] the two are equivalent because they are the two basic human perspectives on the very same thing and on everything (Matza, 1969: 127).

Thus Kuhn's 'neural programme' that he sees as underlying conversion (Kuhn, 1962: 204), Wittgenstein's contexual implications of seeing a duck-rabbit (Wittgenstein, 1953), Ryle's abrogation of a mental theatre of operations (Ryle, 1949) and the neurological and chemical changes occurring in the cortex, are synthesized in Matza's two possibilities of *essence* and *relation*.

Alternation or conversion takes place either within or towards a value-oriented setting. Such settings may be carriers of dominant or of deviant values and often such values may mesh badly with those of society at large. When they do, they are said to be uncomplementary and incongruent (Brim and Wheeler, 1966: 100). When the value-system espoused is generally acceptable then the settings

> act as catalysts and miniscule mirror images of the ideologies which are reflections of the formal catechism of society, while others are clearly performing a function of chism and differentiation at variance with the formal catechism . . . The belief systems to which individuals are converted do not exist in some disembodied state but are tangible in some organisation or group which are an integral part of the larger social system (Jones, 1977).

The process of sacralization, as Mol (1976) states, is enshrined within the dilemma of a permeating dialectic or dichotomy, weaving a difficult path between external and internal significations of fission and fusion, integration and disintegration, and conflict and harmony. Mol sees the mechanisms through which identity is sacralized, that is, objectification, commitment, ritual and myth, as instances of the specifically integrative contribution of religion to the 'fusion' aspect of the dialectic. Consequently, various nuances of contact occur between personal, group, and social identity along the levels of congruence and incongruence.

O'Dea (1966: 15) argues that by accepting the values of religion and a cosmological catechism individuals develop areas of their own understanding and self-definition. Furthermore, the ritualistic aspect enables them to enact particular elements in their own identity. During rapid social change and social mobility religion can function as an 'identity anchor'. However, it must be argued that the fragmentary nature of religious action begins by its location in 'this' world as opposed to the 'other'. We cannot say that religion 'supports' the social system as some religious systems advocate the destruction of both capital and consumer goods while others advocate a radical redistribution (Goode, 1973: 205). The support of some political and economic systems by some religious institutions is not a unitary phenomenon, but varies enormously. Dysfunctions of religion occur quite frequently (a) between different religious groups; (b) by ascription to differing values; and (c) by a conflict between religious and secular values. Religion not only reinforces the moral norms and prevailing sentiments of society but also instigates rebellion and canalizes behaviour towards the eventual modification of social structure. (The Marxists stress that religion does affect behaviour and that it has, as Weber held also, differential consequences for different social strata: Merton, 1968: 98.) Again, though, it is quite clear that religion affirms identity by regulating individual commitment (although such commitment is regulated also by secular agencies). Simmel (1955: 12) argued that man constructs religion out of his own experiences, selecting those aspects that enable unity to be maintained and, indeed, attained in the first instance.

The dialectic between integration and disintegration is, like all dialectics requiring choice between one process and another, merely a matter of taste (although a taste which is firmly rooted in our own sociological placenta). But the dilemma of the fragmentation of commitment to a belief system, whether secular or transcendental, remains, for it is embryonic to disintegration that there will emerge a separation of what is to be believed and not believed; a separation of what is henceforth to be regarded as pure and not pure; a separation of the saved from those who are not; and an erection of boundaries which will demarcate both cognitive and physical territories of interaction.

We have attempted to examine some of the implications of the term 'identity', concluding finally that it is firmly rooted in social interaction and manifested in role performance. Such role performance, taken in a 'motivational' context rather than a 'behavioural' one (Garfinkel, 1956), led us to the conclusion that 'identity' could embrace the 'ultimate grounds' for behaviour in addition to the behaviour itself, i.e. the motives or reasons for the behaviour — although this approach is open to several philosophical objections (White, 1967). Nevertheless, it does help us towards reconciling Wheelis's (1958: 200) definition with a sociological approach. Bellah's (1965: 173) approach, regarding identity as fixed and virtually unaltered, is thus rejected. Recognized in external performance and validated by action, identity tends to be less a concept which emphasizes its reflective nature than a social interactionist concept which flourishes in the human scene of cynicism and pretence.

The examples of various secular and transcendental settings, together with the Kuhnian thesis in the sociology of science, made us conclude that these overtly dissimilar settings were, in respect of organization and structure and by the very processes which they engendered, in fact similar; the adoption of new paradigms was a process common to that following the crisis in 'normal' science and also to other more obvious areas such as the conventional conversion setting. The sacralization of identity at a personal and a group level entailed, both in secular and transcendental settings, an elevation and transformation of those involved, and the emergence of ostensibly new beings.[10] The presence of commitment in the conversion process, defined as an emotionally heavy investment, was most likely to occur (Becker, 1960: Matza, 1969) although this view was not unanimous (Brittan, 1973). The presence of a firmly established belief system is common to both religious and secular sacralization processes (Jones, 1970, 1972, 1974, 1975) as is also an element of ritualization.[11] The possibility of both an incongruous and uncomplementary mesh between the values of settings and society at large merely emphasizes that such settings are an integral part of a larger social system. There is no static process at work here, as the element of social control by the social canopy can coerce groups, individuals, and settings holding incongruent ideologies, at the very worst modifying and changing them. Sometimes, but very rarely, various organizational and group ideologies have threatened the values of the social canopy and some modification has resulted in the latter. When this occurs it usually means that such ideology has become transformed into political action.

NOTES

1. For example, James (1902), Starbuck (1899), and Greeley (1975). Perhaps more has been done on the psychology rather than the sociology of conversion but psychological studies range from psychoanalytical fantasy such as Allison (1968, 1969) to work such as that of Salzman (1953). The former writes that, '... the conversion experience adaptively facilitates the emergence of an adolescent into adulthood by replacing a weak, ineffective or absent father ...' (Allison, 1969: 37).

2. See Sargant (1957), Berger (1966) and Berger and Luckman (1967). The term 'alternation' was probably first used by Berger (1966; 65): 'Instead of speaking of conversion (a term with religiously charged connotations) we would prefer to use the more neutral term of "alternation" to describe this phenomenon. The ... situation ... described brings with it the possibility that an individual may alternate back and forth between logically contradictory meaning systems'.

The social psychological view would suggest that the factors involved in identity change include transformations in knowledge structure, performance, attention deployment, and somatic processes, but other factors have been suggested such as a resulting reduction in dissonance arising from inconsistency between behaviour and belief, adoption of a new reference group, improvization of arguments, reinforcement of behaviour, and selective scanning of information (Lindzey and Aronson, 1969: 550-57). The social interaction perspective of identity theory maintains a constructional view of the nature of identity as being built up from a series of interactions. A social ecology of identity is concerned with the placement of the self within a concomitant network of social systems, and this enables us to place or locate the individual along a number of dimensions such as involvement, value, and status (Lindzey and Aronson, 1969: 551).

3. Examples of the term can be found in Swift (1969: 44-47) and Brim and Wheeler (1966: 56 ff.).

4. We could extend the notion of conversion in the sociology of medicine to that of assuming the role of the sick person. See Jones and Jones (1975) and Robinson (1971).

5. The notion of boundary is an important one. It is discussed in Homans (1951), Denzin (1970) and Krupp (1961).

6. A considerable amount of work has been done in examining the way in which paradigms are related to the structure of the scientific community. For example, Hagstrom (1965), Crane (1969, 1972), Price and Beaver (1966), and Barnes (1972, 1974). The debate between rational objectivists and their opponents can be found in works such as Hempel (1965), Popper (1956), Hanson (1958), Polanyi (1958), Feyerabend (1962, 1971), Scheffler (1967) and Quine (1953). A sustained attack on Popper can be found in Bartley, III (1968).

7. In addition to Wittgenstein (1953) see also Bartley, III (1974: 125-29), Wittgenstein (1966) and Hudson (1969: 36-51). For a philosophical development of the concept of identity see Hunter (1973). See also Williams (1973) especially

'Personal Identity and Individuation', pp. 1-18, and 'Bodily Continuity and Personal Identity', pp. 19-25.

8. See also White (1967) and Wood and Pitcher (1970).

9. See Urban (1971) and Jones (1977).

10. Mitchell (1973: 137) writes:

It is worth emphasising once again the extent to which problems which we tend to associate uniquely with religious belief arise also in a secular context; in particular those which have to do with the process of conversion and tension between faith and reason. Conversion from liberal democracy to Marxism or from humanism to naturalism . . . involves as radical a transformation as conversion to or from Christianity and is equally unlikely to occur as a result of a single argument or series of arguments; it involves, intellectually a massive shift in the overall appreciation and assessment of an immense range of facts and experiences and, with this, a new pattern of feeling and acting.

11. Four secular instances of a 'massive shift in the overall appreciation and assessment' merit inclusion. First, John Heilpern's interview with the artist Lowry in the *Observer Review,* 9 November 1975: 21:

The turning point in his life came when he was 22 and his family moved to the grime of Salford . . . For six years he disliked the area intensely. It was as if he suddenly awoke to a vision of life. 'I *saw* it,' he told me, lighting up again. 'I saw its beauty! I was with a man and he said, "Look!" ' And then I realised there was this wonderful subject I'd never seen before. I felt *compelled* to paint it . . .'.

Secondly, Patty Hearst's conversion to the self-styled Symbionese Liberation army may, if we analysed the transcripts, illuminate the area under discussion. *The Sunday Times* for 28 September 1975: 13 quotes from the affidavit:

All sorts of fantastic shapes and images kept coming and going before her eyes, so that the faces of the kidnappers and jailors appeared to her as weird and horrible masks . . . her mind became more distorted and confused . . . She finally came to the realisation that she was becoming insane.

Thirdly, Heilpern's interview with Artur Rubinstein, recorded in the *Observer Review*, 23 May 1976: 26, describes a crisis moment as follows:

Rubinstein left Warsaw for Paris, running out of money on the way. Stranded in a Berlin hotel, he decided to hang himself with his belt. But the belt broke and he crashed to the floor. He cried a little, comforting himself on the piano. Then he felt hungry, went out into the street – and discovered the world.

'I was born again! After you are dead you are born again. I looked at the world with completely new eyes and saw what a damned fool I'd been. It was a beautiful world, full of women, full of flowers . . . there was nothing to stop me from being happy. To be happy to live, whatever comes, whatever there is. I started to be happy from that moment on.'

Lastly, Russell's (1967: 220-21) description of his conversion to pacifism is pinpointed to a particular day in 1901 when he experienced a peculiarly mystical illumination:

> 'Suddenly the ground seemed to give way beneath me, and I found myself in quite another region ... At the end of those five minutes, I had become a completely different person. For a time, a sort of mystic illumination possessed me ... having been an imperialist, I became during those five minutes a pro-Boer and a pacifist.'

These quotations were included as note 46 in Jones (1977).

BIBLIOGRAPHY

ALLISON, J. (1968) 'Adaptive Regression and Intense Religious Experience', *Journal of Mental and Nervous Disease*, 145: 452-63.

——, (1969) 'Religious Conversion: Regression and Progression in an Adolescent Experience', *Journal for the Scientific Study of Religion*, 8 (1): 23-38.

BARNES, S. B. (1972) 'The Reception of Scientific Beliefs', in S. B. BARNES (ed.), *Sociology of Science*. Harmondsworth: Penguin.

——, (1974) *Scientific Knowledge and Sociological Theory*. London: Routledge & Kegan Paul.

BARTLEY, III, W. (1968) 'Theories of Demarcation Between Science and Metaphysics', in I. LAKATOS and A. MUSGRAVE (eds.), *Philosophy of Science*. Amsterdam: North-Holland, pp. 40-119.

——, (1974) *Wittgenstein*. London: Quartet Books.

BECKER, H. (1960) 'Notes on the Concept of Commitment', *American Journal of Sociology*, 66: 32-40.

BELLAH, R. N. (1965) 'Epilogue: Religion and Progress in Modern Asia', in R. N. BELLAH (ed.), *Religion and Progress in Modern Asia*. New York: Free Press, pp. 168-229.

BERGER, P. (1966) *Invitation to Sociology*, Harmondsworth: Penguin.

——, (1973) 'Identity as a Problem in the Sociology of Knowledge', in G. W. REMMLING (ed.), *Towards the Sociology of Knowledge*. London: Routledge & Kegan Paul, pp. 273-84.

——, and T. LUCKMAN (1967) *The Social Construction of Reality*. London: Allen Lane Penguin Press.

BIDWELL, C. E. (1962) 'Pre-Adult Socialisation'. Paper presented at the Social Science Research Council Conference on Socialization and Social Structure.

BRIM, O. G. and S. WHEELER (1966) *Socialisation After Childhood*. New York: John Wiley & Sons.

BRITTAN, A. (1973) *Meaning and Situations*. London: Routledge & Kegan Paul.

CRANE, D. (1969) 'Social Structure in a Group of Scientists: a Test of the Invisible College Hypothesis', *American Sociological Review*, 34: 335-52.

——, (1972) *Invisible Colleges*. Chicago: University of Chicago Press.

DAVIS, F. (1966) 'Professional Socialisation as Subjective Experience: The Process of Doctrinal Conversion Among Student Nurses', in H. S. BECKER, B. GEER, D. REISMAN and R. WEISS (eds.), *Institutions and the Person*. Chicago: Aldine.

DENZIN, N. (1970) 'Symbolic Interactionism and Ethnomethodology', in J. DOUGLAS (ed.), *Understanding Everyday Life*. London: Routledge & Kegan Paul.

FEYERABEND, P. K. (1962) 'Explanation, Reduction and Empiricism', in H. FEIGL and G. MAXWELL (eds.), *Minnesota Studies in the Philosophy of Science*, 3. Minnesota: University of Minnesota Press.

——, (1965) 'Problems of Empiricism', in R. COLODNY (ed.), *Beyond the Edge of Certainty*. Englewood Cliffs, New Jersey: Prentice-Hall.

——, (1971) 'Problems of Empiricism, Part 2', in R. COLODNY (ed.), *The Nature and Function of Scientific Theory*. Pittsburgh: University of Pittsburg Press.

FORT, C. (1923) *New Lands*. New York: Boni and Liveright.

——, (1974) *The Book of the Damned*. London: Abacus Books.

GAGNON, J. H. and W. SIMON (eds.), (1967) *Sexual Deviance*. New York: Harper & Row.

GARFINKEL, H. (1956) 'Conditions of Successful Degradation Ceremonies', *American Journal of Sociology*, 61: 420-32.

GOFFMAN, E. (1959) *The Presentation of Self in Everyday Life*. New York: Doubleday.

——, (1960) 'Characteristics in Total Institutions', in M. STEIN, A. J. VIDICH and D. MANNING (eds.) *Identity and Anxiety*. Glencoe, Illinois: Free Press, pp. 449-79.

——, (1961) *Asylums*. New York: Doubleday.

GOODE, W. J. (1973) *Explorations in Social Theory*. Oxford: Oxford University Press.

GREELEY, A. (1975) *Ecstacy – A Way of Knowing*. Englewood Cliffs, New Jersey: Prentice-Hall.

HAGSTROM, W. O. (1965) *The Scientific Community*. New York: Basic Books.

HANSON, N. R. (1958) *Patterns of Discovery*. Cambridge: Cambridge University Press.

HEILPERN, J. (1975) 'Lowry', *Observer Review*, November.

——, (1976) 'Rubinstein', *Observer Review*, May.

HEMPEL, C. (1965) *Aspects of Scientific Explanation*. Glencoe, Illinois: Free Press.

HOBSBAWN, E. J. (1959) *Primitive Rebels*. Manchester: Manchester University Press.

HOMANS, G. (1951) *The Human Group*. London: Routledge & Kegan Paul.

HUDSON, W. D. (1969) 'Some Remarks on Wittgenstein's Account of Religious Belief', in *Talk of God*. London: Macmillan, pp. 36-51.

HUGHES, E. (1958) *Men and Their Work*. Glencoe, Illinois: Free Press.

HUMPHREYS, L. (1970) *Tearoom Trade: Impersonal Sex in Public Places*. Chicago: Aldine.

HUNTER, J. F. M. (1973) *Essays After Wittgenstein*. London: Allen and Unwin.

JAMES, W. (1902) *The Varieties of Religious Experience*. New York: Longman.

JONES, R. K. (1970) 'Sectarian Characteristics of Alcoholics Anonymous', *Sociology*, 4 (2): 183-95.

——, (1972) 'The Catholic Apostolic Church: a Study in Diffused Commitment', in M. HILL (ed.), *A Sociological Yearbook of Religion in Britain*, 5. London: SCM Press.

——, (1974) 'The Swedenborgians, a Case of New Wine and Old Bottles: An Interactionist Analysis', in M. HILL (ed.), *A Sociological Yearbook of Religion in Britain*, 7. London: SCM Press.

——, (1975) 'Some Sectarian Characteristics of Therapeutic Groups with Special Reference to Recovery, Inc. and Neurotics Nomine', in R. WALLIS (ed.), *Sectarianism: Analyses of Religious and Non-Religious Sects*. London: Peter Owen.

——, (1977) 'Some Epistemological Considerations of Paradigm Shifts: Basic Steps Towards a Formulated Model of Alternation', *Sociological Review*, 25: 253-71.

——, and P. JONES (1975) *Sociology in Medicine*. London: University of London Press.

KOESTLER, A. (1951) *The God that Failed*. London: Hamish Hamilton.

——, (1954) *Arrow in the Blue*. London: William Collins.

KRUPP, S, (1961) *Pattern in Organisational Analysis*. New York: Holt, Rinehart and Winston.

KUHN, T. (1962) *The Structure of Scientific Revolution*. Chicago: University of Chicago Press. 1970.

——, (1963) 'The Function of Dogma in Scientific Research', in A. C. CROMBIE (ed.), *Scientific Change*. London: Heinemann.

LAKATOS, I. (1968) 'Criticism and the Methodology of Scientific Research Programmes', *Proceedings of the Aristotelian Society*, 69: 149-86.

——, and A. MUSGRAVE (1970) *Criticism and the Growth of Knowledge*. Cambridge: Cambridge University Press.

LEWIN, K. and P. GRABBE (1948) 'Conduct, Knowledge and Acceptance of New Values', in G. W. LEWIN (ed.) *Resolving Social Conflicts*. New York: Harper & Row, pp. 56-68.

LINDZEY, G. and E. ARONSON (1969) *Handbook of Social Psychology*, 3. Reading, Mass.: Addison Wesley.

LOFLAND, J. and R. STARK (1965) 'Becoming a World-Saver: a Theory of Conversion to a Deviant Perspective', *American Sociological Review*, 30 (6): 863-75.

MASTERMAN, M. (1970) 'The Nature of a Paradigm', in I. LAKATOS and A. MUSGRAVE (eds.), *Criticism and the Growth of Knowledge*. Cambridge: Cambridge University Press.

MATZA, D. (1969) *Becoming Deviant*. Englewood Cliffs, New Jersey: Prentice-Hall.

McCALL, G. J. and J. L. SIMMONS (1966) *Identities and Interactions*. New York: Free Press.

McHUGH, P. (1966) Paper delivered at the American Sociological Association, 1964. Appearing in O. BRIM and S. WHEELER (eds.), *Socialisation After Childhood*. New York: John Wiley & Sons, p. 116.

MERTON, R. K. (1968) *Social Theory and Social Structure*. New York: Free Press.

MITCHELL, B. (1973) *The Justification of Religious Belief*. London: Macmillan.

MOL, H. (1976) *Identity and the Sacred*. Oxford: Blackwell.

O'DEA, T. (1966) *The Sociology of Religion*. Englewood Cliffs, New Jersey: Prentice-Hall.

PARSONS, T. (1968) 'The Position of Identity in the General Theory of Action', in C. GORDON and K. J. GEGEN, (eds.), *The Self in Social Interaction*. New York: John Wiley & Sons.

−−, and E. SHILS (1951) *Toward a General Theory of Action*. Cambridge, Mass.: Harvard University Press.

POLANYI, M. (1958) *Personal Knowledge*. Chicago: University of Chicago Press.

POPPER, K. (1966) *The Logic of Scientific Discovery*. London: Routledge & Kegan Paul.

PRICE, D. J. and D. de BEAVER (1966) 'Collaboration in an Invisible College', *American Psychologist*, 21: 1011-18.

QUINE, W. V. (1953) *From a Logical Point of View*. Harvard: Harvard University Press.

ROBINSON, D. (1971) *The Process of Becoming Ill*. London: Routledge & Kegan Paul.

RUITENBEEK, H. (1970) *The New Group Therapies*. New York: Discuss Books.

RUSSELL, B. (1967) *Autobiography*, 1. London: Allen and Unwin.

RYLE, G. (1949) *The Concept of Mind*. London: Hutchinson

SALZMAN, L. (1953) 'The Psychology of Religious and Ideological Conversion', *Psychiatry*, 16: 177-87.

SARGANT, W. (1957) *Battle for the Mind*. London: Pan Books.

SCHEFFLER, I. (1967) *Science and Subjectivity*. New York: Bobbs-Merrill.

SCHUTZ, A. (1953) 'Common Sense and Scientific Interpretation of Human Action', *Philosophy and Phenomenological Research*, 14 (1): 3-47.

SHELLY, J. A. and A. BASSIN (1965) 'Daytop Lodge − A New Treatment Approach for Drug Addicts', *Corrective Psychiatry*, XI: 186-95.

SIMMEL, G. (1955) 'A Contribution to the Sociology of Religion', *American Journal of Sociology*, 60, May: 1-150.

SLATER, P. E. (1968) 'Religious Processes in the Training Group', in D. R. CUTLER (ed.), *The Religious Situation*. Boston: Beacon Press.

SMELSER, N. (1962) *Theory of Collective Behaviour*. London: Routledge & Kegan Paul.

STARBUCK, E. D. (1899) *The Psychology of Religion*. London: Walter Scott.

STONE, G. H. W. (1970) *Social Psychology Through Symbolic Interaction.* Massachusetts: Xerox College.

SUGARMAN, B. (1967) 'Daytop Village: a Drug Cure Co-Operative', *New Society*, April: 526-29.

――, (1968) *Daytop* (unpublished manuscript).

――, (1974) *Daytop Village: A Therapeutic Community.* New York: Holt, Rinehart and Winston.

――, (1975) 'Reluctant Converts: Social Control, Socialisation and Adaption in Therapeutic Communities' in R. WALLIS (ed.), *Sectarianism: Analyses of Religious and Non-Religious Sects.* London: Peter Owen.

SWIFT, D. F. (1969) *Sociology of Education.* London: Routledge & Kegan Paul.

TIEBOUT, H. (1949) 'The Act of Surrender in the Therapeutic Process with Special Reference to Alcoholism', *Quarterly Journal for the Study of Alcoholism*, 10: 48-58.

――, H. (1961) 'Alcoholics Anonymous: an Experiment of Nature', *Quarterly Journal for the Study of Alcoholism*, 22: 52-68.

TOULMIN, S. (1970) 'Does the Distinction Between Normal and Revolutionary Science Hold Water', in I. LAKATOS and A. MUSGRAVE (eds.), *Criticism and the Growth of Knowledge.* Cambridge: Cambridge University Press.

URBAN, G. (1971) *The Miracles of Chairman Mao.* London: Tom Stacey.

VOLKMAN, R. and D. R. CRESSEY (1963) 'Rehabilitation of Drug Addicts', *American Journal of Sociology*, 69: 129-43.

WARNOCK, G. J. (1958) *English Philosophy Since 1900.* Oxford: Oxford University Press.

WARREN, C. A. B. (1973) *Identity and Community in the Gay World.* New York: John Wiley & Sons.

WATKINS, J. W. N. (1970) 'Against "Normal" Science', in I. LAKATOS and A. MUSGRAVE (eds.), *Criticism and the Growth of Knowledge.* Cambridge: Cambridge University Press.

WHEELER, S. (1966) 'The Structure of Formally Organised Socialisation Settings', in O. BRIM and S. WHEELER (eds.), *Socialisation After Childhood.* New York: John Wiley & Sons.

WHEELIS, A. (1958) *The Quest for Identity.* New York: Norton.

WHITE, A. (1967) *The Philosophy of Mind.* New York: Random House.

WILLIAMS, B. (1973) *Problems of the Self.* Cambridge: Cambridge University Press.

WITTGENSTEIN, L. (1953) *Philosophical Investigations.* Oxford: Blackwell.

――, (1966) *Lectures and Conversations on Aesthetics, Psychology and Religious Belief.* Oxford: Blackwell.

WOOD, O. P. and G. PITCHER (1970) *Ryle: A Collection of Critical Essays.* New York: Doubleday.

4

IDENTITY AND COMMITMENT

Bert L. Hardin and Guenter Kehrer
University of Tübingen, West Germany

Hardin and Kehrer interpret their research on the small German branch of the World Unification Church (Rev. and Mrs Sun Myung Moon) in terms of its identity provision for individuals. They look upon the sect's demand for total commitment not as a means for strengthening group identity, but as a heaven for lonely individuals. Consequently, ritual and objectification are less relevant than commitment and belief system. Although they provide good evidence for commitment being prior to belief, they follow Borhek and Curtis in stressing the importance of the belief system and treat it as synonymous with identity (a person is what he believes). As a result, conversion is thought of in terms of a cognitive changeover rather than an emotional stripping and welding.

This paper does not pretend to put forth a complete theory of either identity or commitment. Instead, the aim is to describe, with the aid of some of the concepts now in vogue in the sociology of religion, a sect which has been active in Germany for several years. Because of the nature of this symposium particular emphasis will be given to the concept of identity, but we reserve the right to bring in other concepts which may or may not prove to complement the 'identity theory' put forth by Professor Mol. The religious group which we observed has also been studied in the United States (Lofland, 1966). It is one in which total commitment is a prerequisite for protracted membership. As Howard Becker said almost two decades ago, the concept of commitment has received ever-increasing attention and often is used to cover a diverse number of phenomena (Becker, 1960). This may still be the case in our study, but at least we will limit our comments to situations where total commitment is necessary.

BELIEF – IDENTITY – COMMITMENT

A positive identity, as presented by Mol, is reinforced by a sacralizing process which, in turn, has four basic components: (1) objectification; (2) commitment; (3) ritual; and (4) myth or belief system. We wish to take no basic issue with this choice of components. Rather, we wish to concentrate on just two of these. It seems to us that the four components are not equally important for shaping an identity or effecting a conversion from one identity to another. Instead, we feel that the components' *belief system* and *commitment* deserve special attention.

These two components, as used in this chapter, borrow heavily from Borhek and Curtis (1975), but in several respects we have added our own interpretations. Of course Borhek and Curtis had no expressed interest in making contributions toward an 'identity theory'. Rather, they were concerned with the development of a theory of belief systems.

Their definition (Borhek and Curtis, 1975: 5) is as follows: 'a belief system is a set of related ideas (learned and shared), which has some permanence, and to which individuals and/or groups exhibit some commitment'. Belief systems have an existence independent of the individual and are tied to some social carrier. Furthermore, one can say that belief systems provide the answers to the age-old questions of Who am I? What am I? and Why am I? They can be empirical or non-empirical, sacred or secular, this-worldly or other-worldly, and they provide the basis for social action. One could suppose that if the level of commitment were great enough they might be considered to be sacralized in Mol's sense of the term.

The concept of belief system as used by Borhek and Curtis is rather complex and includes the following elements (all of which need not be present):

(1) values (used in the commonly accepted sociological sense);

(2) criteria of validity (the means a believer is to use to determine the validity of any particular statement);

(3) logic – 'the rules which relate one substantive belief to another within the belief system';

(4) perspective (usually how one group of believers see themselves as differing from, or relating to, others);

(5) substantive beliefs (e.g. Jesus Lives!);

(6) prescriptions and proscriptions (in the sociological sense of norms); and

(7) technology — 'associated beliefs concerning means to attain valued goals'.

Their theoretical model deals neither with the believer nor with the validity of various beliefs, but rather with 'how humans come to be so firmly attached to [beliefs] and how that attachment functions in social organisations'. We feel that, viewed in this light, belief systems may be seen as the cognitive aspects of identity.

Going a step further one may say that commitment includes at least two components: (1) action, or perhaps better stated, investment — either of time, energy, or emotion; and (2) the valuation of the investment. Thus, we can say that the degree of commitment may be viewed as the amount of personal identity ascribed to a given belief system. This is in line with what Mol says of commitment as being the '. . . focused emotion or emotional attachment to a specific focus of identity' (Mol, 1976: 216). In other words, one way of viewing identity is to think of it as consisting of a particular belief system and the mechanisms the individual has for maintaining the belief system. To us the major factor involved in acceptance and maintenance is commitment. Very simply stated, our model is as follows:

(1) there are any numbers of belief systems to which a person can be committed;

(2) each system has its own requirements for commitment (Borhek and Curtis, 1975);

(3) in Kornhauser's terms 'to incur a commitment is to become more or less unavailable for alternative lines of action' (Kornhauser 1962: 321);

(4) the social carrier, i.e. the individuals, group, or organization of the belief system, provides the focus of identity for the individual convert;

(5) at any one stage commitment may be more important than the substantive beliefs;

(6) the totally committed person has little identity other than the belief system to which he is committed; and

(7) whether in Festinger's terms of cognitive dissonance (Festinger, 1957), or in Homans's terms of investment and cost (Homans, 1961),

or in Becker's terms of a side-bet (Becker, 1960), once certain actions have taken place certain others must follow and these actions must be validated. This could be argued for in terms other than those of symbolic interactionism if there were time.

In the case we have studied it is not the elite leaders through socialization (Keniston 1968; Kalberg 1975) but rather the ordinary individuals through structural conduciveness (Smelser 1962) or through Kornhauser's 'force of circumstances' who provide the impetus for the initial commitment. Unlike Lofland, who studied the same group earlier in America (Lofland and Stark, 1965; Lofland, 1966), we find that his seven factors for conversion provide an inadequate explanation for the membership in Germany, although his funnel model is useful.[1] For example, we feel that 'seekership' in Lofland's sense does not exist. Although we do not have the hard data to prove it, we hypothesize that the factor of commitment is so important that the particular belief system becomes secondary. In a sense, ideas-values follow actions once the initial stage has been set. This is not meant to deny the existence of goal-oriented actions, but rather to emphasize that a person may well become a member of a sect and adopt a particular belief system (or shape an identity) without this being the result of goal-directed behaviour. Mol's factor of ritual exists, but only as a supporting mechanism for commitment.

The relationship between commitment and identity can be illustrated by the following hypothetical example of political participation. Since beliefs are tied to social carriers and the latter provide the focus of identity, and since beliefs validate commitment, one may assume that the degree of commitment decreases as the focus moves from self to a group to total society. This is because the specific content of the beliefs becomes 'watered-down' and the focus of identity more diffuse, and because commitment is related to action and interaction. Thus, if we take an individual with a high amount of commitment to political participation, we may assume that his identity is related to a local party organization rather than to the total national political system. This is because there is little opportunity for activity in relation to the carrier, 'total society'. This activity can only be displayed on the group level in a local party organization.

Local party identification becomes more important to the involved individual. This identification serves the interests of the carrier, 'total society', which does not define what political commitment is (other than in very general terms), and offers, generally speaking, only the opportunity to act during the occasional elections. On the party level, if this carrier has a belief system which requires little commitment (national party) our highly committed individual may well move into a leadership position. On the other hand, if a belief system requires a high amount of commitment (e.g. a radical party in Western societies) the same activity may be only adequate for membership. A belief system requiring total commitment can only have a limited membership because of the mechanisms required for the maintenance of the belief system. Total commitment, as we view it, would mean total identification with a smaller carrier and limits the possibility of identification with the total society. This can result in isolation, on the one side, and ostracism, on the other. It would mean that at the least the membership of this group would be non-integrative, and at the most, conflict-producing (see the example cited by Mol (1976) where religious participation in Africa seems to work counter to the goals of forming a new national identity). Since the believer sees individual beliefs as part of a total system, and since many beliefs are so widely accepted (sacralized) that they can be found in almost any belief system (e.g. humanism, democracy, and freedom) most partial identities (such as a Christian, an American, a Democrat) may be seen by the individual as a whole (each of these requires little commitment). On the other hand, a belief system like that of the World Unification Church requires what seems to approach total commitment. The amount of personal identification left over for other foci of identity is minimal. Toleration of the group by the society is based on commonly shared beliefs (religion, peace, good works, etc.), but conflicts with other areas because of the almost total denial of the existence of other identities. We will attempt to make this clear by taking a closer look at the World Unification Church in Germany.

THE WORLD UNIFICATION CHURCH

The Unification Church, founded by Reverend Sun Myung Moon, has received widespread publicity in German newspapers and been the subject of extensive discussion by officials of the major established churches in Germany. The publicity did not deal with religious issues, but almost entirely with the forms of commitment required by the Unification Church and with the methods of proselytizing. The aim of the Unification Church is to build a new identity for the proselytized member. This aim must be attained within the conditions of religious life in Germany, which obviously differs from the religious 'scene' in the United States. The material from which we draw our conclusions was gathered during a participant observation study in 1972 and 1973.

In the German established churches committed membership is confined to a minority of the population. Although more than 90 percent of the population are members of the Protestant or Catholic Church, only 1-5 percent regularly attend church. Committed membership in small religious bodies appears to the German as deviant. In this situation there was little opportunity for the first missionaries of the Unification Church to proselytize within existing religious groups. The first missionaries for Moon came from the United States, and even they were native Germans. It was perhaps because of this fact that they did not try to repeat the strategy of proselytizing which they had used in America (Lofland, 1966).

Religious themes are not part of normal communication in Germany. The religious 'seeker' who is always looking for religious novelties can hardly be found in German society. Therefore, the missionaries of the Unification Church had to search for members among the religiously uncommitted. Although the German religious situation is different, we think that our remarks concerning the interdependence of commitment, belief system, and identity are of equal theoretical relevance. Hans Mol points out that identity tends to become sacralized (Mol, 1976). This process of sacralization takes place in every form of identity building. It can be observed when identity is rebuilt in the proselytizing process. The World Unification Church provides a good example for the interdependence of commitment, belief system, and identity, because it has to manage problems of identity-building under conditions which are in some respects extraordinary in German society.

For the well-socialized religious person commitment is the normal consequence of strong faith in the belief system of the group. As Borhek and Curtis have shown, there are rather plausible reasons for assuming that there might be an inverse process, i.e. people may believe because they become committed (Borhek and Curtis, 1975). We do not deny that particular requirements of the belief system will produce particular forms of commitment, yet commitment can also be a prerequisite for acceptance of the belief system. Portions of the belief system consist of what can be called the results of objectification (Mol, 1976). These objectifications are necessary conditions for reinforcement of commitment, though they need not be starting points of commitment at all.

The Unification Church crystallizes the identity of the group's members around the foci: the 'Parents' (Rev. and Mrs Moon), the Church, and Korea. These foci of identity do not only play a role as objects of sacralization, but require active commitment of the group's members. As a religious group the Unification Church possesses a rather elaborated theology linking the foci of identity. This theology is fixed on the basic assumptions, but can be altered in detail as the several editions of the 'Divine Principles' clearly show. The Church does not teach a genuine Doomsday theology yet insists that the final struggle between Good and Evil will occur in this world. For this purpose the forces of Good must be gathered; the Church is the leading power in this process of gathering the positive elements in the world. Thus, proselytizing is the most important job for the average member. We shall consider this point below. For the purpose of this chapter it is important to know that the official doctrine of the Church stresses the fact that commitment can only follow from understanding the truth of the 'Divine Principles'. The missionaries refuse to give rules of life even when the person who is a possible proselyte asks for them.

H.: You want to know how to live. Nobody can tell you. You must try to understand the Principles, later on everything becomes evident. We have complete liberty (in the Church), but everybody who understands the Principles knows what he has to do.

In fact, no one will be able to deduce from the 'Principles' the rigorous rules for conduct even when these rules are compatible with the doctrine of the 'Principles'. Even persons who have been members for many years stress in conversation that they do not understand everything of the doctrine. They know that they are on the right path and in following this path they will understand more and more (see also

Lofland, 1966). Mere cognitive acceptance of the doctrine is insufficient; to become a follower of the truth one must become a
committed follower. This is the crucial point in the proselytizing
process. Unlike the established churches in Germany and most of the
smaller religious denominations, the Unification Church requires total
commitment and not just acceptance of a particular belief system.
Total commitment means that the member must centre his entire life
on the requirements of the Church. And so jobs and families may have
to be abandoned. All foci of identity that were previously taken for
granted must lose their claim. The new member must orient himself to
the new foci of identity.

Our observations and reconstructions of members' lives showed that
conversion is not the necessary condition for the process of building a
new identity around the foci of the Church. Since the aim of the
proselytizing process is the totally committed member, the amount of
time the possible member is spending in the group and with group
activities is a valid indicator of success. The amount of time spent is not
a result of sudden or slow conversion, but depends on variables which
have little to do with cognitive acceptance of the group's doctrine.
Measurement of different degrees of committed time may be possible,
but unfortunately we do not have the hard data. One can view the
process of committing more and more time to the group's activities as a
form of resocialization. Normally there is little re-socialization to be
done, because the potential member of a religious group requiring total
commitment is a person of diverse commitments. The case of an
individual leaving one high-commitment group for another high-
commitment group is not under discussion here. We certainly did not
find any in the German group. In everyday life a person is committed
to those foci of identity that are taken for granted by the dominant
culture. Families, clubs, and professions can be considered as such.
They use up a great deal of the time of the well-socialized individual.
Potential members of a high-commitment group seem to be individuals
in whose identity some of these elements are missing. This leads to
considerable amounts of 'idle' time. 'Idle' time means time not structured by any active commitment. In other words, the lonely person. In
the literature, lonely persons were shown to have a great affinity to
religious groups requiring high commitment (Borhek and Curtis, 1975,
Lofland, 1966). The life histories we could obtain of members of the

Unification Church show that these people had great amounts of uncommitted time just before becoming a sect member.

> G. was a decorator. She worked in West-Berlin. Her parents lived in a small town in the Federal Republic. G. could not find an appartment in Berlin and lived for several weeks in a small hotel. She had no contact with colleagues outside her working schedule. She spent every evening alone. In this situation she met two missionaries of the Unification Church. G. followed the invitation into the Berlin mission centre and spent every evening there. After a week she left the hotel to live in the mission centre.

Fortuitous events are often responsible for the initial commitment to a deviant group. With time and increased commitment a new identity begins to emerge. If the new member is afraid of losing the developing identity, he or she must be prepared to learn something about the belief system which validates the commitment.

Commitment has to do with emotional attachment to something, but to use the conception only in Mol's sense would mean to exclude social action. The difference with Mol's definition lies only in paying less attention to the objectifications to which commitment is attached, but we prefer the opinion that commitment in any way needs social carriers functioning as foci of identity.

That conversion is nearly always experienced within a group, or that no true believer can stand alone, fits this view well. *Unus christianus nullus christianus* was an expression in the first centuries of Christianity. The dominant factor in building a new identity is the group, though of course the group's belief system is important for the validation of commitment and consequently for the forms of commitment. The proselytized member of a religious group is in no position to affect the belief system which all members have in common. This does not mean that the belief system is the cause for emotional attachment. Emotional attachment is rather to the group that holds this belief system fortuitously. The belief system legitimizes the attachment to the group. The more committed a person becomes, the more elaborated the belief system will be that links the foci of identity. The sectarian personality is characterized by attachment to one primary focus of identity to which the minor foci of identity are subordinated. This is the reason why religious groups requiring high commitment dislike interdenominational marriages. In a belief system that subordinates the various foci of identity to one primary focus the degree of *system consistency* tends to be rather high (Borhek and Curtis). There is a correlation between the degree of *system consistency*, as we used it, and the degree of required commitment.

Our observations showed that strength of commitment to the Unification Church correlated with 'higher' foci of identity. They were never cognitive, but always represented persons and groups with significant meaning within the Church. Thus the foci of identity typically build a hierarchy immune to arbitrary alteration. The first focus of identity is the local mission centre, i.e. the members of this centre. This group is normally small (three or four persons). Commitment to this group can be shown in the time being spent with this group. The individual to be proselytized is expected to spend every evening in the centre studying the 'Divine Principles'. If the members of the centre are successful in motivating an individual to spend every evening with them, competing commitments will be rendered innocuous. Since the staff of the centre functions for the new member as 'significant others', he begins to identify with them rather than with the unknown doctrinal quantity. Commitment in this first phase of becoming a sect member is superficially compatible with the situation of the average member of German society. The member may be working at his job during the day and may be slowly losing contact with friends, although in most cases there has been little contact with friends in the first place. A crucial stage in the proselytizing process is reached when the new member is prepared to accept that the Church requires a stronger commitment. This stage is marked by the recognition of Rev. Moon as Messiah. The hints of this are hidden in the 'Divine Principles' and the new member has to find it out by himself, but he is aided by the older members. It is a common strategy of the mission of the Unification Church that the all-deciding fact does not stand at the beginning of the mission but marks the end of the first phase. When asked why they do not openly speak about a fact of greatest importance there is always one answer:

> D.: We cannot tell the people in the street: 'listen, the messiah is on earth.' People would think that we are crazy. Everybody has to find out for himself what the truth is. We can only help.

This answer contains a well-calculated strategy adjusted to the specific German situation. Yet this strategy is not malevolent but typical for every proselytizing process which aims at building a new identity. In the first phase there must be commitment to a small group. The next phase will be to know what belief system the group has for its validation. Only in cases where the potential member is a genuine religious 'seeker' can the cognitive element be the first word, but this situation is extremely rare in Germany. Recognition of Rev. Moon as Messiah means a shift in the focus and locus of identity. The new member is expected to spend a weekend within the major German mission centre which is also the headquarters for the German branch of the Church. This weekend is the crucial period for joining or not joining the sect.

In the first phase of proselytizing, the possible new member is a sectarian only in his spare time. In the major mission centre with about fifty full-time members everybody expects the newcomer to spend several weeks in learning and training. In order to fulfil these expectations the member must quit his job, and break the contacts with his family. Since the members of the local mission centre, where the newcomer has had the first contacts with the Church, are normally not part of the major mission centre, the proselyte has to change the carrier, i.e. the focus of identity. In this phase of proselytizing the Church as a whole functions as focus of identity, but this focus is personalized in the German leader of the Church who is the representative of Rev. Moon for Germany. All actions are oriented towards his person. The training programme in the centre aims at inculcating the new member with the doctrines of the Church and at subordinating all activities to the Church's doctrine as formulated by the leader of the German branch. The member must be ready to 'surrender to a higher, eternal power' (James, 1902: 108). The surrender is in fact to a higher, eternal power, yet not to ideas about eternity, or God, or anything else, but to the group. In this sense, Durkheim's (1912) view of religion is validated by our observations. Faith in the Church's doctrine is the consequence of surrender to the group, rather than surrender to the group being the consequence of faith in the group's doctrine.

Since the Unification Church does not want commitment in a verbal sense, but insists on active commitment, it is able to manage the problem of hypocrisy from the beginning (Mol, 1976: 216-17). As Lofland shows, it was one of the crucial problems of the first American followers of Rev. Moon to distinguish between true proselytes and hypocrites. The German followers have solved this problem very efficiently. Only those who are willing to commit themselves entirely belong to the Church. Though the process of total commitment is not sudden, but takes place in several phases, the most important step (in the major mission centre) requires commitment *before* learning the essentials about the Church's doctrine.

Every observer who manages to come into the major mission centre is surprised that more stress is laid on activity than on doctrine. Commitment is more to activity than to faith. The primary goal is proselytizing. The 'higher' foci of identity, i.e. Rev. and Mrs Moon, the Church (in a nearly universal dimension), and Korea (as the place where the final struggle between Good and Evil will take place), legitimize the active proselytizing and excuse the failure to do so efficiently. The results of the proselytizing work of the German branch compare quite favourably with other small sects in Germany. Since 1970 the group has tripled the membership, although the total number is still below a thousand. For the average member it is a very common experience to fail to win even one member per year for the cause. Thus, there must be frustration. The belief system has a two-fold function for the average member: it legitimizes the necessity of doing the proselytizing work and it helps to manage the failure to do so successfully. There are two major strategies in the management of failure for politically or religiously deviant groups, as follows.

(a) Having no success is to be expected. In this world success is impossible. But the truth will be revealed one day, and then the small number now will be the first men and women in the new era. 'The last shall be first and the first shall be last'.

(b) There is no success here and now, but success will come at a definite time in the future or success has already occurred in another place where mission work is being done. We have to work harder in order to have the same success.

Since the Unification Church does not teach a genuine Doomsday theology there is no possibility of relating the experience of success to the Final Judgement. But it is interesting to see that elements of strategy (a) can be found among the members.

> H.: Nowadays the Master knows the names of everyone of his followers. But when the whole world knows that He is the master and the Messiah, everybody will come to him. Then he will not be able to know everybody, but we, the first followers, will be known to him.

Remarks of this kind are, however, of minor significance for the group members. Strategy (b) is more often found in conversations. The theology of the Church is not very definite about the time when the final struggle between Good and Evil will occur, which incidentally is a change from the original teachings (Lofland, 1966). Though it will occur within the near future, there are ways open to postpone the date. Predictions about success within a definite time are therefore not available for the management of failure. The way is open, however, for belief in success in other parts of the world. In this context Korea has a key function, and in some smaller degree the United States. Since Korea is the localized focus of identity as the country where the Messiah is coming from and as the place where the final struggle will take place, it must be the place where success is of crucial importance. The average member does not have exact figures about the Church's strength in Korea or in the United States, but he 'knows' that in these places the Church is an important factor in societal and cultural life. He has little knowledge of the work done in Korea, but he 'knows' that important work is done there. This attitude can be compared to the faith of committed Maoists in Western societies who have never had the opportunity to see China but hold the strong belief that in China their ideas about the nature of men and society are the motor of politics and economics.

When the member is willing to proselytize on a full-time basis or to accept a job arranged by the Church, to which all other activities are subordinated, he has reached a point of no return. The only way back will lose him his identity. Since commitment is only to the Church and not divided into a lot of disparate foci, there is no chance of breaking up the identity by strengthening one minor focus of identity. A sectarian of this type could possibly change to another high-commitment group, but this possibility rarely exists in Germany.

We have shown that there is a hierarchy of foci of identity for the group's members. Though the highest foci are on a nearly universal level this does not lead to a 'watering-down' of commitment. We think that the reason for this is to be found in the fact that even the highest foci on a nearly universal level (Rev. Moon and Korea) are linked to carriers which allow intimate interaction. Sects, parties, etc. which require total commitment and do not succeed in building strong groups on a local basis are not able to have members who sustain a high level of commitment over any period of time. This may be true despite the degree of commitment which is deduced from the sect's or parties' belief system.

NOTE

1. Lofland's seven factors are: tension; type of problem-solving perspective; seekership; the turning point; cult affective bonds; extra-cult affective bonds; and intensive interaction (Lofland and Stark, 1965).

REFERENCES

BECKER, Howard S. (1960) 'Notes on the Concept of Commitment', *American Journal of Sociology*, 66: 32-40.
BORHEK, James T. and Richard F. CURTIS (1975) *A Sociology of Belief*. New York: John Wiley & Sons.
DURKHEIM, Emile (1912) *Les Formes Elémentaires de la Vie Religieuse. Le Système Totémique en Australie*. Paris: Alcan.
FESTINGER, Leon (1957) *A Theory of Cognitive Dissonance*. Stanford: Stanford University Press.
HOMANS, George C. (1961) *Social Behavior: Its Elementary Forms*. New York: Harcourt, Brace & World.
JAMES, William (1902) *The Varieties of Religious Experience*. New York: Modern Library.
KALBERG, Stephen (1975) 'The Commitment to Career Reform: The Settlement Movement Leaders', *The Social Service Review*, 49 (4): 608-28.
KENISTON, Kenneth (1968) *Young Radicals*. New York: Harcourt, Brace & World.
KORNHAUSER, William (1962) 'Social Bases of Political Commitment: A Study of Liberals and Radicals', in Arnold M. ROSE (ed.), *Human Behavior and Social Processes*. Boston: Houghton Mifflin.
LOFLAND, John and Rodney STARK (1965) 'Becoming a World-Saver: A Theory of Conversion to a Deviant Perspective', *American Sociological Review*, 30: 862-75.
LOFLAND, John (1966) *Doomsday Cult: A Study of Conversion, Proselytization, and Maintenance of Faith*. Englewood Cliffs, New Jersey: Prentice-Hall.
MOL, Hans (1976) *Identity and the Sacred*. Oxford: Basil Blackwell.
SMELSER, Neil, J. (1962) *Theory of Collective Behavior*. London: Routledge & Kegan Paul.

5

CRISIS, IDENTITY, AND INTEGRATION IN AFRICAN RELIGION

Max Assimeng
University of Ghana, Legon, Ghana

As can be expected, Assimeng is particularly interested in the religious provision of a stable meaning system at times of change in Africa. There are the crises of sickness and death, natural disasters, birth, but above all, modernization. Religion puts these crises in a larger perspective and thereby restores personal identity. He finds that on the group level tribes are no longer capable of moral regeneration, in contrast with the sects which he sees as modernized versions of tribal groupings. On the national level, the author cites the instances of the Convention People's Party of Ghana and the United National Independence Party of Zambia becoming objects of worship, or the association of the nation with deity.

RELIGION AND THE SENSE OF IDENTITY

Although there are several senses in which the nature and function of religion may be analyzed, it seems that perhaps the intrinsic role of religion, in maintaining identity and integration in the face of perceived chaos, disorder, and fear, has been taken for granted for a long time. Probably because this identity-integration nature of religion appears obvious, analyzing religion as an institution with such perspectives has perhaps not been given much conceptual clarification and theoretical underpinning.

In Africa, revivalist developments in religious behaviour since the days of intensive white contact have been seen principally as a response to acculturation and the search for cultural and psychological renewal.

Yet 'identity' as an analytical tool has not been specifically operation-alized and used as a central interpretative hypothesis or paradigm in studying such phenomena.

Among other things, this chapter discusses aspects of the content of belief and ritual practice as these are experienced by traditional persons undergoing social and cultural transformation. It is hoped that the features of religious life that obtain for individuals in such circum-stances may be typical for religiousness in a number of African social and religious systems. Furthermore, it is hoped that such differences as may be encountered elsewhere in black Africa may be in *form* rather than in *substance*. In such a discussion it is essential that stress be laid on the traditional, the changing, and the contemporary religious beliefs and practices; what should also be emphasized are the dynamics of interaction of individuals and social groups with the changing belief systems attendant upon changing social realities. It is thought that the items so chosen for discussion would help to highlight the extent to which religion could be discussed from the point of view of man's perennial search for selfhood, and for identity with time and space.

Identity as a concept that relates to religious behaviour may be analysed from the following perspectives: identity may be conceived as 'soul-seeking' that animates behaviour in diverse circumstances of social interaction. In that sense one could consider the relationship between identity and the problem of wholeness. One possible way of under-standing this relationship may be to perceive man as a human being only in so far as he has a sense of selfhood. This selfhood has meaning for him in terms of his interconnection with other men, and with his habitat of natural and man-made environment. In this regard, one could also postulate that an analyzable relationship subsists among identity, disorganization, and cognitive vacuity as these phenomena are experienced by the individual.

Identity crisis should also be deemed to have manifestation at different levels of expression. Different amounts of psychic energy are thus expended in seeking restoration of personality structure when that structure experiences disorganization. Owing to the kind of inextricable dependence that the living in Africa acknowledge to have upon nature, empirical evidence would perhaps confirm that any fundamental search for identification would usually be with the sources of creation and the ultimate destiny of created forces. Another perspective that would require probing is the relationship among the variables of identification, charisma, and the problem of modernization. And, on the supposition that the foregoing indications have any central position in the religious behaviour of man in Africa, we should be able to comment further upon some of the contemporary expressions, and directions, of the quest for identity in black Africa.

A generally recognized function of religion in traditional African communities has been seen in the integration of symbols and values around problems of communal life and social order. This is related to the nature of interpretative and ethical values that relate to, and sacralize, the day-to-day thoughts and actions of community living. Central to these values are the many taboos that surround social life, the punishments that are visited on those who cause infractions in taboos, and the restitutive rituals that purify such individuals or social groups who break taboos. Religion in such societies serves to define the individual in the group; it also makes his own presence in society as a living being, and his activities in such a community, meaningful to him. A starting point in any such analysis of the religious person in a tribal setting might be to locate the nature and network of traditional tribal communities. This involves typification of those structural elements which make tribal communities survive and persist together, and which call for the constant enactment of ritual acts around social and cultural life.

A tribal society, such as African communities have been despite the surge of nationalism and ideologies of nation-building that have made the term 'tribe' perjorative, is made up of clusters of corporate lineage groups. These groups are interrelated with one another in affinal, juridical, economic, political, and religious-mythical orders. Such groups live in localities of adjoining and socially interrelated homesteads. One way to identify an individual in such societies is to ask from what 'house' does he come, or as the Akan of Ghana would ask: *ofi ofie ben mu?* Collectively the living believe that they are also dialectically linked in some metaphysical oneness with the ancestors of the community 'who have lived before and gone beyond'.

In an earlier comment on religion in traditional Ghanaian society (Assimeng, 1976), I have posited that there are certain primordial questions in all human societies for which answers become imperative. The point was also made that if such societies have very shaky and irregular control over their natural environment, as is the case with pre-industrial societies, the problems would be much more acute. Also, answers to such problems often admit to little objectivity and impersonality. It may well be true that the longing for extra-natural entities as objects of worship is steeped in the very structure of human experience; but when the human experience is within the context of inexplicable forces of recurrent nature, perhaps the longing becomes more urgent.

The problems that arise in primal societies may then be said to relate to questions of origin, of structure, and of interconnection of tangible and intangible properties in the day-to-day span of human experience in society, and of human destiny. Then there is the issue of integration. This is related to the integration of the individual with his own soul or essence; it hinges upon the anxiety that concerns, for instance, what it is that makes me *me*; and it also concerns integration with members of one's own immediate community. One should thus think about identity at the following levels with differential intensity: man with his *self*, his *sibling*, his *lineage*, his *clan*, and the *tribe* to which he belongs. Then, as we shall see in our discussion of the theme of 'political religion', there is also the problem of the individual's identity with the *nation* and its unifying and meaning-providing and sacralizing symbols.

STRUCTURE OF TRADITIONAL RELIGION

In such a chapter one cannot help being very brief in the presentation of the central tenets of traditional African religion. Suffice it to state that there is belief, throughout traditional black African religious systems, in a Creator who set in motion the entire creative process. Men, animals, trees, rocks, rivers, and innumerable entities that are seen and unseen in the universe are said to have been created by God. All this animate and inanimate matter possesses a mystical bond of kinship. Man, being a reasoning and questioning being, reflects on several questions with regard not only to his own origin, but also his nature, circumstances, and destiny. When man's relationship with these entities becomes disturbed, purification rituals are gone through in order to restore the poor and disjointed relationship to a pure and proper situation.

But, although the Creator continues to keep watch over the affairs of mankind, this interest is of a universalistic nature; it is deemed to be the kind of interest which the Creator has for all His creations everywhere, and at all time. But the particular and specific needs of men are catered for with the aid of God's many and diverse spiritual intermediaries. At Akim Anyinase, a village about nine miles north of Akim Oda in the eastern region, for instance, one such spiritual intermediary is the main river in the village from which drinking water is drawn for domestic use. This river, called *Asu Kɛse* (literally 'Great River'), is regarded as a goddess, and is the object of worship. Taboos surround the relationship of human beings to this river. Once a year, during the annual *Odwira* festival, sheep are slaughtered for the river, and mashed yam, eggs, customary drinks, and other items are presented to her.

Although there is no priest or priestess who serves as a mediator between the goddess and human beings, the goddess occasionally possesses persons when she wants to communicate with the living. Her help is sought when people are embarking upon various hunting, farming, and commercial ventures. The village is a farming community, with agriculture centered on the cultivation of food crops such as plantain, yams, cocoyams, cassava, corn and rice. Cocoa is also cultivated. Another river which is believed to be also a goddess, although probably of less communal significance, is called *Aworabo*. While people at Anyinase do not take this particular river seriously, local inhabitants claim that in moments of physical and spiritual misfortune when they have visited certain shrines elsewhere for cure they have actually been told that remedies to their ailments could be better provided by propitiating *Aworabo*.

Apart from these rivers there is also the notion of ancestors. The ancestors are divided into meaningful categories. There are, on one hand, the clan ancestors, the leading ones of whose blackened stools are kept in the *abusuafie*, or lineage house. The *abusua*, or lineage, has a head who, for purposes of the ancestral cult, is the officiant, and propitiates the ancestors for the well-being of the lineage. To be excluded from ancestral veneration at the lineage level means being cut off from the lineage. This has sociological connotations because, as I have intimated earlier, a crucial question that confronts a tribal African is 'which house does he belong to?'.

Then there are the tribal ancestors, i.e. ancestors from the chiefly clan. The blackened stools of such ancestors are kept in the stool room at the *ahenfie*, or palace. Sacrifices in the form of food and drinks are offered to these ancestors, through the mediation of attendants to the stools, during the principal cycles of sacred days. The role of the stools, and their relationship with the living and the dead, has been extensively studied by Sarpong (1971). As far as the living are concerned, perhaps the moral significance of ancestor veneration is contained in the classification of the dead into 'good ghosts' and 'bad ghosts'. Good ghosts qualify for periodic propitiation. Bad ghosts are deemed to be those of people who had not lived and died according to the conformist and traditional prescriptions of communal living as the ancestors had bequeathed these to the living.

As in the case of several villages in southern Ghana, Anyinase now has the modern varieties of Christian religious expression. Catholicism, Protestantism in the form of historical churches, the Salvation Army, and spiritual movements of one type or another, and of varying degrees of recency, now abound in the village. Except in a very vague manner that relates to membership statistics, adherence to these movements is not mutually exclusive, and several instances exist whereby a person belongs to different denominations and sects at the same time. In addition, there are residents at Anyinase who are of northern and upper Ghanaian extraction. These are mainly Islamic, and their presence has made people in the village aware of the role of talisman and Koranic incantations which are believed to be able to offer aid in situations of helplessness.

A village in a rural area, such as Anyinase, is not likely to contain many people who profess ostensibly chiliastic and revolutionist teachings of the Watch Tower type, although the experience of this situation in central Africa is different (Assimeng, 1970; and forthcoming). Villagers in West Africa have been much more concerned with magical protection from evil, than with the radical overthrow of the social structure. Nevertheless, a citizen of Anyinase who may have been to an urban area in Ghana could have encountered the teaching or literature of Jehovah's Witnesses' missionaries. Or he may have occasionally drifted to a Watch Tower open-air assembly, and heard something akin to what Cunnison (1951: 459) encountered in Zambia:

> We do not have big people and little people in the church. We are all brothers and sisters. We do not have fathers — there is only one father and He is in heaven. So we talk with each other instead of listening to laws given by someone greater.

One specifically traditional cult, which is a by-product of general spiritual and cultural crisis, is the *Tigare* movement (Christensen, 1954; Ward, 1956; for Nigeria, see Morton-Williams, 1956). Often people in the villages have felt that the gods had become less potent. Such feelings frequently give rise to the emergence of religious enthusiasm and renewal. In Nigeria and Ghana the outbreak of influenza soon after the First World War gave rise to considerable social and psychological ferment. It is, therefore, important to mention that several varieties of faith-healing cults, often on the inspiration of tractarian evangelization from North America and Britain, abound in the Akim Oda area. One should also take note of the existence of wandering *thaumarturges*, and the boom during the period of the Second World War, of what the *Eastern Nigerian Guardian* (16 February, 1943) described as 'Astrologic Frauds'. As the newspaper editorialized,

> By close survey we observe that a new field of profession is slowly rearing up in our Society. This profession is that of the so-called problem solvers, interpreters of dreams, and foretellers of the future who claim to be astrologers and thus prey on the gullible with their supposed interpretation of the occult influence of stars on human affairs.

The newspaper appealed to 'those who indulge in this empty charlatanry to find honest means of earning their livelihood'.

Within this plethora of religious world-view, the spiritual portrait of a typical Anyinase citizen could be impressive. He may have been baptized as a Methodist during infancy. Later, if he attended the local Roman Catholic School, it is probable that he also became a Catholic, took classes in religious catechism, and was baptized and confirmed; this was a sure way then of guaranteeing that he would continue to have a place in the Catholic missionary schools both during the primary stage and (until a middle school was established at Anyinase) at the Akim Swedru post-primary level.

The spectacle of drumming and dancing that accompanied the

enthusiasm of the Tigare days may certainly have appealed to him as a young school pupil; certainly he remained aware of the cases of individuals – mainly women – who were 'caught' by Tigare, and who 'confessed' to terrible offences; or he may himself have been taken occasionally by his parents to the Tigare priest or priestess in the night for protection against bewitching, and certain kinds of kola may have been given to him to chew. Inexplicable dreams usually needed explanation for adults, as Field (1958: 1048) noted: 'Dreams are regarded as highly important and when vivid or frightening give the dreamer great anxiety till a satisfying interpretation is found. Such interpretation is a part of the work of the shrines.'

Related to the search for meaning and integration, one should also look at religion in terms of its expression in moments of life-crises. These crises, as they are given public acknowledgement through ritual, go through several stages. In Africa such rites begin from the period of pregnancy, when taboos surround the life and movement of the pregnant woman. When birth has taken place there is an outdoor ceremony on the eighth day, during which the new-born baby is ritually incorporated into the community of the living. Not all African societies have elaborate ceremonies to mark initiations into age sets, as in some East African societies, or into secret societies, as in West Africa. But all tend to have female puberty rites of varying degrees of elaboration. In marriage, too, the gods are invoked to serve as witnesses to the ceremony and are asked for blessing, success, and prosperity.

But undoubtedly it is funerals which provide the one glaring and spectacular opportunity for human beings to raise anew the question of the purpose of existence, the nature of death, and the possibility of immortality. It is occasion for contemplation, and this is expressed in the content and style of open wailing that takes place during such funerals, as well as in the items with which the dead are buried. Among the Akan of Ghana, for instance, death is perhaps the greatest of the crises that confront man. This is especially so when death has appeared unusual, as, for instance, when a person dies suddenly in the prime of his life, either through snake bite, a mysterious fall, or from a falling tree or wall; or when the nature of sickness is unclear and obscure, as most sicknesses are, considering the development of health care and medical delivery in the country. In such circumstances funerals are accompanied by divination. This involves the search, from the gods, for intimations that would provide meaning and interpretation of such mysterious events.

There is even a notion of proper sequences in death according to generations. As the Ghanaian 'high life' music composer stressed the point recently:

Please Death
Allow me to bury my mother
Before I die.

Even when death has become easy to explain within the context of what Berger and Luckman (1966: 56) regard as 'recipe knowledge', there is the added desire to understand and to soothe people that death is not — and should not be — the end of existence. One way of emphasizing this continuity of life, some feeling of immortality, is found in the insistence that the dead person be buried in his home town, on his ancestral land. The symbolism entailed in this belief would be interesting to explore, from the point of view of psychoanalysis, but the Akan of Ghana believe that, as much as possible, 'where part of the umbilical cord is, there must the dead body of the person be buried also'. The traditional belief is that this would ensure that he really joins those members of his lineage 'who have gone before'. Traditional religion thereby provides the framework of continuity of existence, through the positing of the ancestral world. The qualifications for gaining entry into this world are clearly spelt out, and the supreme wish of many a traditional African is that on death he would not be found wanting as far as such qualifications are concerned.

The range of appurtenances with which the dead are buried is connected, as we have noted, with a set of interrelated ideas and practices concerning traditional views on what things look like 'beyond thanatology', as Vrasdonk (1972) calls it, and which can be understood only within the context of the world-views of the specific peoples concerned. According to Vrasdonk (1972: 283):

Man overcomes his fragmentary contingency by conceiving himself as relating to eternal life. It may be the Nirvana of Buddhism, the Kingdom of God according to the Judea-Christian tradition, the Vedic aspects in Hinduism, or the heaven of the Platonic ideas.

He could well have added to this catalogue the wish of the traditional African to join his ancestors.

A point that should be stressed, as deriving from our discussion so far, then, is that if the social collectivity is generally stable, with a very piecemeal and predictable rate of change, the individual's connection with such collectivity, which is a fundamental pillar of his identity, is assured of stability, continuity, and meaning. But if the collectivity begins to experience rapid and sudden change, then the question of meaning and structure becomes a major problem, as we shall discuss in the following section.

RELIGION AND THE CHALLENGES OF MODERNIZATION

It is worthy of note in this connection that African peoples have experienced the inevitable process of urbanization, and that religiousness and religious participation have been influenced thereby. This, in turn, is related to a general phenomenon of social change that is affecting the very structure of social reality and man's understanding of, and adaptation to, this reality.

Although the sources of change have been various, perhaps for the purposes of our discussion the role of missionary evangelization and the colonial experience have had the most lasting and revolutionary impact. These are the forces that seriously questioned cultural identity — and, in the view of their respondents — challenged the very right-to-exist of Africans. These forces also sought to provide — though it was later recognized that Africans too had religion, and culture as well — new cultural and spiritual values that would serve as mainsprings of social and psychological action. Christian evangelization, in particular, was accompanied by a whole network of new cultural baggage, including literate education, the emergence of new men and women into positions of eminence and authority, new conceptions of technology or adaptation to the natural environment, and new political structures and incumbents to office and power.

In brief, African social structures came to embrace, at varying levels of congruence and disharmony, the modernizing features of monetized economy and its implications: individualism and economic and status competition; urbanization and the relatively permanent physical and psychological movement of people from their places of birth and nurturing, to new centres of population aggregation; secondary relations becoming dominant as an imperative of bureaucracy; new patterns of social stratification, with wide divergence in 'who gets what' and the variation in access to the market; and differential experience of fortune and misfortune, etc.

It is part of this process of modernization that the goals of society — originally simple, mythically chartered, and clear within an ahistorical framework — have become confused and diversified, with no specific agreement among even the smallest unit of social grouping. There is a clear shift from the conceptual cyclology to lineality in time, as Ruch (1973: 116) has specified:

> the cyclic time of myth gives way to the lineal time of conscious and planned progress. The stability and perennity of mythical life, in which the individual was perfectly and harmoniously integrated with his physical and social surrounding, disappears. Man is now torn between his own rapid individual becoming and the slow growth of society: two lineal times running at different speeds.

Because the modernization process has not had its origins principally in the indigenous institutional orders, one witnesses haste for modernization without adequate understanding of its base and contingency. The new emergent *tradition of change* has given rise to acute tensions. For instance, one now finds competing loyalties among sib, kin, tribe, nation, and a trans-national entity designated pan-Africanism. A similarly significant central ideological problem has also come to center on what to revive, and what to discard, in a situation of *sankofa* or meaningfully reinterpretative vein. Dean (1956) sees this in the form of 'Anti-Westernism', and Matossian (1958) has analyzed the situation as concerning 'Ideologies of Delayed Industrialization', with 'tensions and ambiguities'. A more psychiatric study of this situation is that of Sachs's (1937) *Black Hamlet, The Mind of an African Negro revealed by psychoanalysis.*

The foregoing experiences may be better gauged from the angle of a small village. Again, let us look at Anyinase. The people of this village are now part of a larger national community in search of goal and direction. It may well be, therefore, that the kinds of problems that they face, and the responses that they try to offer, could be regarded as part of the general dilemma of modernization in Africa. Since about 1940, through missionary activities, there has been a primary school in the village. From its humble beginnings this school has turned out a number of 'graduates', some of whom are now in diverse spheres of occupational responsibility. Eight miles south of Anyinase a secondary school exists at Oda, the capital town of the Akim Kotoku Traditional area.

A more recent factor of modernization has been the establishment of a health post at the village since April 1975. Thenceforth, the village has become a lively and busy center of health care for the surrounding villages of the area. An electricity plant for the village is projected, and it is hoped that a water project, also billed for the district as a whole, will embrace the village also. Now, with the new health center and the prospects of good water and electricity in the village, the conception that the villagers will have of the traditional river goddess, the ancestors, the witches and wizards, and the fear of ghosts, would be a rewarding field for research in future.

THE CHALLENGE OF CULTURAL RENEWAL

Our discussion so far may be summed up in the following way: the people of Akim Anyinase can be likened to any other village community in contemporary black Africa that has chosen, consciously and unconsciously, the path of social progress. Although the older generation of the people often wonder about the rate and speed, they scarcely openly question the wisdom that is entailed in efforts to bring the village within the orbit of enlightenment and a qualitatively higher standard of living. Indeed, contrary to the belief that village communities cling adamantly to tradition for its own sake, it may well be that some of the inhabitants have often questioned the traditional ways of doing things; they may also even have challenged the efficacy and worthwhileness of traditional gods. Egharevba (1951: 7) raised similar queries in Nigeria:

> What have the gods done? The gods teach believe, submit and give; Science teaches learn, see and be wise. The gods are darkness, while science [is] radiant light. The gods impart fear and ignorance, while science imparts learning. The gods demand autocracy and adoration, while science demands knowledge, democracy and liberty.

Has the modernizing tempo now taking place in contemporary African social structures affected the nature of religiousness in the villages? Answers to this question would have to be related to several premises, among which are the following:

(a) that the inhabitants of the villages do make distinctions between religious and non-religious activities and modes of thought;

(b) that the act of embracing a new religious formulation constitutes a conversion experience, i.e. the ritual burying and sloughing off of an earlier style of life, and the re-birth of a new one; and

(c) that the constant experimentation with new religious beliefs and practices poses problems in the minds of the religionists in traditional communities concerning the compatibility or otherwise of theological and practical consequences of different religions.

Clearly, if one considers the current pattern of religious life in African societies perhaps the concept of synthesis fits the situation best. This situation was described by Shonle (1924: 262) as a 'mutilation of the old culture to permit elements of the new to enter, the result being a fusion of the two into a third type of culture'. 'Mutilation' is not a happy term that seems apt as characterizing the actual process of acculturation experiences. Fisher (1964: 9) puts it perhaps more aptly as 'a reconciliation between divergent norms. It moves not always towards the African, but sometimes away, according to the imbalance that needs to be righted.' Banton, too, (1956: 354-68) characterizes this as 'adaptation and integration', as this circumstance occurs to migrants into urban centers.

Sometimes responses to what natives see as cultural decay have taken the form of attempts to resurrect past cultic practices which are then given impressive pedigrees.

I do not know of any study of acculturative processes in Africa which have been specifically designated as 'cultural renewal'; my own earlier designation was 'cultural revival' (Assimeng 1969a). Responses to the contact situation have varied even within single social communities, and I conceptually identified the response types in terms of revolutionism, accommodationism, and revivalism. Cognitive behavior during the Mau Mau uprising in Kenya, for instance, has been similarly studied from the point of view of differential cognitive attitudes among the Christian urban Kikuyu and the traditionalist Kikuyu in the rural setting (Schutte, 1973).

One could, for instance, take the case of the revival, among Nigerian Yorubas, of the Ogboni Secret Society. It was then realized that the traditional cult needed respectable re-definition, as in the following description:

> Probably, Ogboni stands in some historical connection with the primitive Assembly of Elders in the Israelite state, as a Court of Law and Authority. In a word, it is the Sanhedrin of the Yorubas.[1]

Another example of the foregoing attitude, also manifested in Nigeria during the early phases of nationalism, is when Marie Ochie offered the opinion that

> A close study of the Pentateuch, with the ancestorial laws and customs in the Ibo tribe, would make one wonder whether the Ibos and some other tribes of Nigeria did not originate from the 'last house of Israel' always referred to in the Bible.

Writing in the *Eastern Nigeria Guardian* of 3 December, 1941, Ochie noted further:

> To an average Bible student, such should not be a surprise when he compares and finds the synchronism of the second table of the laws from Mount Sinai, and the pre-religious laws and customs in Ibo land, which existed for a long time before the advent of Christianity. . . . Is it not, therefore, a challenge to modern Christian civilization that the ancestors, with their primitive ideas of God, excelled modern Christianity in moulding the hearts of man towards the real fear and knowledge of God? Today, most people are taught to forsake the traditions and practices of their forefathers. African sciences, secret societies, et. cetera, are condemned and termed diabolical. How funny.

Or, consider the following editorial, which clearly follows the vein of what I have elsewhere (Assimeng, 1969a) called the 'revivalistic response!'

> The native dweller in Nigeria had a religion before the advent of Christianity. His religion was perfect, and taught him the brotherhood of man and the

fatherhood of God. He lived for the other man, His one sole aim was to carry sunshine and happiness into the home of his fellow man. . . . The African has a religion which, unfortunately, is fast giving place to the imported form of worship. His religion takes him closer to the Divine Presence, and enjoins on him true love for his fellow man. Hence the African has always been found a child of nature, docile and unsuspecting. This copyist attitude in all phases of his life has robbed the African of his innate godliness, and it was time our people turned to find God, to worship Him, and to serve Him in the true African way.[2]

Following on the heels of nationalism and cultural reinterpretation, many African leaders of religious thought now believe, as Kwame Bresi-Ando did (cf. Assimeng, 1975), that for religion to be meaningful it should be authentic and indigenous. Such religion should not impose different and meaningless cultural ethic-ways which have nothing to do with religiousness as such. As Coker (1917: 28) stated during the heyday of religious independentism in Nigeria: 'There is nothing in polygamy to cut one off from Christianity or render one incompetent for all requirements of that Religion. The question of polygamy, I think, should not be left to be settled by Europeans or White concerns.'

But, whatever the ideological or rationalizing underpinning, and irrespective of its ostensibly religious or secular nature, much of the revival or reinterpretative energies are directed towards the re-discovery of selfhood. Often the reaction has been ambivalent and bizarre, as in the case of a Nigerian, Solomon Laka of Eleme, who wrote to Hitler during the Second World War asking the German tyrant to take over his country. Solomon Laka had refused to pay tax, and had intimated that 'if Hitler took over the country, he would pay tax. In fact, he would become the tax collector.'[3]

Indeed, religious and secular life become fused in the attempt to extricate the social and cultural schemes of African people from foreign intrusion and cultural domination. This exercise, on the part of pro-testers against cultural intrusion, has often made use of exaggerated myths of ancient greatness. Thus, according to the teaching of the National Church of Nigeria (Onyioha, n.d.: 7, 8, 9)

Time was when Africa lived in pomp and splendour. She straddled the world known to her. Today Africa is in chains. . . . Beneath the weight of imperialism Africa wriggles in humiliations and misery. . . . And so these imported religious bodies have disintegrated African communities and made it difficult for chained Africa to remuster muscles and nerves to extricate herself. . . . Everywhere the society of man has been upset by religious bodies. The National Church of Nigeria comes to reshape things.

Nonetheless, even within the specifically Christian tradition the process should not be regarded as a return to 'neo-paganism' (cf. Steenberghen, 1959), or even de-christianization. As Hinson (1967: 584), noted ten years ago:

> The new nations of Africa and Asia, as well as many of the older nations of Latin America, are today seeking to discover their peculiar identity as nations. These people feel that their destiny and identity in the past have been determined by a colonial power or powers, and they now want to affirm and define their own selfhood as nations. Believing that they have been living on the margin of history, they wish to discover their own self-identity so as to make their destinctive contribution to history. They want to be free to develop their peculiar national character and way of life.

The result has often been reflected in sectarian participation. Some of the sects perform the kind of functions of moral re-generation which ensure a return to puritanism, simplicity, and frugality; these functions the tribes, as tribes, are no longer capable of performing. This is why the sects could now be seen (cf. Assimeng, 1978) as perhaps modernized versions of tribal groupings. This has been found especially of Watch Tower members, whether in Kenya (Wilson, 1973), Zambia (Assimeng, 1970), or elsewhere. Thus, at a time when men and women in Africa are unsure of the meaning and direction of fads and fashions, mostly imported, some sectarians have, through their social teachings, offered leadership in modesty, sobriety, and the maintenance of personal dignity. Jehovah's Witnesses, for instance, have teaching on even weight problems and expenditure on clothing, a teaching that is related to the movement's missiology. Cunnison (1951: 460) encountered this during a Watch Tower assembly in central Africa, noting in his research dairy:

> The Canadian said we must throw aside all weight because we have a race to run. Can people, he asked, run swiftly if they are wearing tight clothes and heavy boots? What sort of weight can be thrown off, so that we can concentrate on the work in hand?

Then, at the purely personal level, one meets the desire for a kind of religious affinity that satisfies, in the way traditional gods did but in a modernizing social situation, meaningful spiritual and material needs; religion that works, that is. One way of appreciating this phenomenon is to pursue the extant confessions and reminiscences of modern sectarian religionists in Africa. Witness, for instance, Ogbonna (1961: 7) of Nigeria explaining 'Why I joined the [Assemblies of God] Church':

> My fellowship with the Assemblies of God has made Christ real to me. I have known Him as my Saviour, and I follow Him. I have received many blessings from God, both spiritually and materially, since I have been redeemed. . . . This is why I joined the Assemblies of God Church.

POLITICAL RELIGION: DISCUSSION

While religion per se undergoes transformation as a communal pheno-menon and as an agency for the generation and reinforcement of collective sentiments, and while other associative groupings of an apparently secular nature take over some of the traditional integrative functions of religion, it is remarkable to witness the extent to which these secular groupings have themselves either operated as quasi-religious bodies, as in the religion of Godianism in Nigeria (Onyioha, n.d.), or have found it fit to operate with religious symbolism. Apter (1963) views this phenomenon as 'political religion'. In Africa this has been especially the case with political parties and national leadership. The political parties owe their origin largely to the elitist and mass associations which began as a challenge to the colonial situation: they had as their main purpose the liberation of African societies from colonial domination, and from the corresponding feeling of cultural worthlessness. It appears that in some instances these nationalist move-ments virtually became objects of worship, as in the case of the Convention People's Party of Ghana and the United National Inde-pendence Party of Zambia; men and women have been seen to invest the kind of emotional resources which are usually associated with the worship of spirit forces. Indeed, it is remarkable that so enlightened a scholar and politician as the late Dr J. B. Danquah, popularly known as the 'Doyen of Ghana politics', could write on 27 June 1950: 'I cannot think of a greater religion than the worship of my nation. God is in Ghana and Ghana is in God' (Akyeampong, 1971, II: 118).

Nationalism itself was largely a reaction to a condition of social and cultural despair, particularly at the level of leadership. As Johnston (1916: 322) observed long ago:

> More often having acquired the requisite knowledge [in USA, France, Germany, but *not* in England] they return to the colony in which they were born, to find themselves frustrated in almost all directions if they wish to earn a livelihood in the leading professions.

The original search for selfhood, in protest against what Garvey (1927) called *The Tragedy of White Injustice*, continues even after political independence. This is because first, 'all the things' that were promised to be added unto it [i.e. independence] are yet to be evident (cf. Assimeng, 1969b); this has stimulated some people in independent African countries to continue to await a supposedly better second independence, as in the case of the Kwilu rebellion in the Congo (cf. Fox et al., 1965); or because it is now realized that political independence per se does not necessarily lead to economic and cultural self-re-discovery.

Ghana's National Pledge, currently introduced as an agency of social mobilization, and obligatorily recited at all official public gatherings, could be similarly conceived. The words are as follows:

> I promise on my honour;
> To be faithful and loyal to Ghana my motherland
> I pledge myself to the Service of Ghana
> With all my strength and with all my heart;
> I promise to hold in high esteem
> Our heritage won for us
> Through the blood and toil of our fathers;
> And I pledge myself in all things
> To uphold and defend the good name of Ghana;
> So help me God.

'Ghana' now becomes the new, or re-discovered, symbolic mother-figure, to which oaths of allegiance and duty are made in the same way that mother earth used to be propitiated, respected, venerated, and identified with during moments of what people feared to be personality and cognitive disintegration. Perhaps it is pertinent to mention also that on 4 January 1977 the ruling Supreme Military Council of Ghana proclaimed three days of national meditation for the period 7-9 January to seek the help of God — and, no doubt, the ancestors — in Ghana's attempt to surmount economic and social-structural difficulties. In the face of economic chaos and fears of planned strike action in the country the authorities in Ghana found it necessary again to declare the week 27 June — 3 July 1977 as 'A Week of National Repentance and Meditation'.

I would like to think that I have attempted to offer some partial explanation for the kinds of search for meaning and direction that are animating people in black Africa. Any account that deals with religiousness in Africa — traditional, changing or contemporary — is bound to be sketchy and fraught with many short-comings. Africa is a vast continent, and the amount of ethnographic ignorance on the continent is unfathomable, and will continue to be so for some time to come. There is as yet little collaboration among academics on the African continent, so that what one can survey may be only a small part of what is actually going on. A pioneering attempt to bring together academics of religious studies in Africa has been spearheaded by Terence Ranger, a noted historian, and it is hoped that systematic documentation will continue in this direction.

The other difficulty hinges on diversity of interest — and of interpretation. This has meant that views and interpretative models differ, calling forth the need for mutual communicability and interchange of ideas. Religion, especially in Africa, is a field that has attracted scholars from different disciplines. If in this chapter I have chosen for treatment topics which might appear rather peripheral to others, the reason is that my research interests have been mainly concerned with modes of adaptation to changing social and cultural frameworks in Africa, especially through the vehicle of religious beliefs and practices.

Space limitations in a chapter of this kind constrain one from venturing into all the areas of research interest that one would wish to touch upon. Nevertheless, I think it would be pertinent in future studies for one to focus on the implicit similarities between religious groups and political parties, both at the incipient stages of their formation and now, in terms of aims, goals, leadership, membership, hymnology, promises of individual and collective salvation, and responses to unfulfilled prophecies. It would also be rewarding to probe, in such associations, problems of internal dissension and excommunication, and encounters with other groups, religious and secular, such as with the Alice Lenshina Lumpa sect, or with the Kitawala and Watch Tower movements in several parts of central and east Africa.

NOTES

1. 'Osugbo: Yoruba Secret Society', Mss. Afr. s. 662 (5). This anonymous typescript, prepared in 1931, is at Rhodes House Library, Oxford.

2. Editorial in *Eastern Nigeria Guardian*, 30 May 1947, entitled 'Revive Native Religion'.

3. *Nigerian Eastern Mail*, 30 August 1941.

REFERENCES

AKYEAMPONG, H. H. (1971) *Journey to Independence and After: J. B. Danquah Letters 1949-1951*, II. Accra: Waterville Press.

APTER, D. E. (1963) 'Political Religion in the New Nations', in Clifford GEERTZ (ed.), *Old Societies and New States.* New York: Free Press of Glencoe.

ASSIMENG, Max (1969a) 'Status Anxiety and Cultural Revival: Pursuit of the Good Old Days', *Ghana Journal of Sociology*, V (1), February: 8-14.

—, (1969b) 'Religious and Secular Messianism in Africa', *Research Review* (Legon), V (1): 1-19.

—, (1970) 'Sectarian Allegiance and Political Authority: The Watch Tower Society in Zambia 1907-1935', *Journal of Modern African Studies* (Cambridge), VIII (1): 97-112.

—, (1975) 'Methodological Africanism: Bresi Ando as an Episcopus Vagans', *Conch* (New York), VII (1 & 2): 54-79.

—, (1976) 'Traditional Religion in Ghana: A Preliminary Guide to Research', *Thought and Practice* (Nairobi), III (1): 65-89.

—, (1978) 'Sects, Tribes, and Demography in Ghana', *Legon Journal of the Humanities*, III (forthcoming).

——, (forthcoming) *Saints and Social Structures in Africa.* Tema: Ghana Publishing Co.

BANTON, Michael (1956) 'Adaptation and Integration in the Social System of Temne Immigrants in Freetown', *Africa*, 26 (4), October: 354-68.

BERGER, P. L. and T. LUCKMANN (1966) *The Social Construction of Reality.* Hammondsworth: Penguin.

CHRISTENSEN, J. B. (1954) 'The Tigare Cult in West Africa', *Papers of the Michigan Academy of Science, Arts, and Letters*, xxix: 389-98.

COKER, S. A. (1917) *The Rights of Africans to Organise and Establish Indigenous Churches.* Based on a public lecture of 1917. Lagos:

CUNNISON, Ian (1951) 'A Watchtower Assembly in Central Africa', *International Review of Mission*, XL: 456-69.

DEAN, V. M. (1956) 'Anti-Westernism: Cause and Cure', *Christian Century*, LXXII (19), May: 576-78.

EGHAREVBA, J. U. (1951) *Some Tribal Gods of Southern Nigeria.* Benin City:

FIELD, M. J. (1958) 'Mental Disorder in Rural Ghana', *Journal of Mental Science*, 104 (437), October: 1043-51.

FISHER, H. J. (1964) 'Muslim and Christian Separation in Africa' in *Religion in Africa.* Edinburgh: Centre of African Studies, pp. 9-23.

FOX, R. C. et al. (1965) 'The Second Independence: A Case Study of the Kwilu Rebellion in the Congo', *Comparative Studies in Society and History*, VIII (1), October: 78-109.

GARVEY, Marcus (1927) *The Tragedy of White Injustice.* New York: Amy Jacques Garvey.

HINSON, W. J. (1967) 'The Search for Self-Identity in the Younger Churches', *Religion in Life* (Ann Arbor), XXXVI (4): 583-89.

JOHNSTON, Sir H. H. (1916) 'The Bitter Cry of the Educated African', *New Statesman* (London), VII (170): 321-22.

MATOSSIAN, Mary (1958) 'Ideologies of Delayed Industrialization: Some Tensions and Ambiguities', *Economic Development and Cultural Change*, VI (3): 217-28.

MORTON-WILLIAMS, P. (1956) 'The Atinga Cult Among the South-Western Yoruba', *Bulletin L'I.F.A.N.*, XVIII (3 & 4): 315-34.

OGBONNA, A. A. (1961) 'Why I Joined the Church', *Nigerian Evangel*, 13 (6): 6-7.

ONYIOHA, K. O. K. (n.d.) *A New Civilization From Africa.* Enugu: Eastern Nigeria Publishing Co.

RUCH, E. A. (1973) 'Philosophy of African History', *African Studies* (Johannesburg), 32 (2): 113-25.

SACHS, Wulf (1937) *Black Hamlet.* London: Geoffrey Bles.

SARPONG, Rt. Rev. P. A. (1971) *The Sacred Stools of the Akan.* Tema: Ghana Publishing Co.

SCHUTTE, A. G. (1973) 'Mau Mau: the Cognitive Restructuring of Socio-Political Action', *African Studies* (Johannesburg), 32 (4): 215-27.

SHONLE, Ruth (1924) 'The Christianizing Process Among Preliterate Peoples', *Journal of Religion* (Chicago), IV (3): 261-80.

STEENBERGHEN, Rombaut (1959) 'Neo-Paganism in Africa', *Frontier*, 2 (4): 287-88.

VRASDONK, W. G. (1972) 'Beyond Thanatology: Immortality', *Journal of Value Inquiry* (The Hague), VI (4): 280-85.

WARD, B. E. (1956) 'Some Observations on Religious Cults in Ashanti', *Africa*, 26 (1): 47-61.

WILSON, B. R. (1973) 'Jehovah's Witnesses in Kenya', *Journal of Religion in Africa*, V (2): 129-49.

6

IDENTITY-THEORY AGAINST THE BACKDROP OF THE HINDU CONCEPT OF DHARMA:

A Socio-Philosophical Interpretation

S. Gopalan
Dr S. Radhakrishnan Institute for Advanced Study in Philosophy, Madras, India

Gopalan argues that dharma *(order) and identity are equally versatile as basic concepts for the understanding of the individual and society. Objectification as one of four mechanisms of sacralization adequately sums up the transcendental aspects of Hinduism. Dharma is the means of man's self-realization. Yet it also represents the interaction between personal, group, and social identity and maintains social order.*

The complexity of the subject taken up for discussion calls for a few preliminary observations which may help delimit the scope of the paper and aid in indicating our focus of concern. Maybe it is a truism to state even at the outset that the concept of identity has, in the history of the various disciplines concerned with it, acquired such a variety of interpretations and shades of meaning that it needs to be stated that a chapter such as this is presented from *a* specific perspective while acknowledging the possibility of other approaches and the worthwhileness of entering into dialogues and debates with them; yet it is important to underline the fact that this chapter will *not* review (even in passing) *all* the significant contributions to the conceptual clarification of the idea of identity but draw from a *few* which seem to be significant from the perspective proposed to be adopted. It may also be mentioned that the dividing line between adopting and apologetic stance and an interpretative approach is often so thin that the latter may 'degenerate' into the former and that this is particularly the case with regard to the socio-philosophical approach to the concept of identity that we are proposing. Particularly relevant in our context is the fact that the wide applicability of the identity-theory would, on the one hand, require a 'digging in' to study its implications for a social theory and, on the other, vouchsafe a careful appraisal of its limitations. A similar remark would be equally relevant in the context of the analytic-interpretative approach we propose to take while delineating the deeper significance of the key-concept of *dharma* in the Hindu philosophico-religious tradition.

THE ARGUMENT

Our main line of argument, accordingly, is that the cross-cultural implications and applicability of the identity-concept (which is perhaps a presupposition of the symposium itself) can be studied with profit from the Hindu standpoint by examining certain *aspects* of the proteon concept of dharma. The basis for our argument is that the concept of dharma has deep implications for the individual as well as society, from the point of view of both a psychological, religious, philosophical analysis and building a social theory similar to that of the identity-concept. Whether it be that we study 'identity' from the angle of vision provided by the sociology of religion or consider it as meaningful in the context of man's life — *personal* and *inter-personal* — its significance can be better appreciated by considering the other concept which we suggest is equally 'versatile'. Without 'indulging' in a reductionistic approach — reducing the identity-concept in terms of the idea of dharma — we are suggesting that the comprehensive significance of *identity* can be made apparent by considering a parallel in a different culture. If religion is defined in terms of a system of meaning and a theory of reality, we suggest that its significance for man can be made explicit only by considering its built-in value-orientation which provides a frame of reference for the motivational orientation of human life in *all* its aspects — personal, inter-personal, and trans-personal. The thesis that is presented here is that the significance of identity can be explicated thus by studying it as an integral aspect of a sociology of religion that insists on the necessity of taking into account the various dimensions of man's personality. If religion and identity are interpreted in such general terms our submission is that the generality they are deemed to possess (if such an interpretation has any logical validity at all) can be accounted for by the variations in the historical-cultural 'conditioning' observable and that the philosophy of the individual and society that dharma stands for is a clear pointer to the viability of a theory of identity which has deeper implications for the individual and wider meanings for society and humanity. We shall concern ourselves first with the identity concept and next with dharma to substantiate our position.

IDENTITY

From the perspective of social philosophy (which we define as an inter-disciplinary concern dealing normatively with human life in all its aspects) what interests us most in the concept of identity is its being approached from various perspectives such as the psychological and the sociological.

Strauss's (1959) work is a concrete instance of the first. Though the work goes into the implications of the symbolic interaction approach to the concept of identity and attempts also to explicate the role of language, our interest is in sifting out certain other aspects of identity referred to by him, namely, the indeterminacy of human behaviour and the 'self' being no more immune to re-examination from new perspectives than any other object. With regard to (i) he maintains that indeterminacy of human behaviour need not be considered a stumbling block to scientific research (on matters social) but *has to be* taken into account. We would emphasize the underlying implication, namely, that while an empirical approach to the problem of the individual-in-society, and consequently also to the problem of identity itself, has its value, duly conceding the indeterminacy element in human life enhances the value and deepens the significance of empirical research since the core-reality — *man* as a 'carrier of his inalienable identity' — is not ignored in the process. In our present context it is important to notice that such an approach suggests a possible way of making the identity-concept more concrete. The assertion of the self by the individual in social action, which is apparent in the insistence on the indeterminacy-characteristic of human action, would indicate that identity refers to the core-element in man which makes for the freedom of his will. It is interesting to note here that both from the point of view of 'doing' social science and from the point of view of philosophizing on social action — with its well-known normative and idealistic overtones — the free-will element in man becomes highly significant. No doubt, both in the social sciences (in which discussion centres round social action) and in social philosophy (which normatively approaches human action), the free will of man is presupposed, though very often it is not realized that it is symptomatic of the assertion of identity by the individual. Thus, it seems to us that Strauss's stress on the indeterminate element in human action highlights an aspect of identity which helps us to appreciate better the deeper implications of a sociology of religion with an emphasis on the metaphysical dimension of the human personality. Consequently, with regard to the second point that Strauss makes, namely, that the self cannot be 'exempted' from re-examination from new perspectives, our comment is that it is highly suggestive of the fact that the identity-concept itself need not be considered a purely meta-physical one with accessibility to it denied from all quarters. In effect it provides a rationale for the philosophic approach which stresses the basic element in human action by reiterating the projection of self. From the viewpoint of sociology the implication seems to be that taking into account the role of the self widens rather than narrows the scope of the discipline. If the philosophic approach is to be at all meaningful, reference to the self needs to be considered *not* in abstract terms but concretized in terms of the projection of the human personality in social action. Similarly, the term 'sociological' obtains a significance which does not preclude the 'inner' dimension of human action. The area of intersection between philosophy and sociology so considered yields a realm of analysis in which the concern is as much philosophical as it is sociological. Whether we refer to it as laying an equal emphasis on the social aspects of philosophy and philosophical aspects of sociology or describe it as being concerned with the personal (which does not exclude the metaphysical as unimportant) as well as the social, the socio-philosophical approach takes due note of the wider connotations of the terminology of the self — and consequently also of identity — and the deeper implications of the sociological approach.

It is this aspect of Strauss's theory that interests us and also provides us with a cue to approaching a sociological theory of identity. It offers a further support to our own surmise that a sociological theory of identity need not necessarily dwell all the time on the more tangible, observable, empirical, and social aspects of human action. Mol's theory of identity is a clear case in point. One of the major concerns of Mol (1976) in his recent book is to make concrete the concept of identity by looking at it through the perspective of sociology of religion. The perspective he takes, when analysed carefully, reveals certain metaphysical strands of thought which are significant in our context, as will be evident from the sequel. The concept of identity is concretely analysed by Mol by defining religion as sacralization of identity. His main thesis is that man's attempt to sacralize self-identity, group-identity, and social-identity results in transformation of personality. From this point of view the relevance of religion is perennial and the categories employed by various religions need not be understood as abstract — taking man's thoughts and aspirations away from society.[1] The sociological perspective that Mol adopts is evident from the emphasis he lays on the *process* of sacralization without disregarding the sacred. Mol's contention, thus, is not that the sacred is of *less* value but that the process of sacralization is *more* important from the point of view of the day-to-day living of man.

What interests us most in Mol's theory is his concept of objectification which is referred to by him as one of the mechanisms of sacralization. From the perspective of this chapter, in which we want to bring out the wider implications of the identity-theory, 'objectification' as a 'mechanism' of the *process* of sacralization is quite significant. We are not suggesting that the three other mechanisms of sacralization about which Mol writes are not relevant from our point of view. Concerned as we are with finding out whether (and if so, how) the wider implications of the identity-theory can be illustratively interpreted from the point of view of Hinduism, the mechanism of objectification seems to hold great promise and suggest, in more general terms, the lines on which identity

can be understood from the point of view of both individual growth
and social development.

Since identity is interpreted by Mol in the context of religion, his
concern with what it *does* rather than what it *is* (Chapter 1, p. 3) offers
us a cue to a more concrete interpretation of *identity* that he attempts.
It seems to us that his basic thesis that there is a fluid (and, we may
add, natural) transition from the profane to the sacred — a position
which he acknowledges as being different from that of Emile Durkheim
who considers the sacred to be antagonistic to the profane — stems out
of the significance he attaches to religion.

In support of Mol we would like to suggest that the sociological
significance of religion can be appreciated fully only when religion is
not considered merely as a *product* (of human thinking and social
interaction) but looked at also as a *process* (whereby human thinking
shapes personality-development in the individual and establishes inter-
personal relationships which evolve and ultimately 'expend'). The
dynamics of man-in-society are seen here to offer an insight into the
way religious phenomena need to be analysed and religious processes
understood and interpreted. More often than not it is forgotten that the
individual is not a static entity, being completely determined by the
society in which he lives. Hence the dynamic nature of the individual is
worth reiterating in the context of understanding religion; the concept
of identity aiding the process by concretely visualizing the *personal* and
social aspects of the dynamism.

It may not be an exaggeration to suggest here that both sociology
and philosophy, in an important sense, presuppose the dynamism of the
individual. This is *not* to suggest that the perspectival differences
between sociology and philosophy of religion can either be obliterated
or disregarded in a meaningful analysis of religion as a product and as a
process, but rather to emphasize that the dynamic-individual concept is
the 'prime-mover' in both the disciplines. It is worth noting that but for
the 'dynamics of the individual' being granted, philosophy would not
have transformed (however imperfectly) human life, and progress in
sociology in unravelling the dimensions of religiosity (not used here in
the technical sense of current sociological literature) would not have
been registered.

Paradoxically, this very dynamism of the individual proves to be an
advantage as well as a disadvantage with regard to the effectiveness of

religion — and has a corresponding effect on the possibility of achieving identity. In view of this it seems to be as unrealistic to hold that *religion* has always helped mankind in achieving personality-integration, group-cohesion, and societal unity as it is to point an accusing finger at religion and condemn it as having thwarted individual growth, marred group-consolidation, destroyed human unity, and effectuated alienation and anomie in the individual.

The process-idea of religion suggested earlier in this section, coupled with our comments above regarding the realistic appraisal of the function and significance of religion, would imply that religion can certainly be considered to hold within it the *potentiality* for helping man to achieve identity, and to the extent identity is achieved we can maintain that the potentiality is actualized. In this sense religion is neither an abstract and transcendent entity nor a concrete process which can be 'proved beyond doubt' like certain mechanisms in society. The difficulties in comprehending religious phenomena stem from this and, while referring to *religion*, it is well to bear in mind that since it is not a 'tangible entity' interpretation of reality necessarily creeps in. This may be due to man's nature itself which is amphibious in character — revealing its 'participation' in the world of concrete reality and in a transcendental realm of meanings and system. The restlessness of man as a religious being, observable even in our contemporary society, is symptomatic of this aspect of man and provides an important dimension of analysis and interpretation.

We digressed on a reflection about religion and its significance to the individual and the group to interpret Mol's theory of identity as integral to his sociology of religion and more specifically to study the wider implications of the concept of identity through an analysis of *objectification* as a mechanism of sacralization. It seems to us that in and through the concept of objectification Mol takes note of the transcendental implications of morality and also indicates the metaphysical roots of social life (and naturally also of the social institutions). Though Mol's discussion of objectification is in the context of explaining the various mechanisms of sacralization, our specific interest in the objectification-mechanism is to visualize the way in which ideals are conceived and hence also the significance of idealizations of interpersonal relationships. Mol defines objectification as 'the tendency to sum up the variegated elements of mundane existence in a transcendental frame of reference whereby they can appear more orderly, more consistent and more timeless' (pp. 264-65). Mol maintains that the process of objectification is symptomatic of man's progressive capacity for abstract thinking and ability to use symbols.

It is important to note here that Mol differs from sociologists by taking the position that the emotive-integrative aspects of religion as a symbol-system are as important aas the differentiation-adaptive aspects. The incomplete picture of religion which is concerned only with the differentiating perspective is counter-balanced by Mol's consideration of integration. This concern to make good the 'imbalance' by presenting the integration-potential of religion seems to be at the basis of Mol's theory of religion as sacralization of identity.

In Mol's theory the integration-aspect (the identity-aspect) is thus a potential which needs to be actualized and the process of actualizing this potentiality may be referred to as the process of sacralization. We do not, by this interpretation, fail to notice that in Mol's view sacralization is a more advanced stage than that of integration i.e. sacralization consists in preserving what already has been integrated. But, in so far as visualizing a potential is symptomatic of a projection of an order which is obviously and significantly absent at the mundane level, we may refer to it also as an ideal-construction-process or as a direct consequence of the idealizations of the existential (i.e. the actual) conditions of man at the mundane (profane) level.

It seems to us that the thrust of both the approaches — the psychological and the sociological — to identity is to suggest that identity is neither to be construed as inexplicable from the standpoint of man 'in search of it' nor considered as being exhausted in the *institutional situation*. The wider applicability and the deeper dimension of identity, and the reciprocal relationship between, and the 'wovenness' of the personal and social aspects of identity point to the fact that 'identity' permits manifold languages and terminologies which are *all* expressive of the core-idea; and it is because of this that we maintain that the Hindu concept of dharma is highly suggestive of the implications underlying the identity-theory.

DHARMA

For the purposes of this chapter, in which we want to study the viability of the identity-theory from a cross-cultural point of view, we deem it necessary to confine our attention only to the psychological and social significance of dharma. For one thing it would 'match' the treatment we gave above to identity and for another it is in and through these two aspects of dharma that the significance of the identity-theory can be interpreted. Furthermore, the personality-integration idea inherent in the philosophy of dharma is such that the inner and outer aspects as also the empirical and metaphysical dimensions of man as a *person* are clearly seen reflected in it, thus offering us a 'corraborative evidence' for our understanding and interpretation of identity.

It is indeed significant that the psychological basis of personality-development and the social significance of such a personality-development actually achieved are both connoted by the proteon concept of dharma in the Hindu tradition. And, when we remember that the term personality-development in the Hindu tradition does not merely point to the individual's maintaining 'psychological health', but to a stage which transcends the stage of attaining the 'state of restfulness', a stage in which the true identity of man is realized, the deeper and wider significance of dharma are clearly seen. Notwithstanding the plethora of meaning that the term personality-integration has acquired in the various schools of Hindu philosophy it may be pointed out that there is a general consensus of opinion that integration of personality has a deeper significance than what 'mental equilibrium' connotes. Maybe the deeper meaning of *personality* is attributable to the non-acceptance of mind *(manas)* as the ultimate category. The term *self* *(jiva, atman*, etc.) (in spite of the varying approaches and definitions that the Hindu tradition offers us) gives us an insight into the fact that real integration connotes the transcendence of the level of the mind.[2] The significant point to notice here is that self-realization or realizing man's true identity is possible through the instrumentality of dharma. The deeper significance of dharma consists thus in providing the psychological base for the actualization of a potential in man which is trying to find expression by enabling him to find his true identity. The actualization can well be referred to as the *ideal* for man.

No doubt it may be argued that dharma, as ordinarily understood, is an ethical category in the Hindu tradition — underlying the fact that it connotes the general moral sense that man is considered to possess. We certainly concede this basic meaning of dharma, but even a moment's reflection would suggest that this points to the uniqueness of man as well. The insistence on the distinctness of man, the emphatic assertion of the characteristic emblem of the human species, by the Hindu philosophers points also to an ideal which can and ought to be realized. The Hindu tradition, however, clearly points out that man's distinctiveness does not consist in his being totally different from the animal but only in his possessing moral sense in addition to all the features of animal existence so that man's *identity* becomes a potentiality merely to start with, a potentiality which needs to be actualized. Needless to say the actualization of the potentiality is the result of a conscious and deliberate attempt on the part of man and it presupposes, on the one hand, a self-conscious phase of man's development and, on the other, the possession of a free will which can be 'exercised'. We would like to maintain here that the ethical connotation of dharma is helpful also to point out that achieving the true identity of the individual is, psychologically speaking, a potentiality in one sense and an ideal in another. Our further suggestion here is that whether we look at the concept of dharma as standing for the moral sense in man or as providing the psychological basis for the identity-realizing potential with which man is endowed, the personality-integration idea of dharma is indeed deeper than it may appear on the surface, and also its social implications can be better appreciated by reflecting on it.

In its psychological aspects dharma is considered as essentially a principle of growth embedded in the life of each individual. It is intrinsic to the proper growth of man. Dharma is said to be the law of one's being. But, since no individual can grow apart from or outside his society, the personality-growth of the individual necessarily involves his growing *with* society. In terms of the identity-theory it seems to us that the intimate relationship between the psychological and social aspects of dharma thus understood offers us an insight into the way in which personal identity, group identity, and social identity are understood in the Hindu tradition.

The dharma of an individual is, in its psychological sense, his innate nature — the law of his being and development. In the moral (ethical)

sense it stands also for an ideal of development, signifying righteous-
ness. But it cannot be the same for all (for the simple reason that
individuals differ in temperament) or the same for one individual all the
time (since, during the various stages of development the individual's
inclinations, aspirations, and ideals are different). It is determined by
the total situation which is undetermined. It is thus indefinite and
indeterminate. Thus, dharma is seen to be a dynamic principle, con-
tributing to the development of the individual's personality and to the
maintenance of social order. The term *svadharma* (one's own duty) is
made use of to indicate that the dharma of the individual during
different periods in his life and of different individuals in a society
differs.

The celebrated theories of *Asrama* and *Varna* adumbrated in the
Hindu tradition which provide the basis for our interpretation of the
welding together of personal, group, and social aspects of the identity
problem, are based on this principle of svadharma. It should be
mentioned however, that the concept of svadharma is generally understood more in relation to the varna scheme than with reference to the
asrama scheme and that, because of such an interpretation of
svadharama, the closely-knit scheme of the personal and social aspects
of realizing identity is often overlooked. Hence we deem it necessary to
briefly comment on the asrama and varna schemes.

Looked at from the point of view of the individual's personal
development, the asrama-dharmas (the duties prescribed for the
individual during the different stages of his development) point to the
way in which the individual's identity as a person can be aimed at and
achieved. Looked at from the point of view of social groups or society
at large, the varna-dharmas indicate the conditions under which the
individuals can make their contribution to the group or society really
worthwhile. The asrama scheme lays emphasis on enlarging the area of
social concern in such a way that it helps the individual, ultimately, in
realizing his true identity. Similarly, though the varna scheme may be
interpreted as offering us a blueprint for an ideal social order, the
importance accorded to the subjective aspect of the individuals' contribution to the social weal should not be overlooked. The obvious
significance of such an intertwining of the subjective and objective
aspects of the asrama as well as the varna scheme is that the ultimate
ideal of the individual (realizing his true identity) does not consist in

realizing a state in which the internalization of the individual reaches a 'point of no return', making him a 'world unto himself' with no concern or care for 'others'.

The *varnasrama* scheme is 'designed' in such a way that the full flowering of the individual's personality entails simultaneously a natural and intensive concern for society and humanity. The clear recognition of the fact that cultivation of such an attitude towards 'others' can neither be achieved all at once nor without a process of widening one's area of concern gradually through the 'more immediate' social groups is probably the reason why the varnasrama scheme is invariably considered to contain the quientessence of Hindu social philosophy. The traditional analysis of the whole scheme as helping the individual to progressively overcome his egoistic predicament also reveals, when studied more carefully, that the 'expansive attitude' advocated serves also to enable the individual to realize his true identity.

CONCLUSION

We have thus suggested that the universalistic implications of the identity-theory can be corroborated by a study of the concept of dharma in the Hindu tradition. In our first level of analysis we were concerned to indicate our own criteria of a universally applicable theory by selecting the psychological and normative-sociological approaches to the concept of identity. If identity is not a mere academic abstraction but is well-grounded in human nature we have maintained that the natural consequence that its correlates in other cultures can well be expected is obvious. On the sociological front too our view has been that as long as the metaphysical underpinnings of the institutional situation of man are accepted as valid, similarity of approach to the problem of man-in-society, far from coming to us as a surprise, must only be expected. In our second level of analysis we have specifically pointed to the psychological and social aspects of the concept of dharma and have argued that the careful working out of the integrated schemes of asrama and varna indicates a clear recognition, in the Hindu tradition too, of the significance of the various 'levels of identity'. We have, however, not considered, even in brief, the subtle (though significant) points of differences in emphases that are apparent even in the terminological differences, this being conceded as one of the presuppositions of this paper. Our accent of emphasis has mainly been on the 'commonality elements' rather than on the divergences of approach. Needless to add, this was not with a view to diluting down or explaining away the differences between the approaches of the identity theory and the varnasrama theories, to the significance of society in general, but with a view to highlighting the 'areas of intersection' within the page-limits suggested by the organizers of the symposium.

NOTES

1. The implicit suggestion here seems to be that a reference to the essence of religion does not connote simply dwelling on certain metaphysical aspects of human life which have no relation to life in society. It is obvious that neither the more purely individualistic aspects of human life nor the predominantly social aspects are disregarded. The close correlation between the two is no doubt more obviously evident when we speak of the inter-personal aspects of human living. Though not so evident, the integral relationship between them is equally significant even when the focus of attention is shifted to realms of analysis which may seem to be non-social. The most significant point here is that this realm of analysis points to the metaphysical roots of society itself by going into basic issues like *integration, harmony, cohesiveness*, etc. As these concepts yield their truer meaning when employed at the individual level, i.e. for discussing the *inner core* of personality, the term identity – in the context of an analysis and interpretation of religion – has the advantage of synthesizing the psychological and metaphysical dimensions of human personality and hence also the deeper implications of inter-personal relationships.

2. T. W. Organ (1970: 89-91) analysing Hinduism as 'the quest for integration' observes: '. . . there is one factor within Hinduism upon which she can build, and that is the integrating quest itself. Inclusiveness, not exclusiveness, is the principle of Hinduism . . . The great strength of Hinduism as integrator of the life of man is its deep sense of the relatedness of things rooted metaphysically in the concept of *jiva* which vitalizes all living forms.' Though Organ's observations are made in the context of explaining 'the quest' in Hinduism, they *are* relevant in our context inasmuch as they are aimed at explaining that the quest reveals depths which are not readily apparent and point to an underlying state which may be referred to as self-realization or attaining one's true identity.

REFERENCES

MOL, Hans (1976) *Identity and the Sacred*. Oxford: Blackwell.
ORGAN, T. W. (1970) *The Hindu Quest for the Perfection of Man*. Ohio: Ohio University Press.
STRAUSS, A. L. (1959) *Mirrors and Masks*. Illinois: The Free Press of Glencoe.

7

WAYS OF YOGA AND THE MECHANISMS OF SACRALIZATION

Manju and Braj Sinha
The College of Wooster, Ohio, USA

Manju and Braj Sinha's chapter is the more sociological of the Indian contributions. It traces the mechanisms of sacralization through the various systems of yoga and finds strong similarities between objectification and Jñāna Yoga, commitment and Bhakti Yoga; and ritual and Tantra Yoga. In all three they find the mythic symbolism of the opposing, and yet also complementing, dialectic between Purusa *(being, the static) and* Prakriti *(becoming, the dynamic), with* Isvara *at the synthesizing apex. They suggest a fifth mechanism of appropriation, congruent with Karma Yoga, which signifies the tendency of the sacred to assimilate all that comes into contact with it and which provides an impetus for active participation in the social process.*

Any system of meaning or value orientation constituting the frame of reference for motivational orientation of its adherents is a sociologically analyzable phenomenon. Yoga is no exception in this regard. This is the basic assumption of this chapter. Against this background the chapter attempts to bring out both the strengths and limitations of the identity model for analyzing the sacralization process. The scientific value and heuristic utility of the conceptual scheme under investigation depends on its cross-cultural applicability and a generality that can account for varieties in the historically and culturally conditioned responses to the ever-felt need for sacralization. Our analysis of the ways of Yoga is one step in this direction.

YOGA AND SELF-INTEGRATION

Functional indispensability of religion is the basic presupposition of the identity perspective on religion. Religion as the repository of institutionalized beliefs and ritual practices guarantees the cohesiveness of the social whole. It provides a frame of reference for individual's self-expression. The expressive orientation of religious symbol systems have integrative consequences for the self. Religion, by providing individuals with an interpretation of existence, performs the invaluable task of resolving the problem of meaning. 'In a world whose purpose cannot be ascertained by reason, religion stands ready with an explanation, however partial it may be, to fill the vacuum' (Glock and Stark, 1969: 5).

The problem of identity consolidation or self-integration is the primary concern of Yoga. Despite the use of the term Yoga in varying contexts it has retained its original meaning, etymologically derived from the sanskrit *root yuj* meaning 'to bind together', 'hold fast', 'yoke', etc. Diversity of opinion may occur as to what needs to be bound together, or to what one has to hold fast, or where the yoke lies. Whether it is communion of the self with Isvara that motivates the aspirant or the restoration of 'wholeness' of self by uniting the *Śiva* and the *Śakti* in *Kundalini* that drives the incumbent on the path of Yoga, the ultimate end of all Yogas is self-integration or the restoration of the self. It is to this self-integrative aspect of Yoga that a modern interpreter of Yoga draws our attention:

> Yoga thus literally means union . . . It implies union of the mind with the inmost centre of one's own being, the self or atman-union of the conscious mind with the deeper levels of the unconscious – resulting in the integration of personality. That is indeed the chief objective of Yoga (Chaudhari, 1965: 21).

The basic assumption of Yoga is that an integrated self is essentially sacred. The purpose of Yogic techniques is to unify the spirit; to do away with the dispersion and automatism that supposedly characterizes the profane consciousness. Self-integration implies bringing home to the self the fact of the essential duality of the self and not-self. Meaninglessness and arbitrariness that infest human existence and constitute pain and suffering have their source in the forgetfulness of the self's essential freedom from the not-self; in its alienation from the ground of its own existence. Alienation of the self consists in its identification with not-self (Larson, 1969: 185).

The bringing together of self, the 'bond' in which the action of binding is to result, presupposes as its preliminary condition breaking the 'bonds' that unite the spirit to the world. Detachment from one focus of identity must precede attachment to another. It is in this emphasis on the detachment and attachment that the sacralizing function of Yoga techniques lies. In the traditional interpretation of Yoga this detachment element has been over-emphasized; the other-worldliness of Yoga, in particular, and Indian philosophy, in general, had been a favorite pastime of scholars in the nineteenth and the first half of the twentieth century. However, the identity perspective that we are employing in this study has the advantage of bringing to the fore the primacy of the attachment or integrative element of Yoga techniques.

It is equally important to note that the Yogic experience is different from conversion in the sense that it is not a detachment from one sacralized perspective and attachment to another that is implied here. Rather, it is detachment from a profane and attachment to a sacred mode of life that distinguishes Yogic experience from the more traumatic conversion experience (James, 1902; Boisen, 1936). Moreover, the new focus of identity is not considered as altogether new. Rather, it is restoration of one's identity or realizing one's true identity. One might suggest that the success of Yoga in certain segments of the modern West resides in this very orientation of Yogic techniques. It is not accidental that modern protagonists and propogandists together (including Indian philosophers, swamis and gurus) have emphasized the non-theistic aspect of Yoga philosophy. From this point of view Yoga is the universal religion, for it is not a religion centered around a conception of a personal god (Chaudhari, 1965: 22-23; Eliade, 1971: 73). Understandably then, despite these expostulations, Yoga has not been able to make inroads into the committed segments of Christian population. Yogic techniques are not developed to suit the needs of a conversion mechanism. They can be successful only where the 'sacralized' identity is already grounded in the secured foundation of tradition, or where the sacralized identity does not have to compete with an already sacralized, and thereby secured, identity. Success of Yoga in the non-

committed, unanchored, 'lost' youth of the modern West is to be
accounted for by the fact that it is eminently suited for identity
integration where the emphasis is on dissociation from a profane
existence, an existence which is utterly meaningless and full of contradictions.

JŇĀNA YOGA AND OBJECTIFICATION

Mol defines objectification as 'the tendency to sum up the variegated
elements of mundane existence in a transcendental point of reference
where they can appear more orderly, more consistent and more timeless' (Mol, 1976: 13). Thus, the function of objectification is to project
a conception of reality, a system of values or a meaning structure in a
transcendental realm. This serves the double purpose of guaranteeing
the incorruptibility of the transcendental order as well as providing a
point of reference in terms of which the corruption, the contingencies,
the chaos, and the inconsistencies of the mundane realm come to be
interpreted and appropriated.

The corresponding concept to objectification in Yoga is the way of
knowledge (Jñāna Yoga). It would seem to be a contradiction to claim
that any concept emphasizing knowledge as a way to ultimate union
with the supreme is comparable to the objectification process. The
contradiction would appear to be more telling if we use the term
knowledge in its current connotation with the instrumentive-adaptive
symbol system. However, in order to understand the way of knowledge
one has to keep in mind that knowledge here refers to a state of being.
To know is to be in a particular state of being. It is that state of being
which coincides with intuitive awareness of the essential nature of
things. As Bahm puts it:

> As one proceeds along the path of knowledge, after distinguishing all dif-
> ferences between things experienced, he progressively realizes their lack of
> ultimacy and withdraws his attention from them as distractions preventing
> him from enjoying the ultimate intuition. The path of knowledge leads
> beyond knowledge to a Yogic intuition in which awareness and being are
> identical (1961: 18).

The mystic overtones of Yoga reflected in this position notwith-standing, we can clearly discern that it corroborates Mol's distinction between the expressive and the adaptive aspects of the symbol system (1976: 3 ff.). Yogic awareness of the ultimate nature of things coincides with coming to terms with the essence of one's own being. The goal of Jñāna Yoga is not to manipulate the structures of the psyche or categories of thought to enable the self to adjust and adapt to the changes in the environing conditions. Its aim is to develop that frame of mind which enables the self to come to terms with itself despite the contingencies, contradictions, and arbitrariness of existence.

Thus, while for Mol objectification serves the purpose of minimizing the disruptive influence of the meaninglessness of existence on the self, Jñāna Yoga proposes the mechanism of discrimination *(viveka)* and the expressive longing for freedom *(mumukṣatā)* to protect the self from the onslaughts of mundane existence (Sinha, 1975). The scheme involving the dialectic of discriminative reason (viveka) and expressive orientation (mumukṣatā) confirms Mol's crucial hypothesis about the conflicting and yet complementary relationship between the discursive-adaptive reason and the expressive-integrative symbol system.

The path of knowledge includes a quest for knowledge both of self and objects as ordinarily experienced and of self and object as they ultimately are. Discrimination (viveka) is that mode of understanding which is employed by the self to comprehend the distinction between the self and the not-self. Discrimination (viveka) means clear under-standing of the distinction between the real and the unreal, the permanent and the transient (Sen Gupta, 1969). Once this distinction is brought home to the self through discursive reasoning and rational analysis it gives rise to the longing for freedom, which for Yoga implies withdrawing *(vairāgya)* from the world of not-self to the self.

Through a clear understanding of the distinction between the *Puruṣa* (being) and *Prakṛti* (becoming), the permanent and the transient, a breach with the immediacy of things temporal, transient, and con-tingent is accomplished. A breach with immediacy is considered as an essential condition of the spiritual quest (Eliade, 1971: 33-34).

One might suspect that this breach with immediacy implies a com-plete rupture between the mundane and the transcendent. However, Jnana Yoga has a different explanation to offer. Jnana Yoga does not aim at the negation of the mundane. Rather, it is the realization that the mundane cannot provide the ground for its own existence, that it draws its being and meaning from the transcendent that constitutes the goal of Jñāna Yoga. The mundane perceived in its own right is full of contradictions, arbitrariness, and cannot defend its purpose and meaning. Perceived in the context of the transcendent the contradictions, the arbitrariness, and the contingencies of the mundane acquire a new meaning and purpose. Transcendent is the meaning and purpose of this mundane existence. It is for the sake of Purusa that Prakriti exists. The way of knowledge aims at this realization.

Mol has argued that the function of objectification is to guarantee the incorruptibility of the transcendental order as well as to provide a point of reference in terms of which the corruption, the contingencies, the chaos, and the inconsistencies of the mundane realm can be interpreted and appropriated (1976: 265). Mol's emphasis on the latter aspect of objectification is not without significance. An extremely interesting example is presented by the Gita in Chapter XI when Krsna unfolds to Arjuna that dimension of Krsna which embraces the whole universe not excluding either of the parts of opposites, good and evil, beautiful and ugly, sweet and terrible, pleasant and painful. Arjuna who was initially reluctant to fight because he was appalled by the ugliness, the horrific vision of the ways of a world which prompt brothers to fight brothers and kinsmen to kill kinsmen, sees Krsna providing the meaning and purpose of human existence. The feeling that all this is not ultimately meaningless, that there is an order and purpose behind the arbitrary and the contingent enables the self to absorb and digest the frustrations and contingencies as not altogether meaningless, but as part and parcel of an orderly world. Through viveka and vairāgya, Jñāna Yoga strengthens and consolidates one's belief in the transcendental order as the ground of the mundane existence.

BHAKTI YOGA AND COMMITMENT

The emotional component or the feeling aspect of the sacralization process is called commitment. Commitment is defined as the focused emotion or emotional attachment to a specific focus of identity (Mol,

1976: 216). Thus, it is the anchoring of emotions in a salient system of meaning. Inevitably, then, commitment reinforces identities, systems of meaning, and definitions of reality. The reinforcing process is seen as guaranteeing consistency and predictability of motivation and behavior. Thus it has a stabilizing effect on systems of meaning and actions and thereby ensures personality integration and social cohesion. Commitment is primarily affirmative and identity-consolidating.

The correlate to the mechanism of commitment in Yoga is the Way of Devotion *(Bhakti Yoga)*. Bhakti Yoga as a way leading to union with the Supreme lays emphasis on the significance of the emotive content of the belief system. Elaborate and extensive discussion of the nature and orientation of Bhakti Yoga is to be found in the Bhagvad-Gitā. However, the earliest expression of the cult of devotion is to be traced to Ṛg Veda where it is recorded as *Śradhā-Bhakti*. Śradhā, defined as faith or preferably commitment to believing in order to realize, is described as the necessary element in all ritualistic activities. (Edgerton, 1965: 32). To quote from the text:

> Śradhā lits the fire, Śradhā pours out the oblation; it is śradhā that the god takes cognizance of in prayers; is she not then the spirit of the ritual? Yes she is the embodied spirit or goddess at whom the whole devotion is aimed; ... let her inspire the worshipper with the spirit of faith (Ṛg Veda).

Later, in the Mahābhārata, of which the Gitā forms a part, it is stated that the sages, full of faith *(sradhadhanaḥ)* and self-controlled, recognized Śradhā as a mighty instrument; every man was indeed as powerful in his spiritual disposition as was his faith, the śradhā in him that according to Bhagvad-Gitā was itself Man (Bhiksu, 1930: 22). *Yo yat sradhāḥ sa eva saḥ*, 'every one is as his faith and truly is he of that faith'. Nothing goes more to the real make-up of man but the commitment (Sradha) and the content thereof; the ideas that he has made his own by his commitment thereto.

Aurobindo, a modern exponent of Yoga, has recognized the significance of the emotional component in the process of sacralization. Commenting on the nature of Bhakti Yoga he maintains:

> ... All is supported here by the primary force of the emotional union; for it is by love that the entire self-consecration and the entire possession is accomplished, and thought and action become shapes and figures of the divine love which possesses the spirit and its members (Sri Aurobindo, 1965: 535).

Aurobindo goes on to explicate the theoretical refinement and conceptual clarity involved in Yogic understanding of the stages and levels of commitment. The emotional attraction or the emotional focusing towards the divine involves three stages of (1) adoration; (2) consecration; and (3) sacrifice. Adoration wears the form of external worship and corresponds to something really felt within the mind, some genuine submission, awe or spiritual aspiration. Adoration leads to consecration, i.e. self-purification so as to become fit for divine contact. Consecration implies becoming like the divine. Consecration leads to a fullness of commitment implying a total devotion of the whole being of the aspirant to the divine. This is described as sacrifice of love where the 'bhakta (devotee) offers up his life and all that he is and all that he has and all that he does to the Divine' (Aurobindo, 1958: 534). Aurobindo's suggestion that this self-surrender, or sacrifice of the Bhakta, may take an ascetic form prompting the individual to renounce all personal possessions and devote his time solely to prayer confirms Mol's observation that 'asceticism is usually a way of clarifying personal priorities and purifying one's loyalties' (Mol, 1976: 229).

The most significant point that Mol makes in his formulation of commitment relates to the priority-setting function of commitment and its relevance for the sacralization of a system of meaning or value structure. Yoga recognizes the importance of setting one's priorities for integration with the Supreme. Accordingly the Hindu Yogic philosophy insists on the inestimable contribution of Sradha in setting such priorities for spiritual realization. Hence, it is maintained that the Bhakti Yoga must be one pointed *(ekānta)*; never attentive to anything else *(ananya)*; never adulterated *(avyabhichāri)*, etc., for in the inner life that is a sacrifice *(antaryajña)*, where the soul is the sacrificer, Sradha, oneness, non-divergence in the Will is the ultimate helpmate of the sacrificer, the Atman (Chaudhari, 1965: 24).

It is the priority-setting function of the commitment link that on a different plane enables the aspirant to perceive immense possibilities for union with the Supreme in self-sacrifice. Self-sacrifice is guided by the intense need to find oneself in the company of the divine, whose constant companionship the devotee always desired, and the certainty born of commitment that death, instead of being an end to life, is the beginning of a more meaningful life in the fellowship (Sakhā) of the divine. Thus sacrifice is a form of commitment which reinforces a system of meaning or identity by clarifying priorities.

TANTRA YOGA AND RITUAL

The sacralizing potential of ritual has been recognized by many scholars. Durkheim acknowledged the capacity of rites to sacralize:

> A rite can have this character; in fact, the rite does not exist which does not have it to a certain degree. . . . If the Vedic sacrifice has had such an efficacy that . . . it was the creator of the gods, and not merely a means of winning their favour, it is because it possessed a virtue comparable to that of the most sacred beings (Durkheim, 1965: 52).

When Jung maintains that in the rite of the Mass 'the Eucharist transforms the soul of empirical man' (Jung, 1958: 273) he is attesting to the essentially sacralizing function of rites.

What does the rite do to sacralize a system of meaning? In Mol's formulation of the problem, again the integrative, identity-consolidating dimension of the sacralization process becomes the pre-eminently important contribution of ritual practices. Thus, he writes:

> Ritual maximises order, reinforces the place of the individual in his society and strengthens the bonds of a society vis-a-vis the individual. Through repetitive, emotion-evoking action, social cohesion and personality integration are reinforced — at the same time that aggressive or socially destructive actions are articulated, dramatized and curbed (Mol, 1976: 13).

By representing sameness in action the rites consolidate the sameness of a system of meaning. Each ritual activity involves, in some way or other, a recommitment to memory of a system of meaning. Ritual as the repetitive enactment of a certain system of meaning tends to strengthen the 'don't touch' sentiments in the same way as sometimes personal habits through constant repetition become so meaningful for the individual that he never thinks of changing them. In both cases the fundamental need for identity is expressed in one's acceptance of the invincibility of the system of meaning constituting the motivational orientation of repetitive actions. It is to this identity-consolidating function of ritual activity that Durkheim draws our attention in his observation that 'through (ritual) the group periodically renews the sentiment which it has of itself and of its unity; at the same time, individuals are strengthened in their social nature' (Durkheim, 1965: 375).

Tantra Yoga in the Yogic scheme operates on the basic assumption that the ritual aspect of the belief system is extremely important for the realization of spiritual communion. Most of the modern literature on Yoga distinguishes between Haṭha Yoga and Tantra Yoga, the latter being the extreme form of ritualism in its most concrete aspect. However, in the ancient Sanskrit writings they are placed together, Haṭha Yoga being a part of Tantra Yoga (Eliade, 1971: 227).

The emphasis in Tantra is on the restoration of the wholeness of being (Dasgupta, S. B., 1974). According to Tantra Yoga the ultimate goal of all Tantric ritual is the union of the dynamic and static aspects of personality. These two aspects are frequently described as the polar opposites of Śiva (the timeless perfection) and Śakti (the dynamism of time) (Chaudhari, 1965: 59). The two are united in Kundalini to restore the 'wholeness' of the 'being'. Symbolically it is represented as a sort of supreme marriage *(mahāmaithuna)* between the feminine and the masculine aspect of personality, between the principles of basic energy and pure existence. The same idea is expressed in the Yogic notion of the synchronization of breath or the respiratory rhythm when the Haṭha Yogi attempts to realize 'totality' or 'wholeness' of existence by uniting the *HA* (the breath of the right nostril representing the sun) and *THA* (the breath of the left nostril representing the moon). In this dialectic of opposites the Yogi 'realizes' the state of *sahaja* (the equilibrium) by transcending the dualities. And as Hevarāja Tantra points out: 'the whole world is of the nature of sahaja — for sahaja is the quintessence *(svarupa)* of all' (Eliade, 1971: 269). Thus the wholeness or totality accomplished in Tantra Yoga is both personal and cosmic.

Rites of Tantra affirm the need for intelligent and organized fulfill-ment of natural instinctual desires. It tends to undermine any basic antagonism between nature (society) and self; and self-mortification is considered contrary to the functional orientation of nature (society). Rites emanating from the Tantric theory of the five Ms such as wine *(Madya)*, meat *(Mānsa)*, fish *(Matsya)*, parched cereal *(Mudrā)*, and sexual union *(Maithuna)* are considered valuable aids to the vigorous growth and development of the spirit (Chaudhari, 1965: 60). According to Kundalini or Tantra Yoga these represent different modes of mani-festation of energy. The assumption is that any individual making profitable use of these for a union with the supreme power through consistent development of the 'whole' of human personality, not in isolation from, but in harmony with, the natural existence, is the true Yogi. For the Tantra Yoga implies that

> all these desires (finding expression and fructification in rites), ultimately come from the divine will. In the final analysis they are aids to the process of evolution and progress. The important thing is to fulfill them with that understanding, in a spirit of cooperation with the creative force of evolution ... The more a person cooperates with the evolutionary impetus, the more his desires are purged of the egoistic taint and are transmuted into the pure flame of aspiration for divine life (Chaudhari, 1965: 61).

There is more than one reason for placing Tantra Yoga on a par with the mechanism of ritual. Indeed, its emphasis on the integrative-expressive orientation of repetitive non-logical action is the obvious common ground. Through an organized manipulation of the instinctual energy in Tāntra, as Turner would put it, 'the raw energies of conflicts are domesticated in the service of social order' (Turner, 1970: 172). The function of Tāntric rituals is to adapt and periodically re-adapt, to borrow Turner's phrase, 'the bio-physical individual to the basic conditions and axiomatic values of human social life' (Turner, 1970: 177). The essential element underlying the Tāntric practices is the belief that these rites cleanse or purify mundane or profane acts and in the process sacralize the acts themselves by superimposing certain constraints on them. Hence Maithuna (participation in a sexual act) for a Tāntric Yogi is a rite and not a profane act; since the partners are no longer human beings, but 'detached' like gods, sexual union is elevated to the cosmic plane. Ritual repetition of an act sacralizes it and the performance thereof, instead of being constitutive of bondage, leads to salvation. The Tāntric texts frequently repeat: 'By the same acts that cause some men to burn in hell for thousands years, the Yogi gains his eternal salvation' (Eliade, 1971: 263).

We have tried to see the degree to which Kuṇḍalini Yoga fits into our scheme of things. The problem of fit has been minimized by asserting the element of repetitiveness as well as the 'wholeness' that is accomplished through the expressive-integrative orientation of the repetitive non-logical action. However, the minimization of the problem is not to our entire satisfaction. Indeed, though Kuṇḍalini Yoga lies on the side of the non-logical and tends to stabilize through emotional sublimation of the basic conflict of human existence, at the same time it has contributed to the sacralization of a permanent state of liminality within Hindu society. The paradox of the permanent state of liminality needs to be clarified by stating that throughout the history of Hindu society it is the Yogis with their expertise in Kundalini Yoga, as a group, who have been considered as outside the boundaries of the social whole and threatening the cohesiveness of the society.

MYTHIC SYMBOLISM IN YOGA

A considerable difficulty plagues our attempt to analyze the Yoga system in terms of mythic symbolism. None of the Yogas noted by us can be identified as dealing with the role of Myth as a separate mechanism. Nevertheless, each and all of them postulate a system of mythic symbolism through which a specific interpretation of reality is internalized and assimilated at the emotional level. Thus the basic function of emotional sublimation of the critical conflict situations of human existence is accomplished through mythic symbolism over and against adaptation through the instrumental symbol system. But at the same time the dialectical relationship between instrumental symbolism, on the one hand, and expressive symbolism, on the other, is not undermined. We have noted earlier how the Gita proclaims the complementarity of these two facets of symbol system in the Yogic scheme of things.

What Mol considers critical for mythic symbolism holds true for Yoga in its totality. According to Mol the basic binary opposition or conflict which is emotionally sublimated on a symbolic level constitutes the core of mythic narration (Mol, 1976: 252). The binary opposition central to the theological formulations of all Yoga systems is the conflicting and complementing relationship between the Puruṣa (the principle of being, static, pure, consciousness, the witness) and the Prakṛti (the principle of becoming, change, that which veils consciousness and is witnessed).

In and through mythical reiteration this basic duality is presented to the seeker of ultimate self-integration. For Jñāna Yoga this basic conflict situation is mediated through the myth of Isvara. The removal of *māyā* implies an intense separative perception of the great duality, Soul-Nature, Puruṣa-Prakṛti. However, at the synthesizing apex of this duality stands Isvara, the supreme being who originally was responsible for māyā causing the false identification of Purusa-Prakrti, and who ultimately guarantees removal of this false perception. In Bhakti Yoga the myth of Isvara takes a somewhat different form. The binary opposition between Purusa and Prakriti is felt to be so intense that any attachment or love *(prema)* for things of Prakrti (including one's dearest) must give way to the ultimate love (prema) of Isvara with utter submission and total and unconditional surrender to the divine will. In Tantra Yoga, though Isvara becomes part of the binary opposition, the centrality of wholeness or totality as the synthesizing element at which the aspirant aims, is retained. In Tantra the divine has two opposed yet inseparable aspects: the archetypal masculine (Śiva), the archetypal feminine (Śakti). Śiva is pure being, timeless perfection, eternal wisdom. Śakti is the power of becoming, the creative energy of time, the joy of love of self-expression. The function of maithuna (sexual rites) in Tantra Yoga is to highlight symbolically the integration of these principles; 'the true sexual union is the union of the *paraśakti* (śakti element) with Ātman (the Śiva element); other unions represent only carnal relations' (Eliade, 1971: 262).

Two observations may be offered. First, the basic binary opposition is constantly present in the mythic symbolism employed by various Yogas. Secondly, the distinctiveness of the myth lies in its constant reiteration, and yet ever-changing narration, of a basic truth. It is the constancy of this basic truth underlying various ways of Yoga that provides the ground for the reinforcement of the definitions of reality and structures of meaning that constitute the uniqueness of the Yoga belief system. Yogic myths in various ways state and restate the binary opposition between Purusa and Prakriti with the ultimate primacy of synthesizing unity in Isvara.

KARMA YOGA AND THE DIALECTIC OF APPROPRIATION

In Mol's formulation of the process of sacralization he refers to the two-pronged dialectic of the process: the making of the sacred, and the sacred in its turn exercising its capacity for further sacralization.

However, in Mol's explication of the process the second aspect of the sacralization process, i.e. the sacred tending to effect further sacralization has received little attention. This scheme stresses the way, or the mechanism through which, the sacred extends its reign over the profane and moulds and transforms the profane into the sacred. I propose the mechanism of appropriation to make the second moment in the dialectical growth of sacralization process more explicit.

It is intrinsic to the nature of the sacred that it appropriates and assimilates all that comes into contact with it (Durkheim, 1965: 358). In the process the profane becomes sacred and the gradual diminution of the sacred occurs   (O'Dea, 1966: 94).   As one value structure or system of meaning tends to become less relevant because of its concretization, which must take place in order that the sacred may exercise its power for sacralization, new value orientations or meaning structures come to be sacralized. The same mechanisms of objectification, commitment, ritual, and myth remain as relevant for sacralization as ever. But the new systems of meaning or value structure, too, once they have acquired the quality of sacredness in and through these mechanisms, do not remain totally confined to the transcendental locus. If they are to have relevance for human existence they must participate in mundane life. This they do through the mechanism of appropriation.

In Karma Yoga the dialectical relationship of the profane and the sacred emerges in its most pronounced form. For Yoga, self-integration is the sacred mode of being; and in Karma Yoga the problem of self-integration is related to the problem of social-integration. Karma Yoga emphasizes the significance of human volition and natural propensities for action and outlines a scheme of things in which the activities of the mundane world, day-to-day living, acquire a new meaning and provide impetus for active participation in the social process. Significantly, Karma Yoga unequivocally declares inaction or withdrawal from the activities of the mundane world detrimental to the growth of human personality and disruptive for the social whole (Rajagopalachari, 1955: 49). Mol has drawn our attention to the fact that 'the integration/sacralization at the level of self or group may have a disintegrative/desacralizing effect on the wider social whole'. This dialectic of individual and social integration is recognized by Yoga and

Karma Yoga is an attempt to minimize the disruptive, disintegrative consequences of Jnana Yoga and Bhakti Yoga which inevitably lead to a self-centered conception of sacred mode of being. Karma Yoga recognizes the dialectic of the conflict and complementarity between the parts (the individual) and the whole (the society), and accordingly exhorts the adherents to strive for a social integration through spiritual growth. Thus the Gita points out:

> Janaka and others attained perfection only through performance of actions. Looking even to the welfare of society, you should work (perform duties of your station). Whatever way of life the great men (enlightened ones) adopt, the other men copy; the standards the (enlightened one) sets up is followed by the people.... Hence, the enlightened should toil with the motive of the social-welfare without any attachment (Gita, 3: 20-25).

The basic presupposition of the path of action is that self and social integration stand in a dialectical relationship, social control of the individual is indispensable, and although the self suffers precisely because of the experience of meaninglessness and anomie in social existence it must cooperate with the social mode of being to realize its own goal of self-integration. Karma Yoga, fully aware of the problematics of the 'existential' situation and the resultant bewilderment, provides the ideal of a fully sacred life, a life full of meaning and purpose. It encourages the man of action and poses that meaning and value can be realized through participation in the world-process. The Karma Yogi does not encounter nothingness, is not occupied by uncanniness, and is free from confusions and bewilderment because he knows that life itself imposes specific obligations upon each individual and that at every moment of his existence he has a duty that is defined by his existential situation. Karma Yoga does not emphasize renunciation of the world and worldly activities; emphasis here is on the performance of those activities with a mental attitude of non-involvement and non-attachment. Non-attachment in this context implies the sacrifice of personal aggrandizement at the altar of the social good. Probably there is a grain of truth in Durkheim's proposition that the sacred is the mode of society's control on the conflicting interests of individuals. Karma Yoga is a classic case of a religious symbol system performing this function.

In and through Karma Yoga sacredness is extended to human

existence in its entirety. Religion, in order to be relevant to the needs of meaning and order in mundane existence, cannot remain content with articulating a totally other-worldly mode of sacredness. Inner-worldly motivation is not a prerogative of any one specific religious orientation (Weber, 1958). Rather, it is a prerequisite for the survival and successful operation of any transcendentally grounded religion. It is not without significance that even Buddhism, while exhorting the ideals of renunciation in its extreme form, also developed the ideal of Bodhis-attva, the spiritual being who finds it extremely desirable to postpone his own final deliverance in order to be able to participate in the affaris of mundane existence (Conze, 1959: 125 ff.).

It is precisely at this point that universal religions have specific advantages over other elements of culture. Universal religions not only have the privilege of sacralizing expertise within the specific cultural contexts, but they also have the opportunity to be in tune with the demands of the dialectic of integration-adaptation, stability-change. Through prophecy, charisma, conversion, etc. changes are incorporated and assimilated at different levels. While conversion and other rites of passage enable the individual to cope with the moments of change in personal identity, charisma and prophecy are mechanisms developed for the purpose of incorporating changes at the level of social identity (Mol, 1976). Because of this expertise in dealing with the forces of change and adaptation, universal religions have developed a certain amount of immunity to the diminutive effects of appropriation. They tend to assert their relevance even in the wake of continued onslaughts by the forces of change. The point of the argument is that though sacralization through appropriation entails subsequent devaluation of the sacred, this danger is effectively counterbalanced in the context of institutionalized religions. Just as an organism develops immunity to certain bacterial infections through constant exposure to it over a long period of time or an immunity in the organism is developed through injection of the bacteria in the organism under controlled conditions, so have institutionalized religions developed immunity to the desacralizing potential of sacralization through appropriation.

This, however, is not true in the case of the newly-emerging sacralizing catalysts. The plight of the Ānanda Mārga movement in India is a case in point. The movement, as long as it remained a religious movement offering a viable alternative to institutionalized Hinduism, was able to draw a considerable following from the rank and file of the intelligentsia who seemed to be disenchanted with institutionalized Hinduism. However, the movement went astray and suffered inexorable loss in prestige and following as soon as it moved to appropriate the realm of politics in order to influence the course of change in the country. On the other hand, a modern political party, Jana Sangha, which claims to derive its ideological strength from mainline Hinduism has not only grown stronger in the last decade but has forced all the other leftist parties to combine together against this formidable enemy. The association of Hindu religious fervor with a political party has contributed to the strength of the aforesaid political group without jeopardizing the character and strength of the religious fervor. While appropriation of the everydayness of human existence can take place on different levels of economic, political, and cultural or artistic sub-systems, the consequence of such appropriation is always integrative for the group. This is even more true in the context of newly-emerging sacred patterns of meaning structures or value systems. Thus 'without the daily routines, stable hierarchies, the personal loyalties, the emotional satisfaction of speaking on a similar wavelength our technocratic empires would have succumbed long ago to the forces of rationality and efficiency which produced them in the first place. Also semi-sacred formulas such as "free enterprise", "democracy", "rational skepticism", and "objectivity" have emerged at the heart of some of the sub-systems of modern societies, such as the economy, polity and science' (Mol, 1976: 264). How effectively these systems of meaning tend to appropriate the entire realm of human existence is an issue that cannot be settled on a theoretical level. Intensive empirical investigation is required before any incontrovertible conclusions can be drawn. However, on impressionistic grounds it may not be unfair to maintain that these semi-sacred formulae, too, do not lag behind in placing their claims on the everyday mode of human existence.

REFERENCES

BAHM, Archie J. (1961) *Yoga: Union with the Ultimate*, New York: Fredrick Ungar.

BOISEN, Anton, T. (1936) *The Exploration of the Inner World*, New York: Harper & Row.

CHOUDHARI, Haridas (1965) *Integral Yoga*. London: George Allen & Unwin.

CONZE, Edward (1959) *Buddhism: Its Essence and Development*. New York: Harper & Row.

DASGUPTA, S. B. (1974) *Tantric Buddhism*. Berkeley: Shambala.

DURKHEIM, Emile (1965) *The Elementary Forms of the Religious Life*. New York: Free Press.

EDGERTON, Franklin (1965) *The Beginnings of Indian Philosophy*. Cambridge, Mass.: Harvard University Press.

ELIADE, Mircea (1971) *Yoga, Immortality and Freedom*. Princeton: Princeton University Press.

GLOCK, Charles Y. and Rodney STARK (1969) *Religion and Society in Tension*. Chicago: Rand McNally.

JAMES, William (1902) *The Varieties of Religious Experience*. New York: Modern Library.

JUNG, Carl Gustav (1958) *Psychology and Religion: East and West*. New York: Pantheon Books.

LARSON, G. J. (1969) *Classical Samkhya*. Varanasi: Motilal Banarasidass.

MOL, Hans (1976) *The Sacralization of Identity*. Oxford: Blackwell.

O'DEA, Thomas F. (1966) *The Sociology of Religion*. New Jersey: Prentice Hall.

RAJAGOPALACHARI, (Tr) (1955) *The Bhagvadgita*. New Delhi: Hindustan Times Press.

BHIKSU, (1930) *Bhakti Yoga*. Chicago: Yoga Publications Society.

SEN GUPTA, Anima (1969) *Classical Samkhya.* Lucknow: United Press.

SINHA, M. K. (1975) *Glock's Dimension of Religiosity, the Ways of Yoga and the Mechanisms of Sacralization*. Masters Dissertation, McMaster University.

AUROBINDO, Sri (1965) *On Yoga*. Pondicherry: Aurobindo Ashram.

TURNER, Victor W. (1970) 'Symbols in Ndembu Ritual', in Dorothy EMMET and Alasdair MACINTYRE (eds.), *Sociological Theory and Philosophical Analysis*. London: Macmillan.

WEBER, Max (1956) *The Protestant Ethic and the Spirit of Capitalism*. New York: Charles Scribner's Sons.

8

IDENTITY MAINTENANCE AND IDENTITY CRISIS IN MINANGKABAU

Taufik Abdullah
National Institute of Economic and Social Research, Indonesia

Dr Abdullah traces the precarious maintenace and subsequent breakdown of Minangkabau (Western Sumatra) identity. In the nineteenth century there were two pillars to this identity: (a) adat (a pre-Islamic pattern of rules and laws); and (b) Islamic religion. Drastic economic change (the money tax system of 1908) and political upheavals (the various rebellions against the Dutch from 1900 to 1930) upset this delicate balance and as a result a change in identity foci occurred from tradition and collectivity to the present and the self.

The period between 1900 and 1930 was very crucial in the modern history of the Minangkabau people, whose home territory covers most of the province of Western Sumatra (Indonesia). The government of the then Netherlands Indies had by that time consolidated its rule all over the region and had also effectively reorganized the once fragmented administrative system of the region. In this period important economic and political changes took place. New ideas were brought in either by returning Minangkabau *perantau* ('outmigrants'), who were mostly traders, Islamic teachers, and Western-educated intellectuals, or by the Dutch government. In this period Western Sumatra was not only one of the most politicized regions in the Netherlands Indies, but it was also the place where private schools, Islamic or otherwise, developed rapidly.

From 1900 to 1930 two important rebellions broke out: the anti-tax rebellion of 1908 and the so-called communist rebellion, led mostly by Islamic religious teachers, in early 1927. Several minor incidents also took place. In 1904 an orthodox religious teacher led his students in a revolt against traditional (supposedly) indigenous *adat*,[1] and religious institutions which he thought to be contrary to correct Islamic teaching. In 1912 a conspiracy of mystic teachers, still obsessed by the opposition to the money tax system, was uncovered, and in 1915 another mystic teacher led an attack on a police station.

No less important than all these economic and political events were the attempts of the Minangkabau *literati*, most of whom were adat-chiefs *(penghulu)*,[2] and religious teachers *(ulama)* to maintain the sacred notion of Minangkabau identity, which was conceived to be a composite concept of adat and Islamic values. This identity was strongly defended in the face of the ideological and political assaults of Dutch policy. Objectifications of self and the present became more apparent when the alien power was thought to have started to destroy the basic foundation of the Minangkabau world *(alam Minangkabau)*.

A more serious problem emerged, however, when one of the 'pillars' of Minangkabau identity, Islamic religion, responded to its international aspects: the development that took place outside the boundary of Minangkabau began directly to question the continuing validity of the world as being the only locus of attachment. If the concept of history, as expressed by the traditional historiography *(tambo)*, was still valid, then change was not only inevitable, but a necessity. After all, the genius of adat should be found not only in its continuing applicability, but also, more importantly, as some adat theoreticians used to emphasize, in the unfolding of its inherent greatness. But, as the literati and the intelligentsia asked themselves, how could the conflicting demands of change and continuity be resolved? There was a crisis. The content, the configuration, and the understanding of the sacred identity were put into question by the legitimate parts of the identity itself.

This chapter is an attempt to look at the history of religion in Western Sumatra by applying as far as is appropriate the concept of identity developed by Hans Mol (Mol, 1976).

I

Since its inception in the 1840s in Sumatra, *corvée* (*heerendiensten*, obligatory unpaid manual work) was taken to symbolize what was wrong with the world. It was felt to be so diametrically opposed to what the world, *alam*, should be that the people lamented, '*adat* was [then] useful, now, it is *rodi* (corvée), which rules'. But if corvée was the only reality how miserable was this world! How could one bear this life? How could they, the Minangkabau, who claimed to be the descendants of Alexander the Great ('Legende', 1859; Sango, 1955), accept the humiliation from the people 'who came from the country above the wind'? It was too much indeed.

But then it was also a fact that they did not have to pay taxes. Nor were they directly ruled by the Dutch. As the Dutch Commissioner General once stated in the famous *Plakat Panjang* (*Lange Verklaring*, Long Declaration), issued during the Padri War[3] in 1833, the people did not have to pay tax and the Dutch came merely to trade and only asked them to cultivate coffee and sell it exclusively to the company's *pakhuis* (warehouse) (de Stuers, 1849/50: 8-14). And were not the observable rulers of the village, *nagari*, their own penghulu, the traditional adat chiefs? The Dutch administrative policies that tried to balance the need for administrative efficiency and uniformity with the maintenance of traditional polity gave basis to this notion, which was nurtured to mitigate the psychological impact of the corvée.

After a long war, the Padri war, that ravaged the region for more than thirty years (twenty years of civil-religious war followed by a war of conquest when the Dutch intervened; Cuisinier, 1959), the people needed something to hold on to. In spite of corvée they preferred, or perhaps pretended is the better word, to look at the Dutch as the partner who came to trade. The real world of the colonial situation was made bearable by this world of pretense (Abdullah, 1976). It is, perhaps, a truism to emphasize that colonial situations do have a tendency to create contradictions. By maximizing one aspect of a political situation and consciously altering the significance of another the Minangkabau were at pains to stress the subjective meaning of their reality.

In the meantime, after the late 1860s coffee production began to decline and the power of the extra-adat chiefs, who were appointed by the government, continued to grow at the expense of that of the penghulu (Westenenk, 1913: Schrieke, 1927). In the 1870s the judicial power of the village council *(balai)*, whose members comprised penghulu and other adat dignitaries, was taken over by the government. By this action the penghulu lost the most important sanction of their power vis-à-vis the people. More than ever their power became dependent on the government's support. They were, then, virtually recognized only to be the heads of their respective matrilineal kinsmen *(kaum)*, who were responsible for the maintenance of order, custom, and social harmony. In some cases they might be taken as the representatives of the government.

With the growing importance of towns as administrative centers and the increased frequency of contacts with the centers of the Islamic world, the Islamic orthodox movement began seriously to question the legality of matrilineal inheritance law – the heirs were not one's children but one's sister's children. The movement was launched by a Minangkabau ulama, who was an *Imam* of the Syafi'iete school in Mecca. Through his many writings and pupils, who in their own right had already been acknowledged as ulama, religious teachers, his ideals spread out widely in Western Sumatra (Schrieke, 1920; Deliar Noer, 1973).

It seems, as was the case with the Padri movement, that a frontal attack on the whole social structure had been launched. By condemning the religious legality of matrilineal law, the orthodox movement also in effect rejected the legitimacy of the penghulu, whose claims to the chieftainship was, among others, determined by his possession of land-right, and who inherited both the right and the title of penghuluship from his maternal uncle.

By that time, however, with the growing importance of trade and the increasing number of people engaged in the not-strictly-agricultural professions, a very slow process toward a solution of the conflict between adat and Islamic laws was already in the making (Verkerk Pistorius, 1869: 93). The blow of the attack was somewhat lessened by the prevailing ambivalence toward the law – in one situation one could be a son to one's father and in another a nephew or niece to one's uncle.[4] The possibility for a person to play different functions in different legal situations was, and still is, a basis of Minangkabau legal conservatism (cf. Tanner, 1969).

At the end of the nineteenth century a fiercer assault was launched on the heterodox mystic teachings by the Islamic orthodox movement. The idea that man was the manifestation of the essence of God and not merely His shadow, as another orthodox mystic school used to teach, was condemned. The universe as an emanation, instead of the creation of God, was furiously repudiated. With these doctrinal attacks, Minangkabau cosmogony, which had included the idea of *Nur Muhammad* (the Light of Muhammad) as the origin of the world (their world, the alam Minangkabau), was also rejected (Abdullah, 1972: 183-90; 230-31).

Minangkabau at the end of the nineteenth century was, indeed, a very shaky and fragile world. Almost all bases of identity were under serious attack. The only consolation was the fact that the penghulu and the religious teachers thought of themselves as the masters of the situation. However shaky the claim could be, it was not an unimportant psychological defense. But when, in 1908, the Dutch government finally introduced the money tax system, in place of the coffee monopoly, the chips were down. The basis of the newly constructed world was destroyed. Suddenly, the present, artificial as it was and full of dissatisfactions as it might be, was now felt to be the proper legitimate world that was worth fighting for.

Penghulu and mystic teachers emerged as leaders of the anti-tax opposition party. What was now felt to be at stake was not only their positions, or the intellectual and doctrinal legitimacy of the orthodox movement, but something much more direct and immediate. It was something that neither the defenders of the old systems, who led the opposition, nor their critics who were utterly unprepared to face the situation, could take lightly. Isolated from the administrative sphere by the Dutch, the religious teachers, orthodox and heterodox alike, usually gave religious significance to political actions taken by penghulu. With the introduction of the money tax system a strange and blasphemous world was felt to be in the making. Neither adat nor religion, Islam, the two inseparable pillars of the alam Minangkabau, could be used to justify the naked fact that Minangkabau was, indeed, under foreign domination. After all, by tradition taxation had always been a token to signify 'who ruled over whom'. It was a tradition of the 'independent' nagari in the interior (the heartland of Minangkabau) not to pay tax to the king, whose main function was to serve as the sacral equilibrium power. Royalty had jurisdiction only over the *rantau*, newly acquired, territories, which were mostly on the coast (Abdullah, 1966).

Now they had to pay tax. Who were the Dutch to force 'us', the Minangkabau, to pay tax? What about the Plakat Panjang? And history was retold and reinterpreted. Had the Dutch not issued the promise that they did not come to rule, but only to trade, the fight against them would certainly have continued. (In fact it did until 1837, but then it was under the leadership of the Padri ulamas, who were opposed by both penghulu and the mystic teachers.) How greedy the people with the 'green eyes' could be. 'We are not the *kemenakan di bawah lutuik* ('serfs') of the Dutch', people used to say during this period (Scheltema de Heere, 1923).

They had to fight because they were on the right path, *fisabilillah*, on the path of God. As a pamphlet stated, 'those who pay tax are condemned by Allah'. Religious teachers, leaders of the heterodox *Shattariah* mystic school *(tarekat)*, not only gave religious sanctions to the anti-tax opposition and led their students *(urang siak)* but also distributed charms of invulnerability (Van Ronkel, 1916: App.). The 'science' and the charms of invulnerability spread out in the region. If it was true, as the creed said, that nothing could happen unless Allah wanted it to happen, then death, so it was reasoned, was also beyond human control. 'Nature leaves no trace'. It is Allah's power that makes the traces. Therefore, with proper ceremonies and charms God's power could manifest itself in the invulnerability of the believers who were fighting on His path. Religion and magic were, then, converged into one unified whole for the sake of the now-sacred present.

So it happened. From the beginning of March 1908 mass demonstrations and riots took place in some districts. In several villages open scattered rebellions broke out. Several police stations and houses of village chiefs, who were assigned to collect the individual tax, were attacked and burned. Fresh troops had to be sent from Java. With heavy-handed treatment all opposition was crushed by the end of June (Heckler, 1910).

When, finally, adat feasts for expressing regret were held in some nagari, several dozen people had lost their lives; a number of opposition leaders had been arrested; and a few others were about to be exiled. Social integration was ceremonially reestablished by the feasts. Breaches which occurred during the scattered rebellions and mass demonstrations were healed. Order and social harmony were thought to have emerged again (Batuah and Madjoindo, 1956: 66-72). The adat feast is an example of the function of a traditional ceremony in settling a crisis caused by a traditional concern over the continuing penetration of outside elements.

The scattered rebellions and mass-demonstrations were desperate attempts to maintain the existing order. They failed. Individual tax was soon collected. The Netherlands Indies' government, which had just 'pacified' (actually conquered) Aceh (the Northern part of Sumatra) in 1904, had now embarked on a more aggressive consolidation policy in the Outer Islands. The enforcement of the tax system was based on a sound economic rationale. While the overall picture of the economy was improving, the government's income continued to decline because of its dependence on coffee delivery. The rebellions were indicative of an incompatibility of rationalizations.

The people's understanding of their circumstances, the meaning they attached to their social environment, was incompatible with the economic rationalization. It made them see more clearly the shakiness of their 'world' and the fragility of their identity. In other words, they could no longer afford the luxury of being ignorant of the process that was taking place. The critics of the old order, the Islamic orthodox movement, though, privately condemning the use of magic in the struggle (Hamka, 1967), could not oppose the rebellion either.

It was inherent in the Minangkabau traditional concept of history that change was inevitable. 'When flood comes, the bathing place moves', the proverb says. In the same vein, it was reasoned that if money taxation was finally enforced 'we might have to move to the moon', as a leader of the opposition once said. Taxation would certainly create its own realities, realities that the opposition leaders were not willing to accept. The present, however unsatisfactory it might be, should be untarnished.

History did not have to be stopped, but it should be made timeless, eternal – an illegitimate innovation had made its way. History could move, as it should, but let it move in accordance with its destiny, the perfection of society, which did not delineate from the basic foundation of alam Minangkabau.

The opposition did not aim to destroy the power of the alien ruler – as some nationalist historians would like to emphasize – but rather to maintain a world with which they could conduct a continuous dialogue and in which they had always felt at home. The crisis which was instigated by the orthodox movement could still be resolved, so it was thought, for it did, after all, originate from a legitimate part of alam Minangkabau, the Islamic religion.

Adat and religion, which constitute the bases of collective identity, became more real in this time of crisis. Both became the bastion of conservatism in the face of hostility. Commitment (Mol, 1976: 216) to the identity constituted by these pillars was strengthened, for the whole foundation of the world was thought to be at stake. With historical hindsight one can see that this crisis served to enhance the social capacity to face another crisis, a more crucial one, and to maximize self-confidence in reviewing the bases of identity that were to come later.

III

Following the imposition of the money tax system, the government abolished the ban on rice exports and established village banks which were put under the jurisdiction of adat authorities. The positive response to these new economic opportunities was encouraged by the existence of the rotating market system whereby in every sub-district certain nagari held their market days once or twice a week.

On its market day, the nagari became the center for its neighbouring nagari. This rotating system was repeated on the district level. In the meantime, commercial crops became more important. Coffee, rubber and, to a lesser degree, cinnamon and other crops helped to change somewhat the economic status of the population. Towns were no longer simply administrative centers for their surroundings but became economic and educational centers as well. In this situation it was not only the prevailing social hierarchy that was questioned (Wertheim, 1959), but also the validity of Minangkabau cultural paradigm (in the Kuhnian sense) that was scrutinized. The process that was interrupted during the anti-tax movement was now resumed. The time when the old identity was the basis of social integration had, temporarily at least, lapsed. No longer did the world of pretense (thinking of the Dutch as partners) exist in the minds of the critics. Neither did the notion of 'to be or not to be', so obvious during the period of the rebellion, survive. The main issues now were the religious correctness of the old identity and its adequacy in the face of a changing situation. In other words, was the sacred identity really sacred in accordance with the correct religious doctrine? And how could it maintain its validity in the face of structural changes that had been introduced from the outside? It was a debate that focused on the notion of the idea of sacredness itself. As a result, the feeling of certainty that was so prominent during the rebellion lost much of its strength. Social polarization began to occur. The understanding on the substance, the configuration, and the meaning of identity became a matter of personal choice and decision. It ceased to be a certainty. One's social status and affiliation with the several new competing experts of reality-definition determined one's decision. 'Traditionalist' adat-theoreticians and experts, the penghulu, who tried to make sense of realities on the basis of traditional wisdom, and mystic teachers might find common ground on the basically inherent greatness of the alam Minangkabau, which was defined as a manifestation of *the* truth ('the king of *the* nagari, who stands by himself'). They were the literati par excellence of the Minangkabau. But other theoreticians put more emphasis on the notion of the continuous unfolding process of the 'greatness', which, as they stated, was not in contradiction with the 'progressive world' *(dunia maju)*. On this point the 'progressive adat theoreticians' were in alliance with the newly-emerging Western-educated intellectuals and the Islamic reformists, regardless of the fact that these two latter groups preferred to define their cultural orientation beyond the Minangkabau world.

The first important ideological assault on the old identity concept came from the reformist religious teachers, who had been influenced by the Egyptian modernist movement (Deliar Noer, 1973). In the early 1910s they began to repudiate crucial aspects of mystic teachings which, according to them, had failed to practise and to preach religiously correct behavior. They demanded and urged a balance between 'the purity of heart', strongly emphasized by the mystics, and correct behavior. They rejected the notion that if one had reached a certain level of religious experience one could ignore the lower level. To the reformist *syarak*, the legally correct religious behavior, was the foundation, not simply as the mystics (particularly of the Shattariah and other heterodox schools) taught, a stepping stone to the next step, the tarekat (path), which would eventually lead one to agnostic experience.

Furthermore, the reformists sharply criticized the alleged escapist attitude of the mystic leaders who, in their opinion, tended to believe that knowledge of religion was the only thing of importance in this world. 'Islam is not only a religion for the world hereafter, but, more important a guide for life in this world', as one of their spokesmen stated in his book (Ahmad, 1914). In another work he even went so far as to state that, 'in the past our people were trapped in the valley of suffering and destruction, because of the corrupt teachers and traders of religion, who persuaded and tied our people to the religion of ignorance' (Ahmad, n.d.).

The reformist movement was a drive towards religious rejuvenation and rationalization. It stressed the importance of reason, *akal*, and condemned *taqlid*, blind loyalty to established religious authorities (cf. Gibb, 1947). By using akal they appealed for a return to the original religious sources, the Qur'an and *Hadith*, the Prophetic Tradition. By a 'realistic' approach to a world that should be freed from unlawful innovation *(bid'ah)*, such as superstition, and magic escapist attitudes, the Islamic reformist laid down a religious basis for social change. Theodicy (Berger, 1973) as defined by the mystic teachers had to their minds lost many of its credentials. Man could not be judged by what fate had made him. Man should be judged by what he was when he was born — clean, full of potentialities. Man should and could be continuously perfected. Theodicy was only proper when all humanly possible efforts had been considered. Consequently, the reformists raised questions of liberation (Abdullah, 1975).

During the debate the reformists also began to reformulate the collective identity of the Minangkabau. As universalist Moslems they were closely linked to their society and its values. The main question was what should be the relationship between adat law and syarak (religious law) within the social system? Armed with new canon and more rigorous argument they re-emphasized the predominance of the *Kitabullah*, the Book, over adat. Adat was no longer seen as the all-comprehensive system that constituted the foundation of the Minangkabau world, but rather the manifestation of religious teachings

— 'religion designs, adat applies'. This aphorism, which had been controversial since the middle of the nineteenth century, would have structural consequences to the position of religious teachers. It could lead, among other things, to their official predominance. Their political isolation, preserved by the Dutch government, would have to be broken. But, as the history of the nationalist movement in Western Sumatra shows, political activism made the government more aware of the danger that might come from Islamic quarters (Bouman, 1949).

The call for participation in the dunia maju, the modern world, was first voiced in the early 1900s. It was not a surrender to the unavoidable political and economic circumstances but, as the promotors put it, an actualization of the idea that was inherent in tambo (traditional historiography), with its concept of the spiralling rhythm of history. Structural changes could take place as long as they were based on the foundation of the alam Minangkabau.

But how far is enough, asked the young Western-educated intellectuals. Innovation could, and did, create its own realities. The first introduction of structural change in a coastal town had even begun to threaten the position of the promotors by denouncing, amongst others, the coastal aristocratic establishment as being in contradiction with the 'democratic' adat of Minangkabau (Van Anckeveen, 1911). If adat was, indeed, democratic then 'we', the educated youth, should also be heard. But, how could adat custodians and theoreticians accept this when the young Western-educated intellectuals, while continuing to respect adat and tradition, actually preferred to take modern civilization and knowledge as the basis of 'progress'? And how could the Islamic reformists agree with that position?

How about Islam? Both 'progressive' adat theoreticians and Islamic ulama reformists felt that they had unleashed the still-untamed youngsters prematurely. But they still had more pressing issues to settle. Ideological deviation of the very tiny group of young intellectuals — less than a hundred persons — was a matter of time and distance (most of them were trained in Java).

Adat and religion had been, and still are, the pillars of the sacred notion of the Minangkabau world. With the continuing penetration of Islamic orthodoxy into the social fabric, with its growing strength in social and personal conduct, and with the enlargement of its scope of influence (Geertz, 1967), could adat leaders, whose positions were matrilineally inherited, accept the new formula? The acceptance of the new formula would, as has been indicated earlier, question the place of the penghulu in the adat-hierarchy. Adat theoreticians, then, used history to repudiate the new formula. How could one make syarak, religious law, the basis of adat, when adat had already existed even before Islam came to Minangkabau? 'When nothing was existent, the universe did not exist, neither earth nor sky existed, adat was already there.' This was 'adat which is truly adat'. It was, in short, identical with natural law. It was the Nur Muhammad (the Light of Muhammad) itself through which God created the universe. 'Be it', Allah said to the Nur Muhammad, and so 'the earth and the sky' were formed. In their counter-argument, adat-theoreticians did not return to the pre-Padri formula, which stated the complementary nature of the two pillars, the validity of one being determined by the existence of the other. They did, however, show the equal position of the two, for they originated from the same idea; the Idea of Truth: God. The difference between the two was only in their concepts of the nature of the relationship between the idea of God and the universe. While syarak emphasized that all was the creation of God, adat stressed that its existence was the manifestation of the Real Essence, the Nur Muhammad.

On this particular point we find that the so-called 'progressive' adat theoreticians allied themselves with their more conservative colleagues and, more importantly, with mystic teachers, whom they once repudiated for their alleged escapist attitude.

The attempt to understand the world and to find a proper place for one's self are common historical phenomena. Reality becomes 'real' after a meaning is attached to it. Therefore, the framework through which reality could and should be perceived had not only to be found but, if necessary, to be vehemently argued. Too much plurality of framework would not only mean the loss of the plausibility of the framework itself but it might also threaten the integration of society. It has to be argued, for it provides not only an interpretative scheme, but also, in the final analysis, the basis of one's collective identity. Indeed, the conscious attempt to find a commonly agreed formula has been one of the major themes of Minangkabau history since the nineteenth century. In spite of the rhetorics, the critics of the old concept of the Minangkabau world did not aim at the destruction or abandonment of adat. Neither Islamic modernists nor Western-educated intellectuals could or really wanted to fully liberate themselves from the social structure in which they found themselves. After all, that very structure also gave them enormous intellectual and social advantages — they were put at the high echelon of the social hierarchy. The real issue was the ranking of the 'inner hierarchy of significance', as Luckmann would have put it (Luckmann, 1967: 56). How should meaning be structured? And what should be taken as the basis of all norms, which also could give rationality and viability to all? (Glock and Stark, 1966: 171-79).

In the meantime, Islamic and secular schools continued to grow and the number of children in schools increased rapidly. Activities of voluntary associations and nationalist political parties, with their divergent political ideologies and social aspirations, made the residency of Western Sumatra one of the most politicized regions in the Netherlands Indies. The notion of 'greater Indonesia' nationalism, in place of the narrower concept of 'Sumatra nationalism', and Islamic nationalism posed challenges to the old notion of 'Minangkabau nationalism' (Bourman, 1949). The spread of voluntary associations and nationalist parties to the villages made the position of the adat chiefs more crucial. They provided new mechanisms through which one could channel one's aspirations and from which one might receive new ideas. In the process, group identity no longer became a certainty but a matter of choice, a personal decision. Social conflict, if it occurred, was no longer confined to traditional disputes concerning inherited values or senses of propriety, but was also a question of group loyalty and, more often than not, supra-village allegiances. Economic development had its social consequences: the sacred inalienable land in some parts of the region was 'desacralized'. One could acquire property with money earned rather than only inheriting it (Schrieke, 1956). The changes of economic status gradually challenged the existing system of social stratification. But, however fluid the situation, economically and socially, the Dutch were still there to remind all the competing experts of value-formulation that they were not really the masters of their destiny. The so-called communist rebellion of 1927 (Benda and McVey, 1960) ended the debate. The rebellion was crushed and a few dozen were exiled. Subsequently, the main problems shifted more definitively to colonial relationships. With the outbreak of the national revolution in 1945 (after three and a half years of Japanese occupation), the adat chiefs, who were accused of being the supporters of the then Netherlands Indies, were in political disgrace. In 1951 at the congress of adat leaders, ulama, and intellectuals, the three types of recognized social élite, the formula of the predominance of syarak was accepted. Although the legal consequences of this formula were ideologically recognized, legal pluralism still continues (Tanner, 1969).

In his famous book, *Dasar Falsafah Adat Minangkabau* (Philosophical Foundation of the Minangkabau Adat), Nasrun (1957), a lawyer and a former governor, defines more concretely an already widely accepted solution: Islam is the natural perfection of adat: Islam provides a transcendent basis of adat. The sacred identity of the Minangkabau people had returned to its pedestal. The 'Minangkabauness' is definitely determined by commitment to the values that were formulated by Islam and actualized by adat. Such, at least, is the theory.

But the questions of whether this notion of 'Minangkabauness' could find its place within the context of the new nation state, Indonesia, and how this collective identity could maintain its integrity in the plurality of definitions of truth of a modernizing society, remain to be answered. These, however, are beyond the scope of this chapter.

IV

Life goes on and realities can usually take care of themselves. But occasionally one is confronted by the question of one's collective identity. From what has been said above, the problem of identity cannot be separated from one's historical experiences. The anti-tax rebellion of 1908 shows how the present and self were sacralized in the face of a power that was thought to threaten the collective identity. The central issue was how to maintain the familiar world in spite of the fact that some members of society recognized the internal inconsistencies of that world.

The intellectual history of the Minangkabau in the post-rebellion period shows that the notion of the sacredness of identity itself is not enough. Sacredness should be more definitively tied to the definition of truth as provided by Islam, and the capacity and ability of identity to confront the changing historical circumstances.

NOTES

1. Although the concept of adat emerged only after the spread of Islam – it is an Arabic word – it usually refers to indigenous customs and norms. On a more abstract level, adat also refers to an ideal pattern of behavior or, sometimes, to the concept of identity itself, in which adat, as a pattern of behavior, and Islamic prescriptions find their modus (cf. Abdullah, 1966).

2. Penghulu is the head of matrilineal lineage. In the literature penghulu also is usually called adat-chief, although it should be noted that there has never been uniformity of the roles and positions of the penghulu. Adat political tradition of the (more or less) 'independent' villages, nagari, differ considerably.

3. The Padri War began when three zealous reformers, who had just returned from Mecca, where they had observed the early period of the revivalist Wahabist movement, managed to secure the cooperation and support of the growing numbers of young religious teachers and students in the interior of Minangkabau. (It should be noted in passing that since the end of the eighteenth century there has been a strong tendency to transfer the center of religious teaching from the coast to the interior.) The reformers and their supporters attacked existing religious schools for being heretical and for failing to thoroughly Islamize society. They condemned Minangkabau institutions as being the products of the *jahiliyah* ('dark') period. Civil war broke out in 1803. Many villages and village-federations were conquered and large numbers of the Minangkabau royal family were murdered. In 1821 the Dutch who since the seventeenth century had maintained a trading station in Padang, a coastal town, were 'invited' to intervene by some remnants of the royal family. From the early 1830s, however, the war had become a war of conquest. The last king of Minangkabau was exiled to Batavia. And the great leader of the Padri, Tuanku Imam Bonjol, who is now acknowledged as one of the 'national heroes', was exiled to Java and later to Manado (North Sulawesi), where he died.

4. It is unnecessary to emphasize that the position of a son in the Islamic paternal inheritance law is stronger than that of a daughter. On the other hand, a niece, a sister's daughter, has the central position in a matrilineal society. She is the bridge between generations.

REFERENCES

ABDULLAH, Taufik (1966) 'Adat and Islam: An Examination of Conflict in Minangkabau', *Indonesia*, 2: 1-24.

——, (1972) 'Modernization in the Minangkabau World: West Sumatra in the Early Decades of the Twentieth Century', in Clair HOLT et al. (eds.), *Culture and Politics in Indonesia*. Ithaca and London: Cornell University Press, pp. 179-245.

——, (1975) 'Cita dan Corak Reformasi Islam: Sebuah Tafsiran', *Masyarakat Indonesia*, II (1): 103-22.

——, (1976) 'The Making of the *Schakel* Society', in *Conference on Modern Indonesian History* (July 18-19 1975). Madison: Center of Southeast Asian Studies, University of Wisconsin, pp. 13-25.

AHMAD, H. Abdullah (1914) *Pemboeka Pintoe Sjorga*. Padang: Al-Moenir.

——, (n.d.) *Ilmoe Sedjati*, 2. Padang: Sjarekat Ilmoe.

BATUAH, Ahmad Dt and A. Dt. Madjoindo (1956) *Tambo Minangkabau*. Djakarta: Balai Pustaka.

BENDA, H. J. and R. McVEY (eds.), (1960) *The Communist Uprisings of 1926-1927 in Indonesia*. Ithaca: Cornell University, Modern Indonesia Project.

BERGER, Peter (1973) *The Social Reality of Religion*. Harmondsworth: Penguin.

BOUMAN, H. J. (1949) *Enige Beschouwingen Over de Ontwikkeling van het Indonesisch Nationalisme op Sumatra's Westkust*. Groningen, Batavia: J. B. Wolters.

CUISINIÈR, Jeanne (1959) 'La guerre des Padri (1803-1838-1845), *Archives des Sociologie des Religions*, 4, pp. 70-88.

DELIAR, Noer (1973) *Muslim Modernist Movement in Indonesia*. Kuala Lumpur: Oxford University Press.

GEERTZ, C. (1967) *Islam Observed: Religious Development in Marocco and Indonesia*. New Haven: Yale University Press.

GIBB, H. A. R. (1947) *Modern Trends in Islam*. Chicago: University of Chicago Press.

GLOCK, Charles Y. and Rodney STARK (1966) *Religion and Society in Tension*. Chicago: Rand McNally & Company.

HAMKA, Haji Abdul M. K. A. (1967) *Ajahku: Riwajat Hidup Dr. H. Abdul Karim Amrullah dan Perjuangan Kaum Agama di Sumatra*. Djakarta: Djajamurni.

HECKLER, F. (1910) 'Memorie van Overgave: betreffende de toestand van het Gouvernement Sumatra's Westkust' (7 April 1905-2 February 1910), *Verbaal*, April 21 1911 (Archive in the Ministry of the Interior, The Hague, Netherlands.)

'Legende van de afkomst der Sumatranen en van hunne instellingen' (1859) *Tijdschrift voor Nederlandsch Indie*, 30 (1): 378-89.

LUCKMAN, Thomas (1967) *The Invisible Religion: The Problem of Religion in Modern Society*. New York: Macmillan.

MOL, Hans J. (1976) *Identity and the Sacred: A Sketch for a new social-scientific theory of religion*. Agincourt, Canada: The Book Society of Canada.

NASRUN, M. (1957) *Dasar Falsafah Adat Minangkabau*. Djakarta: Bulan Bintang.
SANGO, Datuk Batuah (1955) *Tambo Alam Minangkabau*. Pajakumbuh: Limbago.
SCHELTEMA DE HEERE, G. A. N. (1923) 'De Belastinginvoering op Sumatra's Westkust', *Indische Gids*, 45: 122-56.
SCHRIEKE, B. (1920) 'Bijdrage tot de Bibliografie van huidige Godsdienstige beweging ter Sumatra's Westkust', *Tijdschrift van het Bataviaasch Genootschap*, 59: 249-325.
——, (1927) 'Het Probleem der Bestuursorganisatie ter Sumatra's Westkust', *Koloniale Studien*, 11 (1): 57-106.
——, (1956) *Indonesian Sociological Studies*, I. The Hague/Bandung: W. Van Hoeve.
DE STUERS, H. J. J. L. (1849/50) *De Vestiging en Uitbreiding der Nederlanders ter Westkust van Sumatra*, 2. Amsterdam: P. N. van Kampen.
TANNER, Nancy (1969) 'Disputing and Dispute Settlement among the Minangkabau of Indonesia', *Indonesia*, 8: 21-67.
VAN ANCKEVEEN, G. de Wal (1911) 'Maleische Democratie en Padangsche Toestanden', *Adatrechtbundel*, 1: 114-28.
VERKERK PISTORIUS, A. W. P. (1869) 'De Priester en Zijn invloed op de Samenleving in de Padangsche Bovenlanden, *Tijdschrift voor Nederlandsch-Indie*, 3 (2): 423-52.
VAN RONKEL , S. (1916) *Rapport Betreffenden de Godsdienstige Verschijnselen ter Sumatra's Westkust*. Batavia: Landsdrukkerij.
WERTHEIM, W. F. (1959) *Indonesian Society in Transition*. The Hague: W. van Hoeve.
WESTENENK, L. C. (1913) 'De Inlandsche Bestuurshoofden ter Sumatra's Westkust', *Koloniaal Tijdschrift*, 2, 673-93, 828-46.

9

IDENTITY AND PLURALISM:

A Case-Study

Jan M. G. Thurlings
Catholic University, Nymegen, The Netherlands

Thurlings looks at the history of Dutch Catholicism in the light of an hypothesis that minority group behavior will result from, on the one hand, the group's desire to keep its identity intact and from, on the other hand, its willingness to assimilate with the majority. From 1650 to 1860 Catholics were a persecuted minority torn between the Roman and the Dutch identity. From 1860 to 1930 they became a successful militant minority proud of their Catholic identity within the larger Dutch setting. From 1930 to the present day their militancy declined because they discovered that there was no further threat to their identity. Lately there has been tendency towards disorganization as a result of the internal struggle between the theological and the administrative elites.

The subject of this chapter is 'identity and pluralism: a case-study'. The case is Dutch Catholicism, and more especially the revolutionary changes it underwent (Table 1). The question is: How did these changes come about?

Before going into this question a few preliminary notes may be useful. First, the following exposition only intends tentatively to explain what happened in The Netherlands. It does not rise above the status of a set of hypotheses which are in need of further testing. In addition, I had to devise a conceptual framework and a sociological theory of minority group behavior to aid the explanation. This raises the question as to whether this theory also applies to other minority-group processes — religious or otherwise — elsewhere in the world. For brevity's sake we cannot go into that question now.

TABLE 1

	Resignations from the priesthood		Priests ordained		Sunday Mass attendance		Mixed marriages solemnized in R.C. Church		R.C. christenings		Votes for Catholic People's Party	
	Abso-lute	Index figures	Abso-lute	Index figures	% of all R.C.'s over 7 years	Index figures	% of all R.C. marri-ages	Index figure	‰ of all R.C.'s	Index figures	% of all votes	Index figures
1966	74	100	227	100	64.4	100	8.7	100	20.0	100	30.1	100
1967	155	209	193	85	63.3	98	9.2	106	19.3	96	26.5	88
1968	202	273	143	63	56.0	87	11.0	126	18.6	93	–	–
1969	244	330	110	48	50.8	79	12.4	142	18.6	93	–	–
1970	243	329	48	21	47.2	73	–	–	–	–	24.2	80

Sources: Memorandum 183, Catholic Social Institute (The Hague, 1971), pp. 14, 19, 20 and 27; *De Tijd* newspaper, 29 April, 1971.

* The subject of this article is treated in greater detail by the author in a book entitled *De wankele zuil: Nederlandse katholieken tassen assimilatie en pluralisme* (The Tottering Column: Dutch Catholics between Assimilation and Pluralism; Nymegen, 1971).

Secondly, in building the theory I deliberately restricted the scope of the study. That is, I chose to restrict myself to the factors applying to one minority group. The focus of the theory and of the underlying observations was on this minority group. This implies that I did not go into the problems of other religious groups in Holland, nor into the question of what was happening in the world in this period of history. Even with these restrictions the subject turned out to be very complicated.

In order to grasp what happened in the 1960s one has to go back into the history of Dutch Catholicism as far as 1648, the year of the peace treaty of Westfalen, which ended the eighty-years' war between Spain and the Dutch Republic. At the end of that war the Dutch Catholics found themselves in the position of a victimized minority group the size of which — according to the estimations — ranged somewhere between 47 and 34 percent of the total population.

Of greater importance than the exact size of the Catholic group in Holland at that time was its power-position within Dutch society. The latter was certainly small and precarious. From 1648 until 1795, the year of the French invasion, Dutch Catholics were deprived of the formal rights of citizenship. They had no right to assume public offices, they very often were refused entrance into the guilds, and public assistance was not available for the Catholic poor. Dutch Catholics in that period were in considerable jeopardy. Relatively often they belonged to the lower classes.

Yet, on the basis of my research I feel it safe to say that political and socio-economic deprivation does not in itself provide the key for understanding events. It had influence, but Dutch Catholicism cannot be understood as primarily the result of some sort of socio-economic emancipation movement of a set of people who by sheer accident happened to be Catholics. It was exactly this finding of my research which necessitated me to examine the possibilities offered by a theory that focuses on the relatively autonomous identity-problems of a minority group in a culturally pluralistic society.

The identity-issue, i.e. the issue of preserving, deepening and eventually redefining a group's specific cultural identity, seems to me the vital key to the understanding of what has happened to Dutch Catholics.

The basic point of departure is the general hypothesis that minority group behavior will result from the group's desire to keep its identity intact on the one hand, and from its willingness — prompted by the influence of its environment — to assimilate with the majority, on the other.

Two aspects of this situation can be distinguished. One aspect is the degree to which the group in question feels itself *relevantly different* from its environment. The other aspect is the degree to which this group feels itself *threatened* by the environment. Out of the confrontation of perceived difference and perceived threat will result a certain type of *attitude* towards the environment:

$$\frac{\text{perceived difference}}{\text{perceived threat}} \longrightarrow \text{attitude}$$

The *specific* type of attitude chosen by members of the minority group will have something to do both with the degree to which they think their identity is relevantly different from their environment and with the degree to which they feel threatened by it. Consequently, the theoretically possible attitudes can be located somewhere in Table 2.

TABLE 2

Typology of Attitudes		Perceived difference	
		Large	Small
Per- ceived	small	militancy	openmindedness
threat from		defensiveness	
environ- ment	large	fear, submissiveness	indifference/ defeatism

Accordingly, four types of attitude may be distinguished in each one of the four cells of this conceptual scheme:

(1) an attitude of militancy when the perceived identity-difference is large and the perceived threat is small;

(2) an attitude of indifference and defeatism in the opposite case;

(3) an attitude of fear-submissiveness in the large-large-cell; and

(4) an attitude of openmindedness in the small-small-section.

An interesting attitude somewhere between fear and militancy is defensiveness. These attitudes will determine the *actual behavior* of the minority. They will take into account the possibilities and limitations present in the structural-cultural context of environment.

In the Dutch situation four types of coping behavior can be distinguished. The first one is conflict, the second is deliberate isolation in formal or informal groups, the third is peaceful coexistence and cooperation on practical issues, the fourth is ideological contact either in matters of profane, secular ideology, like liberalism or socialism, or in matters of religious ideology, e.g. contacts between Catholic and Protestant theologians.

To be complete, two other behavior types may be added. The first is flight — but for Dutch Catholics this could, at the most, have been an individual solution. The second is renunciation — but at the very moment that a group chooses this solution its identity is definitely lost. Nevertheless, it seems that this last mentioned behavior type, renunciation, in fact has been chosen by the millions of Catholics who in the course of these three centuries have silently left the church. The four behavior types mentioned above can be combined into different sorts of strategies. In Table 3 those strategies are listed which in the Dutch case were of greatest importance.

It is a logical assumption that there is a systematic connection between the various types of attitude and the various types of single or composite behavior that will be chosen. So, fear would motivate the choice for the clandestine church strategy. Or, to take another example, the attitude of indifference would motivate the type of behavior we termed renunciation [outside the scheme (Table 3)].

In reality, however, this assumed relationship between attitude and behavior is precarious. First, because the choice of behavior types is not solely determined by the attitude preceding it, but also by the possibilities and limitations perceived in the structural-cultural context.

Secondly, because a behavior type, once chosen, tends to continue under its own momentum — for the double reason that it is programmed and that it holds vested interest — and therefore often will continue even though the generating attitude has meanwhile changed.

The next point requiring attention concerns the *effect* of the various strategies. This effect will be two-pronged, bringing about a change in

TABLE 3

Types of minority behavior and composite minority strategies

Behaviour types / Strategies	Fight	Isolation		Coopera-tion	Ideological marginal contact	
		Formal	Informal		Profane	Religious
Clandestine church			x	(x)		
Independence	x	x	x	(x)		
Pragmatic breakthrough	(x)	(x)	x	x		
Ideological breakthrough	(x)	(x)	(x)	x	x	
Ideological dialogue		(x)	(x)	x	x	x

(x) signifies 'only when absolutely necessary'.

the *structure* as well as the *culture* of the minority group. An example of the structural effect is to be found in the large-scale structural segregation, called *verzuiling* ('pillarization') which took place in the first half of the present century. An example of the cultural effect is provided by the past-oriented cultural renaissance experienced by Dutch Catholics in the same period, especially in the twenties.

Figure 1

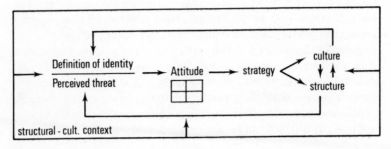

Finally, these structural and cultural changes will not fail to have a *feedback* effect on both the group's definition of its identity and its sense of being threatened. Thereby the wheel has come full circle (Figure 1).

This spiral process model (Figure 2) makes it possible to analyze the history of Dutch Catholicism since 1648. In what follows I will provide a short summary of this analysis. We will concentrate on the attitude part of the scheme. That is, the typology of attitudes will serve as our main frame of reference.

Figure 2

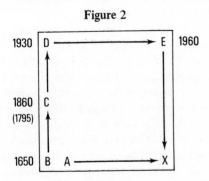

(1) Around 1650 it can be said that most attitudes of Dutch Catholics ranged in a circle which was located somewhere in the lower left of the square. Within that circle two critical positions have to be distinguished, namely, the positions *A* and *B*.

People in position *A* defined their situation as hardly bearable, so that sooner or later they changed their definition of identity in the direction of lower perceived difference; 'are we really that much different from Protestants, and if we are, is that difference really so relevant that we should endure all these hardships'? Very often their answer was 'no'. Consequently, their attitude changed from *A* to *X*, i.e. became indifferent, and sooner or later they left the field. In fact this stream of renunciation has been flowing almost uninterruptedly during all these centuries, be it in different degrees of intensity. The ranks of Dutch Catholics were never closed completely, and their reputation as faithful parishioners is to a large extent due to the fact that dropouts went unobserved, and that those who stayed behind were as prolific as they were faithful, so that they rather easily made up for the losses by relatively higher church attendance and birth rates.

Quite another story has to be told about people in position *B*. Although they were fearful too, they felt strong enough to go on practicing and to stay in the Catholic community. They managed to do so by adopting the type of strategy we called 'clandestine church'. They had a hard life, and time and again they were torn between loyalty to Rome and loyalty to the nation. Yet the strategy was more or less successful. Their situation gradually changed for the better, particularly through the liberalizing side-effects of the French Revolution after 1795. Attitudes changed correspondingly.

(2) Around 1860 we find them in position *C*, characterized by defensiveness, and by the strategy of independence. This strategy was so successful that the situation changed radically. The present crisis within Catholicism is a consequence of this change. Dutch Catholics, precisely because of their success, became gloriously militant somewhere around 1930 and began to adopt position *D*. They paraded in the streets – and made their non-Catholic compatriots rush into panic.

Sooner or later after 1930, however, it became clear that there was no point in being militant if there were no threat. And so it happened that gradually the attitude towards non-Catholics became more friendly. The number of interfaith contacts increased, even though this tendency remained for a long time restricted to the people at the top of the social hierarchy. Small as it may have been in the beginning, the switch was made from militancy towards openmindedness (position *E*). This is where the movement stood around 1960, catalyzed by the Second Vatican Council.

(3) The developments after 1960 seemed in the first instance to consist of a real religious revival in which a relatively large number of church members enthusiastically participated. Yet around 1970 the development seem to take a disastrous turn. What were the causes of this tragic catastrophy? First, the new climate, in position *E*, prompted quite a few Dutch Catholics (and the marginal members in particular) to feel that there was no point in being active while the old norms and old formulas were under discussion – a situation typical for every religious revival. To them Catholicism had lost its identity and consequently they disappeared from the scene. This tendency towards disorganization became stronger after 1965.

Secondly, the revival movement was real enough, and many Catholics took part in it, but at the same time the very movement turned out to be a source of conflict. At the core was the fundamental controversy between the two elites to be found in every religious community as soon as it becomes institutionalized. The one elite consisted of the *theologians*, the other the *curial executives*, or, to put it in somewhat more general terms, the one was formed by the intelligentsia, the other by the administration.

As long as a religious group is fighting on the barricades, it is perfectly within the logic of the situation for the administrative elite to be at the top of the hierarchy, defending the discipline. In this situation the role of the theologian will be an auxiliary one, i.e. auxiliary to the discipline-oriented authority. The theologians' role will be confined to a *guardianship* of the faith. There will be little room for contemplation and for helping others to contemplate about the real meaning of the holy message. His is the task of the cerberus who has to watch the people more than the treasure he is guarding.

When war is over, however, and communication becomes a real possibility again, the theologians will rise in status and the administrator's position will fall. It is self-evident that this circulation process does not go without conflict.

By now this conflict of elites has spread all over the country, involving all active Catholics, for the precise reason thatin the course of this process they found themselves polarized either in the position of those who defined their Catholic identity as the community of Christians united under Roman authority, or in the position of those who defined Catholicism – if they used the word – as the unifying hope for what was promised in the holy message, without being very interested in questions of institutional discipline. The first definition is a static one, the other is dynamic. The most tragic aspect of this polarized structure is that the first group has the power but no future, and that the second group can have future – if there is any – but has no power. So much at least is clear, that within the next twenty years Dutch Catholicism either will manage to find some form of internal pluralism, or will be reduced to a relic.

10

MAORI IDENTITY AND RELIGION

Hans Mol
McMaster University, Ontario, Canada

In this chapter the four sacralization mechanisms are applied to the study of Maori identity in the pre-European era. Objectification *is found to strengthen tribal order by the use of such symbols as canoe, land, and chieftainship.* Commitment *in Maori society took the form of aroha (love) and tapu (awe towards the sacred) which delineated and separated an intricate system of identity boundaries.* Ritual *preserved identity by harnessing and guiding necessary change from one pattern to another. Meeting, eating, and singing together on the marae (meeting place) and the carvings of ancestors on the meeting house reinforced the tribal traditions.* Myths *provided the fitting contour for Maori society. Generally the basic antipodes in the myths related to male and female; sky and earth; war and peace; order-challenge and order-maintenance; and the fixed and the fickle.*

In its pristine form Maori identity was shaped by its opposite, rootlessness. Migration to greener pastures, escape from tyranny, defeat in battle, and trade with other cultures have always tended to destroy roots. Only the strong migrant, the resilient vanquished, or the energetic trader would succeed in forging a new identity out of the destruction of an old one.

If the legends of origins have any historical validity (and they often do!) the New Zealand Maori came to what they called Aotearoa (the Long White Cloud) from the mythical place of Hawaika and Rangiatea (most likely the Cook or Society Islands). The great migration occurred around 1350 A.D. It was the outcome of inevitable dissensions (Buck, 1929: 8) in a society where taboos and military prowess combined to oppress minor tribes. Insufficient crops and population pressure (Buck, 1940: 4) did the rest.

Those who left and survived the treacherous voyage over thousands of miles in primitive craft were physically and mentally vital and courageous, quite capable of coping with any adversity. And yet, no matter how capable of dealing with adversity, they would not seek such innovation and change for its own sake. They would consolidate what was left of their roots and rebuild the very patterns and hierarchies from which they had escaped originally. Change became harnessed, as it always has in history.

What form did this harnessing take? Religion is one of the foremost means of harnessing (making sense of) change. It objectifies order so that temporal dislocations remain manageable (section 1). It strengthens commitment to that order (section 2). It reinforces this order by ritual (section 3) and surrounds it with mythical accounts (section 4).

1. OBJECTIFICATION

Viable religions have generally used symbols which are part and parcel of mundane experiences and yet somehow transcend these experiences. They use materials at hand and weave them into a coherent pattern as ladies do with a quilt. Lévi-Strauss called this process *bricolage* (1962: 26).

In Maori religion the *canoe* is a good example. It was the vehicle of survival during the migrations. It remained an important source of livelihood (fishing) and the equivalent of the Roman chariot in war. It was also a potential disturber of settled existence, the prototype of mobility, somewhat similar to the car in our society. One way of rendering this necessary source of instability innocuous was to make it part of a sacred meaning system, not altogether unlike the car being the holy object of Western teenagers, or even the sting of sin and death being blunted by salvation in Christianity.

And so where Westerners see Pleiades in the sky, the Maoris saw the prow of a canoe, and where we see Orion's belt, they saw its sternpost (Burland, 1969: 10). The Tail of the Scorpion is the canoe of Tamarereti in which the star-children and their elders were placed in mythical times (Best, 1924a, 111).

Where Europeans trace their ancestors by means of a family tree and its branches, Maoris think of themselves as descendants of the various crews of canoes which landed in New Zealand in the fourteenth century (Firth, 1959: 115). And so for the Maori, identity and social status was (and is) determined by descent even more strongly than it is for the First Fleeters in Australia or New Zealand. Visiting groups in Maori society feel honoured when called 'a prize canoe hauled on to the *marae*' (meeting place) (Salmond, 1975: 117). And a person who was regarded as a medium for the gods was called a *waka atua* (a canoe for the god) (Buck, 1952: 473).

Where Westerners see giants in geographical forms, Maoris discern a canoe and so the South Island of New Zealand was known as the canoe of Maui, a demi-god, son of the ocean goddess.

Yet the canoe is not only the symbol for one's personal place or family identity, but also delineates clusters of tribes from one another. In spite of many internal conflicts, tribes that could trace their descent to the same canoe would soon settle their differences so as to stand united against a common foe (Buck, 1929: 6).

The order created by naming the heavenly stars and earthly forms and by delineating individuals and tribes from one another was extended beyond life. Disease and death came in canoes and gathered their victims in a voyage from village to village (Buck, 1929: 6). The spirits of the dead were thought to sail in a silent canoe on a long journey to a paradise beyond the setting sun (Burland, 1969: 45) although others (Metge, 1976: 37) talk about travelling north to a cave at the entrance to the underworld.

Land is another example of a symbol which was both part and parcel of mundane experiences and yet also tied to a sacred order transcending those experiences.

On the mundane level it is very much like the territory for animals: the central place for one's livelihood; the best hope for physical security; and the least hazardous location for perpetuating the species. All nooks and crannies are familiar. It is, therefore, ardently defended.

Yet for man land soon transcends the mundane. The Maoris not only defended their territory the way some birds defend theirs but they also defined their borders carefully and protected them with strict *tapus* (sacred restrictions).

The Maoris fought bitter drawn-out wars (from about 1843 to

1872) with the European settlers who by hook, crook, or legal façade
insisted on a place under the New Zealand sun. When the Maoris lost
these wars they were hardly better of than animals whose territory has
been successfully invaded. After all, death may be preferable to the
humiliation, depression, and decadence which is the lot of the survivor.

Yet the confiscation of land was more than losing a livelihood. It
also meant the destruction of something much more ethereal and
abstract: *hapu* (sub-tribal) cohesion. Land did not belong to the individual, but stood for inalienable hapu identity. It was *turangawaewae*
(literally, a standing-place for one's feet), a collective, rather than
individual, knowledge of place; belonging. It was the place where the
bones of one's ancestors were buried.

And so right up to the present day, older Maoris are often loath to
surrender their individual land-shares, even when the parcels are much
too small and widely separated to have economic utility. Without land
they feel immigrants and strangers. And this means having inferior
status.

Immigrants and strangers (even those born in the district, but unable
to claim common descent) cannot be hosts on the marae and can
participate only as a favour from those who belong. As in the Hebrew
or Roman temple, the rights of strangers, outsiders, or 'those on the
margin', are restricted. And although those who can claim common
descent are themselves subject to restrictions (in some tribes women
and men whose fathers are still alive are forbidden to speak at the
meetings; Metge, 1976: 236), they at least 'belong'.

Tapu did become the guarantor of an order which transcended the
mundane. Not only the territory as such, but even more the meeting
place at the centre of the tribal lands became tapu, to be handled
circumspectly. The ridge pole (*tuhuhu*) and the rafters (*heke*) sym-
bolized the backbone and the ribs of the founding ancestor. The carved
posts around the walls represented famous ancestors, tribal gods and
culture heroes (Walker, 1975: 22). And so kinship and local identity
became indissolubly linked (Sinclair, 1975: 120).

This linkage of land and kinship had important consequences. Inter-
tribal marriages had to be discouraged as they would weaken either
identity. For the same reason a multi-racial marae was very much a
contradiction in terms. Yet intermarriages are now increasing (Harré,
1966) and multi-tribal marae have been successfully established in

urban areas as an antidote to anonymity and individualism (Walker, 1975: 29; Kawharu, 1968: 181). The inevitable differentiation of urban living did even more effectively what the land-wars in the nineteenth century had begun: it dissolved existing identity patterns and substituted others, more specific and more flexibly linked, such as religious denominations, sects, common interest groups, and sports clubs.

To return to traditional Maori society, the congruence of tribe and land was objectified in mythical accounts. The Earth Mother (Papa) and the vegetation which protects and warms her (Best, 1924a, II: 109) is, in Maori myths, contrasted with the male Sky Parent (Rangi). Reminiscent of Yin in Chinese society, she descends from the moon and darkness, whereas Rangi (like Yang) is associated with the sun and light. Out of this union of opposites numerous children are born, separating the parents so that nature can mature and bear fruit and things can stop moving aimlessly about in a realm of darkness (Best, 1924a: 92). We will return later to this important dialectic between conflict (change) and congruence (sameness). Like tapu it objectifies and thereby consolidates order.

A third example of a mundane necessity becoming objectified to reinforce identity is *chieftainship*. Coordination of tribal affairs was a pre-requisite for survival. Whether or not cooperation in the hunt, the provision of food and shelter, and mutual defence was efficient, determined life and death.

The Maori chief was to be adept in leadership. If the eldest son was mentally or physically deficient another relative was selected to be the effective leader, even if the son remained the ceremonial figure-head (Metge, 1971: 32). Continuity of leadership was so important that a smooth hereditary preparation and transition was preferred over achievement alone. Therefore, a chief had more *mana* (sacred influence or prestige) than others (Best, 1924a, I: 345). Egalitarianism might lead to the chaos of disobedience at crucial moments, even if Maori society put high value on a chief who used public opinion. Actually, only in war was the chief's power perfectly absolute (Maning, 1863: 36).

Chieftainship became objectified as tribal order by being posed as the vital link between gods and men, to both of whom the chiefs were related. The ceremonial clothing of the chief (like the well-stocked warehouses) was designed to present an image of communal strength. Impressing visitors from other tribes ensured thinking twice before launching an attack.

The present-day tendency in Maori society to stress achievement more and ascription less means a further erosion of the tapu of chieftainship. Yet in Western society too there is still sufficient recognition of the importance of authority for order to fully understand more ancient Maori traditions.

In these older traditions arbitrariness and devaluation of everything was thought to follow the disappearance of the customs of tapu as 'they are what keeps everything in place' (Johansen, 1954: 198). And so Te Matorohanga, the nineteenth-century Maori sage, could lament:

> '(In the past) *tapu* was all important – the first of all things; without it none of the powers of the gods were available, and without the aid of the gods all things are without authority and ineffectual; now (however, the mind of man) is in state of confusion (literally like a whirlwind), as are all his deeds . . .' (S. P. Smith, 1913: 104).

Yet it was precisely this intricate system of tapu which prevented a view of order in which achievement had a fuller place. For the urban, individualistic, achievement-oriented society to operate successfully it was necessary for the believed-in order to be further objectified, rendered more vague and abstract, in order to keep the mundane more flexible.

In traditional Maori society the elaborate system of tapu which permeated everything and guaranteed identity remained rather close to a this-worldly experience (e.g. canoe, land, chieftainship). Consequently, the transcendental frame of reference had less separate leverage to anticipate or absorb change. Objectification advanced little, thereby leaving the mundane sacralized rather than relativized. Yet Maori society had its own varied ways of de-rigidifying tapu for the sake of plucking the advantage of aggression and change (see section 2 – Commitment).

There was indeed a system of high, or supreme, gods. Yet in pre-European days it remained confined to an elite of experts, priests, and magicians (*tohungas*) who were trained in a sacred *Whare Wananga* (or House of Learning) away from the village and surrounded by fences and tapus. That there was such an ancient independent tradition of Maori high gods is believed by some (Johansen, 1958: 36) while others think that the belief in a supreme God, called Io, the ultimate source of mana in the universe, omnipotent, omniscient, and uncreated, was a later addition (Johansen, 1958: 193).

In particular, Te Matorohanga, a renegade Christian convert and one of the senior Maori folk scholars who met around the year 1860 to unify the shattered cosmology and history, appears to have had a strong hand in these reinterpretations. Certainly the cult of Io was a local New Zealand development and many features of the accompanying cosmogony of separating light from darkness are post-European traditions (Buck, 1952: 536).

At any rate, in traditional Maori society the counter-balance with the transcendental point of reference appears to have been too weak to have had much impact on the relativization of an intricate system of tapus. It is one thing for scholars to provide consistency of a belief-system, but it is quite another for the people to accept it as a basis for motivation. It was the charismatic leaders of Maori society in the second half of the nineteenth-century who would take the weight off a relatively petrifying system of tapus, not the scholars.

But the Maori magical mode of achieving a positive through the negation of a negative (confidence through the removal of evil spells; Smith, 1974: 23) did not provide the more independent effect of higher religions.

The moderately-successful Westernization of the Maori tended to correlate with their capacity to relate their personal, communal, family, tribal identity to a more flexible system of order. To some this order might culminate in the more remote Io of the Hidden Face, of whom no image could be fashioned and to whom no offerings could be made (Best, 1924a, I: 87-90). To others it took a more apocalyptic form, as will be discussed in later work. But to most Maoris in modern times order is the indefinable, unconscious something that Pakehas just as unconsciously brought with them from Great Britain.

2. COMMITMENT

Commitment to a group or social identity or to a system of meaning is a prerequisite for its functioning. Without a feeling of loyalty the beliefs, values, and norms of tribe, family, and community are likely to crumble.

Commitment in Maori society took a variety of forms. *Aroha* (love, warm feeling) bound the individual to his family and community. He was under constant pressure to maintain the aroha for his family and marae. Even if he had become rather Westernized, the average Maori would not want to be accused of having lost his aroha. It is shown in his extensive and seemingly inexhaustible hospitality; in his behaviour, embracing and wailing, at a *tangi* (mourning for the dead); in his sensitive care for both the living and the dead; and in his sympathy for the lost, lonely, and even the delinquent. It stands for 'all those feelings of empathy that link men together and men with God, and provide the basis for and impetus towards social interaction and positive reciprocity' (Metge, 1976: 67).

Aroha is very similar to the Greek *agape* or Christian love. Yet observers of traditional Maori society have pointed to important differences. Maori warriors were appalled by the Christian injunction to love one's enemies. Like Nietzsche they thought a religion exalting this kind of love fit only for slaves (Dumont, 1935, II: 388). Yet these same warriors would certainly practise aroha as described within the family or hapu. The difference, therefore, relates not so much to the meaning of the concept (feeling of concern, empathy) or to what it does (integrate), but to the identity to which it applies. Christianity (often vainly) attempted to give agape universal application; Maoris expressly restricted it to the family or group – it was in no way allowed to interfere with valour in battle, defence of one's territory, or the eating of one's enemies.

Less obvious, but just as powerful as a form of commitment to one's tribe or kinship, is tapu. As we have already seen, tapu delineates and reinforces structure and order. Loyalty to these structures consists of feelings of respect and awe towards them.

Sometimes tapu is regarded as a strictly legal rather than religious concept. It deals with 'that which is forbidden' (Lehmann according to Johansen, 1954: 120). The train of thought seems to be that since the forbidden is negative it must be different from a more positive feeling of awe produced by the sacred.

Actually, it is the separateness which both tapu and the sacred have in common. And it is this separating or objectifying quality which positively rather than negatively establishes the boundary of a particular identity. What is tapu is in our terms usually the sacred quality of an important classification, delineation, or boundary. When things are forbidden they are set apart and thereby classified as significant and worthy of consideration. Contrary to J. Smith (1974: 6) who regards Johansen's view of tapu (requiring consideration) as 'not particularly useful', this definition gets to the core of its sociological significance. Tapu as a noun can often be translated as 'that which is restricted', or when it is an adjective, as 'restricting'. And so the tapu surrounding chieftainship reinforced this particular mode of ordering tribal affairs as compared with meritocracies, oligarchies, or democracies. Or the tapu surrounding the marae strengthened tribal identity and separated it from the formless nothing of the outside world.

The stress here lies on feeling, irrespective of whether it is positive or negative. Negative commitments (or feelings of avoidance and antagonism) can be just as integrative as positive commitments (or feelings of loyalty and worship).

In Maori, as in Hebrew society, a more positive, contractual relationship with the gods was closely intertwined with a more negative system of tapus. To reinforce this covenant relationship certain objects or people were dedicated or consecrated, thereby strengthening and articulating the relationship between the gods and man in the process.

Sacrifice was one mode of clarifying priorities in commitment. In ancient Maori society, slaves were sometimes sacrificed during the erection of major buildings to articulate their importance and to ensure the protection of the gods. The spirits of the sacrificed slaves were regarded as so many messengers to the gods in question. The sacrifice of a small animal (consequently buried in the hole for the ridge pole of a new house) set a smaller building apart from its surroundings and reinforced the specialness and unity of the family to occupy it at a later stage.

Tapu was another way of clarifying priorities and strengthening one's loyalty to the order represented by the gods. One must avoid offending the latter for otherwise the demonic and chaotic would invade one's world and disrupt personality or group. Best's observation (1924a, I: 476) that tapu and other restrictions built up the social fabric and rendered the tribe cohesive and manageable was a perceptive one. Polluting thus was the ever-present potential for invasion by chaos, disorder, and the meaningless.

Tapu then can be regarded as 'the sacred state or condition in which a person, place or thing is set aside by dedication to the gods and thereby removed from profane use' (Marsden, 1975: 197). Metge (1976: 59) implies that there is more to tapu when she says that indeed 'tapu is readily explained as stemming from close contact with God', but that in other cases 'it is rather a matter of pollution, through contact with death, blood or hostile spirit'. Yet Marsden's definition can be defended as being comprehensive enough to include these kinds of pollution. After all, death, and particularly unexpected death, such as the drowning of a promising young warrior, is the chaotic element impinging on the god-protected order. It becomes tapu precisely because the gods use it as punishment for infringement of their order, or because it is to be contained or restricted within the sphere controlled by the gods, but uncontrolled by men and therefore ultimately more orderly.

J. Smith (1974: 39) suffers from a similar narrow definition when she attacks Johansen's identification of tapu with the holy. She feels that 'it is wrong to apply a concept with such an entirely different cultural origin to the Maori'. However, the differences between tapu and the holy are less important than their similarities; both concepts deal with feelings towards a delineated order. One's capacity for intercultural comparisons and generalizations diminishes dangerously if one deals with culture-bound definitions only.

It is this narrowness of definition which prevents Smith's otherwise sophisticated monograph from fully seeing the close intertwining of the social and the religious. 'Among the Maori, passage between the ultra-human and the human worlds are ritualized and passage within the social world was not' (J. Smith, 1974: 21). Yet if it is true that the ultra-human delineations reflect and reinforce the human social ones, there must be more frequent and latent interaction than this sentence suggests. We will return to this interesting problem in greater detail in the next section on ritual and rites of passage (birth, marriage, death) as the stripping of an old identity and the welding of a new one.

This perpetual guarding of order by feelings of separation implies a perpetual dialectic between the sacred and the mundane, or between identity and change. *Noa* is the Maori word for what is common, not restricted, without purpose, boundless (Johansen, 1954: 204) and therefore stands in opposition to tapu. The meeting house on the marae is tapu, but the cooking area is noa. Yet the entire marae is tapu as compared with the outside (Metge, 1976: 232). If there were no separation the significance of the meeting and the ordering function it has for the group would be less and would not stand out from less significant operations or from no operations at all.

The dialectic between tapu and noa, or the sacred and the profane, or sacralization and secularization, occurs in all cultures. Strong feeling or sense of emotional integration is typical for the first item in the dichotomy. Unrestricted manipulation, rational diversification, and scepticism are typical for the second. Both need and oppose one another; both complement and conflict. In a more comprehensive context we have called this the dialectic between integration and differentiation (Mol, 1976: 21). Metge (1976: 60) has the same in mind when she refers to tapu and noa as complementary opposites, 'presupposing and complementing each other, incomplete and meaningless on their own'.

Closely related to tapu is mana. Its efficacy too hinges on a taken-for-granted feeling towards the person or object possessing mana. Mana is generally translated as sacred power, authority. It is often an endowment by the gods. A chief, or tohunga, has mana because the gods have bestowed power on the ancestral lineage. He can squander or augment it to his own detriment or enhancement, but in the last resort it is a supernatural gift.

So *mana whenua* is the power to rule a particular ancestral territory and to hold it in trust for the tribe (Mahuika, 1975: 89). Without that power the fields, the forests, and the fishing grounds would be arbitrary. It is mana and tapu which keep things in place (Johansen, 1954: 198).

Mana was also thought to be transferable as a gift. 'In the heat of battle a chief might seize the mana of a killed foe by swallowing his left eyeball like an oyster' (Burland, 1969: 52).

The difference between mana and tapu seems to consist in the former more than the latter incorporating achievement criteria, such as success in battle or the hunt; the capacity for making one's hapu prosper. Mana could also be destroyed simply by a woman stepping over the head of the possessor. Yet generosity (a less individualistic attribution than achievement) could also augment the giver's mana. And tapu was thought to increase according to one's mana (Oppenheim, 1973: 16).

If a religious system is to remain viable it also has to possess means for desacralization, de-tabooing, or emotional detachment. Change has to be harnessed, modified, co-opted. Room has to be made for new elements by either enlarging the old frame of reference (further objectification of order and relativization of the mundane) or by substituting the new for the old.

In Maori society there were a variety of ways to destroy tapus. Cooking would neutralize the *mauri* (soul, life principle) of a plant. This in turn would displease the gods and make them depart (Marsden, 1975: 198). Desacralization was also used as a way to prevent the order becoming too stultified. In order that the warrior might be in top form, the tapu of evil influences would be removed by the tohunga sprinkling the warriors with water. In this instance the tapu removal can also more latently be interpreted as a detachment from a pattern in which integration, aroha, and conformity were prominent features (the settled society) and an attachment to a pattern in which the opposite values, individual prowess, agression, and fierce cruelty were predominant (the battle). This interpretation gains all the more strength in that the *tohi* (war ritual) also reinforced the war tapu, which consisted of dedication to Tuu, the god of warriors.

A very similar desacralization of one pattern and sacralization of another took place in the *tira ora* (wand of life) rite (Best, 1903: 68-69) in which the tohunga made two mounds of earth, one of which represented the sky, masculinity, and life, and the other the earth, femininity, and death. A branch (the *tira ora* or wand of life) was put in the former mound and another wand, (the *tira mate* or wand of death) in the other. The latter was made to absorb the evil from the warriors, after which it was cast down.

Ultimately, of course, the emotional detachment and emptying of one pattern, in order to facilitate the emotional attachment or filling of another had the purpose of reinforcing a particular identity, in this case a tribal or sub-tribal one. The frightful mistake of aroha being showered on one's enemy and cruelty on fellow members had to be avoided at all costs and tapu attachment and detachment made it abundantly clear which value was appropriate at what time.

Other ways of emotional stripping and welding, or desacralization and sacralization took place during the rites of passage.

3. RITUAL

Rites restore sameness through repitition. They re-commit a system of meaning to memory. They also preserve identity by harnessing and guiding necessary change from one pattern to another.

In Maori society there are numerous examples of the kinds of rites that reinforce sameness through repetition. Tribal identity was re-inforced by the meeting, singing, and eating together on the marae. Offerings to tribal gods were in the same category of ritual. The carvings of the meeting houses reminded the people of the spirits and values of the ancestors. They would be regularly referred to and talked about by Maoris, such as the one who told Best (1924b: 135):

> Our ancestors ever watch over us, see all that we do and hear all that we say. They punish us if we infringe the rules of *tapu* and if we deny the truth of ancient lore as taught by our experts. They appear to us at night, and warn us of threatening dangers.

A fisherman using a line for the first time would roast a portion of the right side gill of the first fish he had caught, would hold it up in his hand and wave it back and forth, calling to his dead male forebears that there was food for them. The other portion of the gill would be offered to the ancestral spirits of his wife (Best, 1924b: 243).

Similarly, there are many examples of the rites that harness and guide change from one pattern to another. These so-called rites of passage would reinforce a special tribal or family identity by separating outsiders from insiders or by delineating the new from the old, thereby minimizing internal stresses through changes in constituency, such as birth, marriage, and death.

Encounter Rites

These rites would begin when outsiders were about to enter the marae. Incantations would clear the path of any supernatural obstacle. A ritual challenge (*wero*) in the form of a fierce war dance, sometimes accompanied with musket firing, would greet the visitors. They would just as energetically respond to the mock-intimidation with a sham fight (Salmond, 1975: 132-33).

These ritual challenges were originally intended to warn the outsiders. The more distant in kinship and the more powerful the other
party was, the more formal and extensive the ritual would be. Speeches
would be more numerous and the mana of the visitors-invaders would
be carefully evaluated and articulated (Salmond, 1975: 116). By contrast, the rites would be minimal when visitors were few and from close
by.

The speeches were part of a 'decontamination process' (Walker,
1975: 24). The outsiders were people with sacred feet (*waewae tapu*)
and through the oratory and chanting, in which copious references were
made to the ancestors, genealogy and beliefs regarding life and death,
common feelings would unite both parties. After the speeches the
guests would shake hands with the hosts and *hongi* (press noses). The
incorporation of the guests into the marae would culminate in a
common meal. The commonness (integrative potential) of the meal is
articulated in Maori society by its being designated as noa (profane) in
contrast with the tapu (sacred, to be carefully handled as potentially
dangerous). At the meal the place of the individual host or guest in the
hierarchy would be scrupulously observed by the food being presented
in the precise order of importance.

Birth Rites

Birth rites deal with internal delineations. They suitably demarcate and
incorporate the new addition in the existing structure.

In Maori society there were a variety of rites, *karakias* (spells,
incantations) related to conception, pregnancy, parturition, and the
severance of the umbilical cord. All these rites were ostensibly designed
for the the woman to conceive; for the pregnancy to be successful; for
the birth to be uncomplicated; and for the child to have a clear mind,
etc. Yet the effectiveness of these incantations lay in the restoration of
confidence, integrity, and trust.

There was much variety in the birth rituals according to region and
tribe, but in all instances there was a phase of separation and one of
incorporation. When the umbilical cord was severed it was sometimes
deposited in a crevice or hollow in a tree on a boundary line (Best,
1924b: 225).

When the child's navel cord fell off, the tohi (separating) or *tua* (*tapu* removing, naming) rite was performed. According to most sources it consisted of 'ritual cleansing involving running water, and a naming and dedication of the child towards the appropriate role for male and female . . .' (Biggs, 1960: 69). According to Maori myths the children not yet born dwelt in the *po* (world of pre-natal darkness, night, the unknown). After birth they would enter the realm of light, the *ao marama* (realm of light) (Best, 1924a, I: 94-95).

Birth ceremonies in traditional Maori society differed considerably according to rank. The lower the rank, the lesser the ceremony. To the aristocracy, on the other hand, a first-born son would be of paramount importance. Gudgeon (1885: 119-23) describes such an upper class rite; Best (1924b: 226-28) has a similar one, summarized as follows: two tohungas would march with the baptismal party to a stream. Here the principal priest would discard his garments and enter the water up to his loins. With a twig in the right hand he would address Io, the Supreme Being, after which he would take the child from its mother, name and immerse it, thereby removing the evil influences. After the infant had been returned to the father, the other priest would dedicate it to Io. Acts of divining would follow and water would be sprinkled over the parents and other relatives. On returning to the village the inhabitants would sing a welcoming song. On the house-porch one of the priests would recite more incantations, followed by speeches and presents. Biggs (1960: 69-72) suspects that at least part of these and other ceremonies were post-Christian, if not fabricated by informants.

Marriage

Marriage involves a change of boundaries around a particular family unit. Depending upon their importance in relation to other identity configurations one can expect rituals to accompany the re-drawing of these boundaries.

In Maori society the degree of formality and ceremony surrounding marriage correlated with two factors, as follows.

(1) The rank of the parties involved. The higher the rank, the more elaborate the ceremony (Best, 1924a, I: 442; Buck, 1952: 366). Yet even among the common people speeches would be made, genealogies

recited, gifts presented, and visits exchanged (Best, 1924a, I: 445; Gudgeon, 1885: 119). In families of high rank there would be more of these. The ceremonies would vary from tribe to tribe. Sometimes separate food would be cooked for the couple and their close relations, setting them apart from others and uniting the families of origin (Best, 1924a, I: 469).

(2) The degree of exogamy. The greater the genealogical and, by implication, geographical distance, the more elaborate the ceremony. A special feature at these occasions was a ceremony (*pakuwha*) at which the groom's family laid their cloaks, clubs, and ornaments before the bride, and the bride's family did the same to the groom.

In an important monograph Biggs (1960) investigates the evidence for the existence of marriage rites in pre-European Maori society. He concludes (p. 41) that the early writers were correct in saying that there were no marriage rites, but then continues to mention (as also did earlier writers) a variety of social observances (falling in the rite category in our large definition) to insure that marriages would not weaken the rank-order or tribal and kinship identity.

One of these marriage customs in Maori society was the extensive discussion between the families involved about the suitability of the link. Detachment from the wife's family of origin and attachment to the husband's family were carefully guided by these meetings until the couple began to live together or until 'the formal ceding of the bride to the husband was completed' (Biggs, 1960: 42). As in pre-European times most marriages would be pre-arranged and the chances of kinship or family disruptions thereby minimized, lessening the need for elaborate delineations and ceremonies.

Particularly when marriage was not arranged a form of institution-alized quarrelling about the value of the girl or the family she was about to join often became a part of the proceedings. It was more often resorted to when rank between the partners were unequal; when the tribal (genealogical) distance was great. Adultery and separation were also often occasions for quarrelling, particularly by the family of the slighted partner. In all these instances the relations of the wronged party would take up the cudgels and negotiate gifts or land as compensation. Sometimes the quarrelling would result in outright plunder or fighting. Plunder was a check on indiscriminate breaking of tribal laws and sanction against adultery (Maning, 1863: 109). Objecting to a match or quarrelling underlined the importance of the event of marriage (Biggs, 1960: 44, 52).

Marriage was sometimes used as a way to cement the peace between warring tribes and to effectively preclude a future war. In early Maori history there were examples of very eligible, aristocratic maidens being lowered from the battlements to the attacking party to relieve the predicament of those inside. Grey (1906: 217 ff.) recounts the beautiful story of the hero Takarangi who had cut off the enemy within the fortress from all supplies of food and water. While they were dying of thirst the aged chief and his beautiful daughter, Rau-Mahora, asked for water from the ramparts. Takarangi fell in love with the girl and brought them water after climbing the battlement. She agreed to marry him and, according to the story, this ended the war between them forever.

Death

Like birth, death to the Maori meant transition. In this instance the transition was to, rather than from, the realms of darkness, the unknown, po. Death was the painful separation from one who was part and parcel of a network of emotionally anchored relations.

Death rites were (and are) relatively more important than those surrounding birth and marriage, probably because of the greater emotional trauma of death in tightly knit communities and families. Yet all rites would have themes of separation and re-consolidation in common.

As with ceremonies and spells surrounding birth and marriage, death rites were spread over time. The mourning period would be followed by separation of the remains or temporary burial. Then after a period of decay the bones would be scraped and decorated. Subsequently there would be another more permanent burial in a secret place. All these ceremonies would be spread over several years.

Tangihanga (funeral wake) is as the word *tangi* (lament, weep) implies, a time of mourning and wailing. All the early observers of Maori society were struck by its high pitch and loudness (Oppenheim, 1973: 37). This ceremonial weeping was not only confined to the nearest relations of the deceased. Visitors would come from great distances to the marae and would engage in it as well. Laceration would take place according to the closeness of the relation (Best, 1924b: 237). The effect of all this emotional outpouring purified the souls of the immediate relatives. It also rallied the community and reinforced its solidarity.

Sometimes, as a final ceremony, the tohunga would thrust a tira mate (wand of death) in the ground by the side of a running stream (Tregear, 1904: 392), running water always being popular with rites of passage because of their visual association with transition. He would then recite an incantation over the wand, saying:

> Thou wand of Po, the great Po, the long Po, the dark Po, the unseen Po, the unsought Po, stand there ye wand, wand of Tane, wand of the Po. Begone for ever to the Po (Best, 1924a, I: 69).

After this the priest would erect the tira ora (wand of life) reciting:

> Thou wand of this world, the great world, the long world, the dark world, stand here, ye wand, the wand of Hikurangi, the wand of this world, of the world of light. Remain in this world (Best, 1924a: 70).

This chant was intended to preserve the welfare of the living.

Apart from the actual mourning, a fundamental aspect of the ceremonies was the speech-making and the singing of funeral songs (Oppenheim, 1973: 57). In the speeches, repeated references were made to extensive mythology. In some of these myths the dead person was portrayed as having been caught in the snare of Hine, the guardian of po. She was the one who wanted man to die and decay, in contrast with Tane (the god of life, the sun, who separated his sky father, Rangi, from his earth mother, Papa). The latter suggested to Hine that man should wax and wane as the moon which tires, but then recovers its youth and strength in life-giving waters. However, Tane lost that battle and with it man's immortality (Best, 1906: 150).

Another mythical version of man losing his quest for eternal life is the story of Maui, a demi-god and trickster who met his end when he tried to steal immortality from Hine. He found her asleep and entered her to gain eternal life. But half-way in the fan-tail bird began to laugh waking Hine who then killed Maui by closing her labia (Best, 1906: 153).

These and other oft-repeated myths about death are typical for an entire genre dramatizing the dialectic between femaleness (death, identity) and maleness (life, change), to be more fully discussed in the next section.

As mentioned before, the body of the deceased would be removed after a few days. Sometimes it would be buried, but in pre-Christian times it would more usually be put on a platform or 'suspended in a tree encased in a canoe, until decay had taken place' (Oppenheim, 1973: 60). After several years' interval the bones would be assembled and displayed in a ceremony called *hahunga*. At this occasion too, lamenting, speech-making and abundant feasting would follow before burial in a concealed place.

In Maori society death ceremonials were the most extensive of any rites. Strong tapus surrounded many of the activities. Death meant both danger and change. The ceremonies and tapus harnessed that change so that the individuals and society could regain the stable posture which had been endangered. By separating the dead from the living mundane existence could rediscover its familiar grooves.

4. MYTH

Myths interpret reality and provide a short-hand for basic personal and social experiences. They provide a fitting contour for existence and hold arbitrariness and chaos at bay. They reinforce man's place by making implicit, or even explicit, statements about it. Often they do so by means of a system of binary, yet congruent, oppositions, in which fundamental notions are hidden behind concrete symbols.

Maori mythology is no exception. 'It divides all of nature into male and female', Biggs (1960: 12) correctly observes.

The popular Maori cosmogonies dealt with an original phase of nothingness, the void (*kore*). Darkness, both mental and visual (po), followed this phase, and earth, personified by the female god, Papa, developed spontaneously during that time (Buck, 1952: 435). Its opposite number, the sky, was personified by the male god, Rangi. Both remained in close embrace and produced as many as seventy children, one of which, Tane (the god of trees, the sun and light), revolted against the cramped, dark space in Papa's armpits. Together with Tu, the 'erect one', god of war, Tangaroa, the god of fish, and Tawhiri-matea, the god of wind, he plotted the separation of their parents. By severing limbs, shoving, and kicking, Tane finally managed to push Rangi upwards so that light could penetrate and nature could produce its fruit. The source of evil is traced to this rebellion and raindrops are the tears Rangi still sheds for his beloved Papa. According to at least one mythical version, Tane, the fertilizer, was also credited with creating, after many failures, the first female.

Another cosmogony was originally confined to initiates of the training school for tohungas, Whare Wananga, the House of Learning. It was quite possibly influenced by Christianity, as mentioned in the section on objectification. This cosmogony centred on Io, the un-created one, who created earth and sky. He dwelt above the highest heaven and sent messengers to earth to carry out his commands. Situated in front of Io was a stone with the attributes of a magic mirror in which the entire universe could be observed. Io would change events by merely thinking about them. Close by was an altar with stones which were highly tapu and possessed great mana. Io's attendants looked after these stones.

It was to Io that Tane went to receive the three baskets of know-ledge (one each for beneficient, ritual, and harmful knowledge) (Best, 1924a, I: 73). He also received two of the highly-sacred stones later used by the tohungas of the House of Learning for impregnating small stones with tapu.

This journey to and from Io was constantly endangered by Whiro (the god of darkness and one of Tane's many brothers). He had opposed the separation of Papa and Rangi and resented being separated from the warmth and comfort of Papa's embrace. He hated the open spaces.

All was not well either among the other brothers. They struggled amongst themselves until finally Tu devoured them all, including Tane (Grey, 1906: 8).

One of Tu's descendants, Maui, in many respects resembled the exuberant, forceful Tane. He was the last-born in his family, but his mother, Taranga, who unbeknown to her children lived in the under-world during the day, denied that he could possibly be her offspring.

Yet Maui managed to persuade her that actually he was one of her abortions, wrapped in a tuft of her hair and carelessly thrown into the foam of the surf. Here he said the tangles of the seaweed caught, formed, and fashioned him. The ever-heaving surges of the sea co-operated in the venture by rolling him about, while the foaming bubbles nursed him. Finally, he was blown ashore where the soft tentacles of the jelly-fish enveloped and protected him. The old sky father, Rangi, subsequently saved him from the maggots and the birds who were on the verge of picking him to pieces.

Maui's mother now favoured him by letting him sleep with her. This made the other brothers jealous since they had never had the privilege. Yet they kept the peace as they did not want a repetition of the fateful wars of their ancestors.

Maui could transform himself into all sorts of birds, but his brothers liked him best when he was a peaceful pigeon sitting quite contentedly, cooing to himself. They hoped that he would guide them to their parents who lived in the underworld and live peacefully with them ever after. Maui indeed found the cave below the earth where his parents lived with their ancestors. He told his brothers about it, but there is no record of his showing the abode to them. Many of his own adventures, however, took place in the underworld.

One of his exploits consisted of tricking an old ancestress into giving him a magic ancestral jawbone. With this and a variety of ropes and nooses, Maui and his brothers managed to sneak up to the sun when it came out of its aperture in the east, and after a fierce and hot battle they finally beat it into submission. Until that day the sun had marched across the heavens much faster and more jauntily, thereby badly shortening the day. But now it could only crawl and limp on its course. Later, in order to slow it down even more, Maui tied it to the moon.

Another ancestress was tricked into giving Maui fire. He also changed his brother-in-law into a dog. His final and fatal trick was the unsuccessful attempt to gain eternal life from another ancestress. If it had not been for his father leaving out a portion of the baptismal prayers, he would have been still alive (Grey, 1906: 11-41).

One of the ways to interpret these popular myths of Tane and Maui is to think about them as dramatizations of the dialectic between the male, aggressive, pole and the female, integrative, one. The heroes in the myths are rebels who both need, but also conflict with, parents and ancestors. They bring about change and in the process destroy the peace of sameness. It is Maui's ancestress who possesses immortality and bestows death on the aggressive trickster. Tane and Tu rebel against the integrative embrace of Papa and Rangi and divide them. It is the god of darkness (Whiro) who prefers the close embrace and who opposes the god of light (Tane) who prefers the movement and action. It is the goddess (Hine) of the dark underworld (po) who conflicts with Maui whose unnatural birth highlights his distance from integrative union between husband and wife, or mother and son. It is in sexual union (where in Freud's term the contrasting modes of intrusion and inclusion are resolved) that wholeness and identity are achieved. It is integration which the spirit of the warrior constantly puts in jeopardy. It is aggression which again and again undermines peace. And it is the fixed which takes the sting out of the fickle and the fickle which loosens the fixed.

A similar interpretation, in some respects, of Maori myths is presented by J. Smith (1974: 87 ff.). She stresses the difference between the order-maintaining first brother and the order-challenging younger brother. The first one stresses ascription to consolidate the gain or primogeniture. The younger son does not have this advantage and is achievement-oriented.

J. Smith's binary opposition, however, rests on a vertical-versus-horizontal criterion instead of an identity-versus-change one. So to her the elder brother; hierarchy; the social status orientation; culture; ritual; maleness; God-derived power; and tapu-keeping are all represented by the vertical life-style. On the horizontal side she has the younger brother; inversion of social order; anti-social and individual behaviour; achievement orientation; lack of culture; vitality; femaleness; nature; human power; and tapu-breaking.

The advantage of adopting a criterion of identity versus change, or order-maintenance versus order-challenge, or the fixed versus the fickle (to J. Smith the fixed is vertical, the fickle horizontal), is the goodness of fit with large-scale theorizing in as varied fields as anthropology, sociology, psychology and historiography. In contrast with 'life-style' one can link the identity-change dichotomy to Parsons's and Toynbee's integration-differentiation model. Another advantage of the identity-change model is the better fit with the actual stories. Contrary to J. Smith's criteria, in the myths femaleness is usually on the side of hierarchy; the social; ascription; and ritual, whereas maleness is on the opposite side of war-like; manipulative; achievement orientation; and vital behaviour.

REFERENCES

BEST, Elsdon (1903) 'Notes on the Art of War', *Journal of the Polynesian Society*, 12: 68-69.

––, (1906) 'Maori Eschatology: 'The Whare Potae and Its Lore', in *Transactions of the New Zealand Institute*, XXXVIII. Wellington: Government Printer, pp. 148-239.

––, (1924a) *The Maori*, I and II. Wellington: Whitcombe & Tombs.

––, (1924b) *Maori Religion and Mythology*. Wellington: Government Printer.

BIGGS, Bruce (1960) *'Maori Marriage: An Essay in Reconstruction'*, *Polynesian Society Maori Monograph*, no. 1.

BUCK, Peter H. (1929) *The Coming of the Maori*. New Plymouth, New Zealand: Avery.

––, (1940) 'Foreword', in I. L. G. SUTHERLAND (ed.), *The Maori People Today*, Wellington: The New Zealand Institute of International Affairs, pp. 1-17.

––, (1952) *The Coming of the Maori*. Wellington: Whitcombe & Tombs.

BURLAND, C. A. (1969) *What Became of the Maori?* Exeter: Wheaton Press.

DUMONT, D'Urville (1935) *Voyage du Monde*. Paris: Tenré.

FIRTH, Raymond (1959) *Economics of the New Zealand Maori*. Wellington: Government Printer.

GREY, Sir George (1906) *Polynesian Mythology and Ancient Traditional History of the New Zealanders*. Auckland: Whitcombe & Tombs.

GUDGEON, Thomas Wayth (1885) *The History and Doings of the Maoris* (from the Year 1820 to the Signing of the Treaty of Waitangi in 1840). Auckland: Brett.

HARRÉ, John (1966) *Maori and Pakeha (A Study of Mixed Marriages in New Zealand)*. Wellington: A. H. & A. W. Reed.

JOHANSEN, J. Prytz (1954) *The Maori and His Religion*. Copenhagen: Munksgaard.

––, (1958) *Studies in Maori Rites and Myths*. Copenhagen: Munksgaard.

KAWHARU, I. H. (1968) 'Urban Immigrants and Tangata Whenua', in Erik SCHWIMMER (ed.), *The Maori People in the Nineteen Sixties*. Auckland: Blackwood and Janet Paul, pp. 174-86.

LÉVI-STRAUSS, Claude (1962) *La Pensée Sauvage*. Paris: Plon.

MAHUIKA, Api (1975) 'Leadership: Inherited and Achieved', in Michael KING (ed.), *Te Ao Hurihuri (The World Moves On)*. Wellington: Hicks Smith & Sons, pp. 86-113.

MANING, F. E. (1863) *Old New Zealand*. Auckland: Creighton & Scales.

MARSDEN, Maori (1975) 'God, Man and Universe: A Maori View', in Michael KING (ed.), *Te Ao Hurihuri (The World Moves On)*. Wellington: Hicks Smith & Sons, pp. 191-219.

METGE, Joan (1971) *The Maoris of New Zealand*. London: Routledge & Kegan Paul.

––, (1976) *The Maoris of New Zealand*. London: Routledge & Kegan Paul.

MOL, Johannis (Hans) J. (1976) *Identity and the Sacred: A Sketch for a New Social-Scientific Theory of Religion.* Oxford: Blackwell.

OPPENHEIM, Roger (1973) *Maori Death Customs.* Wellington: A. H. & A. W. Reed.

SALMOND, Anne (1975 *Hui: A Study of Maori Ceremonial Gatherings.* Wellington: A. H. & A. W. Reed.

SINCLAIR, Douglas (1975) 'Land: Maori View and European Response', in Michael KING (ed.), *Te Ao Hurihuri (The World Moves On).* Wellington: Hicks Smith & Sons, pp. 115-39.

SMITH, Jean (1974) 'Tapu Removal in Maori Religion', *Polynesian Society Memoir Supplement*, (40) (also published in *Journal of the Polynesian Society*, 83 (4) (Dec. 1974) and 84 (1 and 2) (March and June 1975).

SMITH, S. Percy (1913) *The Lore of the Whare-Wananga (Teachings of the Maori College on Religion, Cosmogony and History)*, III. New Plymouth, New Zealand: The Polynesian Society.

TREGEAR, E. (1904) *The Maori Race.* Wanganui: Willis.

WALKER, Ranginui (1975) 'Marae: A Place to Stand', in Michael KING (ed.), *Te Ao Hurihuri (The World Moves On).* Wellington: Hicks Smith & Sons, pp. 21-34.

11

THE AFRIKANER CIVIL RELIGION

T. Dunbar Moodie
Hobart and William Smith Colleges, New York, USA

Civil religion is very much a legitimate part of the identity model of religion. It is less global in that it deals with only one identity focus (the nation) rather than also person and group. Those, such as Dr Moodie, writing in this field also tend to stress rituals and myths reinforcing the national identity rather than objectifications and commitments.

The sacred history of Afrikaners runs from the defeat by the British at Slagtersnek and the suffering of the Anglo-Boer war to the Rebellion of 1915. The commemorations of these events take place in terms of the biblical theme of exodus and deliverance, suffering and resurrection. The first (Great Trek) cycle of suffering and death did lead to a republican restoration. The second (the Boer war) also was a period of great suffering leading to a new republic and freedom from British domination.

This chapter is deliberately descriptive. I attempt to describe a set of beliefs which constitute political reality and a means to political power for the Afrikaans-speaking white group in South Africa. I shall deal also with the ritual and organizational means by which it attained popular acceptance. In so doing I hope to convey a sense of the appeal of the Judaeo-Christian model of salvation-history for a group who see themselves as persecuted, but to stress also the demonic implications of this type of religious identity if such a group achieves political power.

I

That most Afrikaners are Calvinists goes without saying. In this chapter, however, I intend to concentrate not upon Calvinism as such, but upon a Calvinist heresy which I call 'the Afrikaner civil religion'. The period of Afrikaner history which I know well runs from 1929 to 1948. During that era the Afrikaner civil faith was quite as important as Calvinism in constituting the Afrikaner's world view and his self-identity.

In fact, the Afrikaner civil theology states, as did Calvin, that God reveals himself by his actions in history, directing and electing, dealing salvation and damnation from the majesty of his intervening will. But the civil faith also assumes that the history of Afrikanerdom shows God's particular will in the special election of his Afrikaner People as a racial and/or cultural (ethnic) group, with its own God-given language and its own divine destiny — and Calvin knows no doctrine of national election.[1]

According to the civil faith, as preached in the 1930s and 1940s, the sacred period of Afrikaner history runs from Slagtersnek[2] in 1815 to the execution of Jopie Fourie[3] in 1915. This period contained two cycles of death and suffering. The first was at the hands of the British in the Cape and the Blacks inland and is contained in the saga of the Great Trek; the second resulted from the pressures of British imperialism after the discovery of gold in the Transvaal, culminating in the Anglo-Boer war and the Rebellion of 1915. Innocent Afrikaner women and children bore the brunt of the suffering, both in the Zulu massacre at Blaauwkrantz in the first cycle and in the British Boer war concentration camps in the second. At the centre of this sacred period stands a brief pastoral interlude, the republics of the highveld 'where the hills lie like rams along streams which laugh and chatter' (du Toit, 1962, 8: 215).

Such a sacred history — beginning with an execution after an abortive rebellion and ending on the same note, with English suppression of Afrikaans language and culture a constant theme from the anglicization policy of Sir Charles Somerset in 1806 to that of Lord Milner in 1902 — might seem to offer little hope for the continuance of the Afrikaner language and community. Yet this very history was claimed by Dr D. F. Malan[4] as evidence of God's election:

Afrikaner history reveals a firm resolve and purposiveness which makes one feel that Afrikanerdom is not the work of men, but the creation of God. . . . Throughout our history, God's plan for our People is clear, we have a divine right to be because God created our People (Pienaar, 1964: 236).

Faith such as this is not unusual in the Christian tradition since those who are chosen by God suffer even as the People of Israel and God's son himself suffered. The sufferings of the innocent Christian are but 'the special badge of God's soldiery' (Calvin, III, 8: 7). So too for the Afrikaner the past suffering of women and children and the apparent fruitlessness of his cultural and political struggle during the 1930s was but the seal of God's election. One of Malan's favourite quotes was from Langenhoven.[5] 'For a hundred years we were always losing, but while we lost, throughout those hundred years we were winning' (cf. *Burger* 22 July and 16 December, 1933).

Even more important for the civil faith is the Christian conviction that death is followed by resurrection, suffering by glory. Israel was restored after the Babylonian exile; Jesus rose from the dead. Furthermore, the first (Great Trek) cycle of suffering and death *did* lead to a republican restoration. The *via dolorosa* in Natal led out to the highveld republics. And God's intent that Afrikaners should have a republic was confirmed in the events after Paardekraal during the first (1881) Anglo-Boer war, when the Boers renewed their covenant with the Lord and he led them mightily to victory at Majuba.

Thus, the second cycle of Afrikaner death and suffering, it was believed, would also lead to a new republic. Like Christ the republic had come and was yet to come. For Kruger's republic was the first fruits of an even mightier pan-Afrikaner republic which God would bring in his own good time. Afrikaners had but patiently to keep faith, reaffirming their covenant on 16 December each year, preserving their cultural identity and striving to maintain themselves pure and unsullied by close ties with English-speaking and black South Africans alike. Thus, by 1936 the language movement, the establishment of separate Afrikaner cultural organizations, separate schools and separate voluntary charities were all linked to the Afrikaner's vigil, his expectation of the republican eschaton. In the words of Malan:

> One answers the call of God and the People, and undertakes the great task, and even if the People are defeated, he knows that God guarantees the existence of his People. He is not afraid about winning or losing, because he knows that life springs from death and that he has God and God's mandate to support him in the service of his People (Pienaar, 1964: 238).

Throughout the sacred period of Afrikaner history the major political threat was believed to be British imperialism, the major cultural threat the English language and traditions, and the major economic threat British-Jewish capitalism. In the 1920s and 1930s it was the English peril *(Engelse gevaar)* which seemed paramount to Afrikaner true believers. The desire for freedom from British domination, not fear of the Black masses, was the major theme of the mainstream Afrikaner civil faith. On the Day of the Covenant, 1925, for instance, Minister Charlie Malan stated that the native peril was a threat only when Afrikaners could not be true to themselves.[6]

II

The foregoing outline of the civil faith implies a more consciously systematic creed than would have been asserted by most Afrikaners. Although in the 1930s and 1940s many ordinary Afrikaners passionately believed in their national election, their redemptive suffering and the republican eschaton, their response was emotional rather than intellectual. Opperman puts it well when he says in *Joernaal van Jorik*: 'As one sees stars and lights shiver in the depths of the waters of Table Bay at night, so images of concentration camps still move in a dark corner of this People' (Opperman, 1949: 21).

Certain images are uniquely representative of the major themes of the civil faith. Two such composite figures who express poignantly in condensed form some of the most important preoccupations of the civil religion are those of *die Afrikaner in Engelse diens* (the Afrikaner in English service) and *die Afrikanervrou* (The Afrikaner woman).

Jan Smuts epitomized the former figure. His commitment to South Africa's British imperial link and his leadership of the 'pro-capitalist' South African Party with its combined English and Afrikaans-speaking membership made him for many Afrikaners simply the servant of John Bull and 'Handyman of the Empire'. At the mention of the *Afrikanervrou*, on the other hand, 'there stirs in our memory the upwelling of mother's grief and children's sighs. We see once more the strife and struggle, imprisonment and exile, blood and tears, as well as the quiet rise of an insignificant People which made a mighty effort to sustain its right to existence among the nations' (*Volksblad*, 7 October, 1935).

This ability of the civil faith and its most important images to evoke an emotional reaction from deep in the sources of Afrikaner affectivity presupposes very general acceptance by ordinary Afrikaners.

In fact there is a certain inevitability about the Afrikaner civil faith as I have described it above which must give any sociologist cause to pause. It implies not only that all Afrikaners are inheritors of the sacred history but also that Afrikaans-speaking South Africans who deny the civil faith are not true Afrikaners. Thus, the civil faith claims the universal adherence of all Afrikaners but then proceeds to define 'Afrikaner' in civil religious terms. Such a claim to monopoly on Afrikanerdom may appear self-evident today but if it does so it testifies to the success of the civil religion rather than to the historical accuracy of its claims. General Hertzog, Nationalist Prime Minister from 1924 to 1939, for instance, insisted throughout his life that the term Afrikaner be applied to all White South Africans (whether English or Afrikaans-speaking) who accepted South Africa as their sole homeland. So did Tobie Muller, who was one of the earliest exponents of Afrikaner Nationalism (cf. T. D. Moodie, 1975: ch. 5). Throughout the first parts of this chapter I have begged the question of the breadth of support for the civil faith amongst ordinary Afrikaans-speaking South Africans. I shall attempt to come to terms with this matter in what follows.

III

One of the best measures of support for a set of beliefs is participation in ritual. Ritual action not only demonstrates commitment, it also renews the faith of those who participate. For 'the cult is not simply a system of signs by which the faith is outwardly translated; it is a collection of the means by which this is created and renewed periodically' (Durkheim, 1965: 464). In coming together on ritual occasions in order to reaffirm their civil faith, Afrikaners not only demonstrate their attachment to the sentiments and images of Afrikaner tradition, but that tradition is made real for them in their collective enthusiasm. Liturgical re-enactment dramatizes faith in collective action.

The Afrikaner civil religion has its own civil ritual. The Day of the Covenent — 16 December — is a holy day.[7] Afrikaners all over South Africa congregate in churches and in the open air to celebrate their covenant with God which was confirmed at Blood River and reaffirmed at Paardekraal.[8] They meditate upon their sacred history, exhorted by speeches and psalms, ponder their past and steady themselves for the future. A *Burger* editorial for 16 December 1933 captured the spirit of the occasion:

> The way of suffering traversed by the fathers was not for bread; they strove for an ideal — the ideal to be themselves, to be free from foreign bonds. . . . On [the Day of the Covenant] the Afrikaner examines his heritage. . . . The ideal of freedom was handed on to him, and with it a particular national pride, a unique language and culture, his own traditions. . . . In the spiritual life of a People there is no cessation, only growth or decline — and the growth does not come of itself, it demands exertion and struggle and dedication. Today the Afrikaner pays homage to the fathers. In that homage he renews a silent vow to hold to their heritage and to build thereon.

Afrikaners have not only their sacred time but also their holy places. South Africa is dotted with monuments commemorating the themes and events of the civil faith. Foremost among these is the Women's Monument at Bloemfontein and the Voortrekker Monument near Pretoria These are places of pilgrimage throughout the year and ritual centres on the Day of the Covenant.

However, the existence of such holy times and places among Afrikaners does not necessarily imply wide-scale adherence to the civil faith. The Voortrekker monument was not officially opened until 1949, and construction was financed largely by the State despite a powerful drive for public support in the 1930s. In the 1920s the Day of the Covenant was seldom celebrated at the Cape at all. In the Transvaal in the 1920s the only newspaper which regularly made much of 16 December was Smuts's *Die Volkstem*. When Covenant Day celebrations were held they were frequently organized by the government and attended by the Governor-General who addressed the crowd in English and was heralded by 'God Save the King'. As late as 1932 at an Afrikaner Cultural Congress some of the speeches were delivered in English, despite a text behind the dias which read: *Die taal van die veroweraar in die mond van die verowerde is slawetaal* (The language of the conqueror in the mouth of the conquered is slave language) (*Volk-*

stem, 5 January, 1932). Between 1920 and 1938 hardly one of the school magazines extant in the South African Public Library contained student essays on civil religious themes. Indeed, in 1935 the Afrikaans press announced a 'disturbing' lack of interest by Afrikaner cultural organizations in the Federation of Afrikaner Cultural Organizations (FAK) which was to have been the major co-ordinating body for civil religious activities. Only 131 of the many hundreds of eligible Afrikaner organizations had joined the FAK (*Vaderland*, 29 September, 1935).

The implication of such observations is clear. During the 1920s and early 1930s, general support for the Afrikaner civil religion amongst Afrikaans-speaking South Africans was minimal. This was in striking contrast to the moving events at the time of Paul Kruger's funeral in 1904, widespread Transvaal sympathy for the 1915 rebellion, and broad Afrikaner support for the *Helpmekaar* movement.[9] In the 1920s and early 1930s political disillusionment and economic depression seem to have effectively damped widespread civil religious commitment amongst ordinary Afrikaans-speaking South Africans.

But in 1938 enthusiasm for the symbols of Afrikaner exclusiveness rose suddenly to a gigantic crescendo of collective ferment. This new fervour was dramatically kindled by the celebration of the centenary of the Day of the Covenant. Oxwagons, replicas of those which had undergone the Great Trek, left Cape Town in August 1938 en route for Pretoria where the foundation stone of the Voortrekker monument was to be laid on 16 December. By the time the wagons reached their goal, they had visited every town and hamlet in South Africa. At the outset men wore false beards and occasional slightly embarrassed women donned Voortrekker dress; at the end of the trek the beards were real and Voortrekker garb was worn by women in their thousands. Babies were baptized in the shade of wagons; couples were married beside them. Night after night Afrikaners of every class and political description gathered around the wagons to sing traditional folk songs and partake the cook-out and coffee of brotherhood together. Young men and women jostled about the wagons and rubbed souvenier axle-grease upon their handkerchiefs; old folks clambered aboard for brief ceremonial rides – 'Lord, now lettest thou thy servant depart in peace', said one old man. As the date for the final ceremonies drew near, oxwagon speakers began to hint that the republican eschaton was indeed nigh. Even among tough newsmen in the offices of *Die Burger* in Cape Town there was an air of expectation. To the handful of faithful who had struggled through the years of dark night of the Afrikaner soul it must have seemed that the Lord had once more visited his People. Afrikanerdom had returned to the true way, *die Pad van Suid Afrika*.

If a sacrament be defined as 'a significant deed, a particular use of temporal things which gives to them the value of eternal things and thus incorporates and conveys spiritual reality' (Underhill, 1962: 51), then the *Eeufees* (centenary) of 1938 was indeed sacramental for most Afrikaners. In fact, I suggest, following Durkheim,[10] that in any historical faith beliefs and regular rites tend to be supplemented by sacramental moments of collective ferment when great ideals are created or renewed and when 'following the collectivity, the individual forgets himself for the common end and his conduct is orientated in terms of a standard outside himself' (Durkheim, 1953: 91). For the Afrikaner civil religion such sacramental events included the original covenant at Paardekraal in 1881,[11] Paul Kruger's funeral in 1904, the rebellion of 1915, the Eeufees of 1938, the aftermath of the declaration of war in 1939, the Nationalist political victory in 1948, the official opening of the Voortrekker monument in 1949, and the republican referendum in 1961. In such moments the great ideal

> is lived with such intensity and exclusiveness that it monopolizes all minds to the more or less complete exclusion of egoism and the commonplace. At such times the ideal tends to become one with the real, and for this reason men have the impression that the time is close when the ideal will in fact be realized and the Kingdom of God established on earth (Durkheim, 1953: 92).

In South Africa the declaration of war in 1939 followed hard upon the heels of the oxwagon celebrations. Smuts's decision to go to war split the reigning English-Afrikaner fusion party and thousands of Afrikaners returned to the nationalist fold. It seemed that the promise of 1938 had indeed been fulfilled. When Afrikanerdom was reunited, W. A. de Klerk gave ecstatic expression to the glorious sacrament of Afrikaner communality. He called for

> A return to the deep awareness that even as every member of the People carries around in himself a part of the Divine, and is thus a potential God-man, even so the People is a unity and as a whole the bearer of the Divine in its own soul, so that it possesses the potentiality of becoming a God-People (*Stellenbosse Student*, September 1939: 265).

After the events of 1938 and 1939, the Afrikaans newspapers overflowed with accounts of enthusiastic meetings by local branches of the reunited Party, *Reddingsdaadbond,* the *Ossewabrandwag,* and innumerable cultural societies. School magazines were filled with unadulterated civil religious essays. However, as Durkheim points out,

> once the critical moment has passed, the social life relaxes, intellectual and emotional intercourse is subdued, and individuals fall back to their ordinary level . . . All that was said, done and thought during this period of fecund upheaval survives only as a memory, a memory no doubt as glorious as the reality it recalls, but with which it is no longer at one. . . . Between what is felt and perceived and what is thought of in the form of ideals there is now a clear distinction. Nevertheless these ideals could not survive if they were not periodically revived. This revivification is the function of religious or secular feasts and ceremonies. . . . But these means have only a temporary effect (Durkheim, 1953: 92).

Gradually, therefore, the sense of participation in glorious events and the feeling of common Afrikanerhood, began to lose their immediacy. Nonetheless, things could never be quite as they were. On future celebrations of Afrikaner holy days the ordinary Afrikaner ritual would hark back to those sacramental events of 1938 and 1939. In the years to come there was to be profound disagreement about the achievement of the civil religion ideals, but few ordinary Afrikaners could fail to recall that for at least a few enchanted months 'oxwagon unity' had been a genuine reality.

IV

The momentous sacramental events of 1938 and 1939 help us to understand the rapid renewal of civil religious commitment by ordinary Afrikaans-speaking South Africans. Another element which facilitated acceptance of the civil religion is the oligarchal mode of legitimation which is typical in Afrikaner institutions. Afrikaner society was until recently characterized by separation between a small, relatively wealthy and educated elite and the poor white masses. Since the elite was traditionally conscious of an obligation to its less fortunate fellow-

Afrikaners, and since the ordinary man did not query the competence of the elite to assume leadership, there was little conflict between these two groups. Furthermore, a strong belief in democracy and frequent and friendly personal contact between members of the two groups helped to obscure consciousness of conflicting interests.

Whether the oligarchal style of Afrikaner politics goes back to the early *bywoner* (share-cropper) system or to the patriarchal structure of the trek-groups is not at issue here. Whatever the reasons for it the social structure of the Transvaal Republic between 1870 and 1899 is a good example of this typically Afrikaner style of legitimating authority. On the face of it the government of the South African Republic was democratic in the extreme. 'In the voice of the People', said President Paul Kruger, 'I heard the voice of God, King of all Peoples, and I obey' (Kleynhans, 1966: 23). Public opinion in the Transvaal Republic, he believed, was analogous to the word of God received by Moses on Sinai (Smit, 1951: 15). Even the acts of the *Volksraad*, the elected representatives of the People's voice, were in practice subject to review by public petition. In fact most *Volksraad* legislative action stemmed from citizens' petitions (Kleynhans, 1966: 139). Thus, democratic appearances were radically maintained — indeed, Kruger's philosophy of government was Rousseauian rather than Calvinist. Interestingly, in the Free State, which had a more rigid constitution, President Steyn attempted several times to introduce government by plebiscite. He too was a disciple of the doctrine of the People's sovereign will.

When one looks at the actual operation of government in the Transvaal Republic, however, a very different picture emerges. In a recent paper Stanley Trapido has marshalled impressive evidence that the South African Republic was dominated by an elite of officials (*veldkornets* and *landdrosts*) and wealthy landowners. 'In the last two decades of the century', he says, 'the dominant group of Afrikaner landowners had established an informal network which enabled them to accumulate profitable landholdings' (Trapido, 1973: 58). No doubt such a network also helped to establish political influence.[1][2] Government may have been by petition, but in most cases the petitions were compiled by influential men — officials or local leaders such as church ministers (Kleynhans, 1966: 51, 126-27). A local newspaper cynically offered to get up a hundred signatures on any topic within a week. Another newspaper listed a series of petitions obtained in the Zoutpansberg area which in the editor's opinion 'shews that these documents are not the spontaneous utterances of the public' (Kleynhans, 1966: 128-29).

I do not argue that the economic and political elite (the local gentry) in the Transvaal consciously exploited the Afrikaner poor. *Veldkornets* (local administrative officers), who were drawn from families with wealth and local status, no doubt shared the opinion of F. A. van Jaarsveld that they were protectors, overseers and fathers of the People and were not in the first place officials (Trapido: 1973: 63, n. 18). That such officials prospered despite, indeed perhaps because of, their faithful service to the People, would have seemed but their just reward. And the ordinary poor Afrikaner no doubt agreed. The fact remains that political action was initiated by an influential elite group or number of groups whose decisions were simply accepted by the ordinary man. In fact, Trapido gives one example of a case (that of the Mapoch settlers) where petitions that came from the poor were ignored (Trapido, 1973: 59).

A further example of oligarchy among Afrikaners (perhaps it is the normative example) is the organization of the local congregations of the Dutch Reformed churches. Congregations are rules by a *kerkraad* (church council) made up of the minister, the elders and the deacons. This body is not elected by a meeting of church members but elects its own new members, including the minister, as and when it considers necessary. It meets in camera and is not required to divulge details of its proceedings. This overt oligarchy is justified as conforming both to the will of God and the will of the congregation. I quote at length an exposition of the system:

> According to our system the *kerkraad* [church council] is the body which guides all congregational concerns. It keeps all in order and its decisions alone have force ... As Reformed churchmen we see that the *kerkraad* receives all its authority from Christ, the Head of the congregation. It is indeed the congregation that chooses the *kerkraad* through the combined *kerkraad* which acts on behalf of the congregation, but we affirm further that in this fashion the *kerkraad* is chosen by God himself. Thus the congregation does indeed share the government to which the *kerkraad* is called and lives together in that government, but the *kerkraad* does not receive its mandate from the congregation but from Christ who is Head of the congregation ... [However] the *kerkraad* must be aware of that which lies close to the heart of the congregation. And because a *kerkraad* realizes this it will sometimes call a congrega-

tional meeting in order to discover what goes on in the heart of the congregation in regard to important matters and to guage common opinion on them.
But such meetings are not binding on the *kerkraad* (Theron, n.d.: 17-18).

The logic may seem obscure, but the operation of this system of church
government is important for understanding a further oligarchy which
has been essential to the continuance of the civil faith. If the 'Afrikaner
People' (meaning those who affirm their faith in Afrikanerdom's divine
destiny) is taken as one huge congregation, then it is the Afrikaner
Broederbond which has appointed itself church council to Afrikanerdom (cf. T. D. Moodie, 1975: ch. 6). Self-selected from the ranks of the
Afrikaner elite (school-teachers, civil servants, wealthy landowners,
lawyers, academics), the members of the Broederbond meet in secret 'in
order impartially to discover that which is best for the moral, intellectual, social and political progress of our nation' (*Volksblad*, 3
January, 1945). Membership is restricted to Afrikaans-speaking Protestants who believe 'that the Afrikaner nation with its own character
and task was called into being in this land by the hand of God'
(Oelofse, 1964: 28). The standard used in recruitment is 'the zeal and
readiness of members to work for People's causes and regularly to make
sacrifices, monetary or otherwise, without any expectation of
reward'[13] (*Volksblad*, 14 December, 1944).

The Broederbond thus decides what is in the best interests of the
Afrikaner People. Like the kerkraad, however, the Broederbond must
be 'aware of what lies close to the heart of the People'. Hence, when a
particular policy in the interests of Afrikanerdom has been decided, the
Bond will call a *volkskongres* to present the matter to the People and
establish a formal voluntary association to put its policy into operation.
Hence the *Kultuurkongres* which led to the formation of the FAK in
1929, and the *Akonomiese Kongres* of 1939, which established the
RDB and the *Akonomiese Instituut*. These voluntary formal organizations were all staffed by an overwhelming majority of *broers*.

The Broederbond was founded by Henning Klopper, who was also
organizer of the *Ossewatrek* in 1938. Much of the success of that
sacramental event was the result of Klopper's Broederbond contacts in
pastories and town boards throughout the land.[14] When war was
declared in 1939, it was J. C. van Rooy, the Kuyperian Broederbond
chairman, who organized the great Afrikaner reunion celebration at the
site of the Voortrekker movement.

Indeed, in so far as the Broederbond was able to rally the Afrikaans-speaking elite for civil religion causes, it was ultimately assured the support of the masses. For even as ordinary churchmen followed the lead of self-elected elders and ministers, so the Afrikaner masses tended to follow their cultural and political elite, in this case usually self-elected by fellow-broers. The Broederbond became the clearing-house of Christian-National ideology, fomenting practical proposals for realization of the ideals of the civil faith.[15] If we may transpose an earlier citation on church government,

> it is indeed the People that elects the Broederbond through the combined Broederbond which acts on behalf of the People, but we affirm further that in this fashion the Broederbond is chosen by God himself. . . . However, the Broederbond must be aware of that which lies close to the heart of the People. And because the Broederbond realizes this it will sometimes call a *volkskongres* in order to discover what goes on in the heart of the People in regard to important matters and to gauge common opinion on them.

Finally, in examining the background to popular acceptance of the Afrikaner civil faith, one cannot overlook the importance of the schools. The right education in the mother-tongue had long been a rallying-cry for Afrikaners, but in the 1940s this cry became incorporated into the basic tenets of the civil faith. Afrikaans and English-speakers must go to separate schools, Broederbonders insisted, because only then could 'the culture of the nation' carry over 'pure, from one generation to the next' (Nel, n.d.: 13). Leadership of the Transvaal Teachers' Union (TO) had long been virtually synonomous with the Broederbond. Indeed, a wartime Intelligence Report on the activities of the Broederbond mentioned educational institutions as the major sphere of its activity (Vatcher, 1965: 256-76). In the 1940s and 1950s, this Broederbond involvement in education began to bear fruit in two ways. First, a number of Afrikaans school textbooks appeared displaying deep commitment to the sacred history (Auerbach, 1965). Secondly, Afrikaner hold on the provincial boards of education was tightened until Afrikaans-speaking South Africans dominated the entire educational establishment. As late as 1975 a comparative analysis of Afrikaans and English-speaking elementary school pupil attitudes shows strong awareness on the part of Afrikaans-speaking children of the anti-English themes of the civil religion (cf. M. A. Moodie, 1976).

V

I have argued elsewhere the importance of the Afrikaner civil religion in the 1948 election victory of the Nationalist Party in South Africa (T. D. Moodie, 1975: ch. 12). In this chapter, which deals with the Afrikaner civil faith as an example of an identity theory of religion, it is necessary to provide an account not only of the manner in which this identity came to be constituted for ordinary Afrikaners, but also of the way in which this identity has been reinterpreted by different schools of Afrikaner thought. Finally, I shall deal briefly with the current situation in South Africa where the continued existence of the Afrikaner civil religion itself is at stake.

It is tempting to consider the Afrikaner civil religion as analogous to Freud's conception of the dream. All the primary characteristics of the dream-work in Freud's *Interpretation of Dreams* (1900; trans 1955, ch. 6) are to be found here. We have already mentioned 'condensation' in citing images like die *Afrikanervrou* and *die Afrikaner in Engelse diens.* The second characteristic, 'representability', seems to me to be but a particular aspect of condensation. The third of Freud's functions of the dream-work, that of 'displacement', can be said to operate in the civil religion when a symbol such as 'imperialism' arouses anti-English senti-ment, or when the clearly Semitic figure of Hoggenheimer is used to depict capitalism. Indeed, the theory of separate development itself can be used to give moral justification for clearly racist sentiments. How-ever, the Afrikaner civil religion is particularly open to Freud's fourth function, that of 'secondary revision'.

Secondary revision is the process by which an emotionally over-determined set of images and themes is rendered rationally intelligible. The Afrikaner civil faith was reinterpreted to meet the intellectual demands of a number of different philosophical systems. One of the earliest of these philosophies was Jan Smuts's classical liberalism, ex-pressed in his preface to *'n Eeu van Onrecht* (A Century of Injustice) written in 1899:

> Once more the day has dawned in our blood-written history when we are compelled to take up arms and renew the struggle for liberty and existence, and to entrust our national cause to that Providence which has led our people by miracles through South Africa. . . . We have arrived at that point at which it

must be decided whether all the sacrifices which our fathers and ourselves have laid upon the alter of liberty have been in vain, whether all the blood of our people bywhich, as it were, every part of South Africa is consecrated, has been shed in vain . . . By the light of our history alone it is possible to test and judge the motives of the present, and by this means attain to the truth to which our People appeal as its final justification in the approaching struggle (Hancock, 1962: 109).

Smuts thus interpreted the sacred history in terms of the inalienable rights of life, liberty and the pursuit of happiness with which all men had been endowed by their Creator.

A more important revision of the civil religion was the liberal language nationalism of such as Tobie Muller, D. F. Malan and the early Broederbond. Their main emphasis was that the Afrikaans language be preserved and used in church and school, political debate and daily intercourse. However, such maintenance of Afrikaans should come about only through the continued growth of an Afrikaner culture for, as Malan said, 'no language is simply a means of communication between individuals. It is also the bond of unity between the individual and his People. . . .The language is the cement of all which is unique to the People — religion, character, customs, history, art, literature. It binds one to another and gives certainty to the structure of national life' (Malan, 1911: 36). Muller maintained that the existence of separate cultural consciousnesses would strengthen general South African civic unity. Dutch- and English-speaking Afrikaners alike must 'build up our national character in order to influence for the good other nations with whom we come into contact' (Muller, 1913: 32). Such nationalism was not exclusive, he said, but rather was necessary because it strengthened the moral fibre of the individual by means of his membership within the nation.

This liberal nationalism, with its stress upon the moral character of the individual, had strong roots in the long tradition of constitutional government in the Cape Colony (the southern half of the country) (cf. Davenport, 1965). It was headed by Dr Malan and the most powerful Afrikaans newspaper, *Die Burger*, as well as directors of the largest Afrikaner farming and financial interests which, until the late 1950s, were located in the Western Cape. Clergy of the majority *Nederduits Gereformeerde* (NG) church were trained at Stellenbosch, near Cape Town, where, at least until 1928, undergraduate seminarians were subjected to an evangelical Calvinism derived from Scottish Presbyterianism and the Dutch Reveil.

Liberal nationalists of this stamp were uneasy with militant proponents of the civil faith and tended not to be prominent members of the Broederbond although their commitment to the Afrikaans language movement, the National Party and Afrikaner social welfare could not be faulted.

The most important secondary revision of the civil faith, then, was not liberal nationalism, but rather that which has become known as 'Christian-Nationalism'. The Christian-Nationalist ideology stems from two major philosophical strands: Kuyperian Calvinism[16] and neo-Fichtean[17] or integral nationalism. The Calvinism of Abraham Kuyper has been current in South Africa since before the turn of the century, especially at Potchefstroom University which is staffed largely by *Gereformeerdes* members of the minority, strictly Calvinist, Afrikaans church. Yet since many NG theological students who went overseas for higher study attended Kuyper's Free University in Amsterdam, the influence of his philosophical system spread far beyond the narrow confines of the *Gereformeerde* church. The major principle peculiar to Kuyperian Calvinism is its insistence on the central importance of common grace. According to this doctrine not only the realm of salvation (particular grace) but also the operation of the entire cosmos is subject to God's sovereign will. This notion of common grace is supplemented by the doctrine of *sowereiniteit in eie kring* which states that the various spheres of human existence – church, family, economy, state, art, morality, law, science – each have their own purpose and calling, all independent of one another, subject to the sovereignty of God alone.

> Only Calvinism [said L. J. du Plessis] acknowledges the scripturally revealed law of God as universally determinative of all reality and of every aspect of human life and also acknowledges a divine economy *(wetmatigheid)* which is revealed in nature and history and is necessarily determined by the destiny and nature of every sphere of human association (du Plessis, 1942).

Thus, Christians are called, in the words of H. G. Stoker, 'to subjugate the earth, dominate nature, defend order, and so on, in the name of God ... To dominate nature and thereby form it into culture is the glorious task, the calling which God gives to men as individual and social beings' (Stoker, 1941: 222, 224). For Kuyperians like Stoker and du Plessis, the People too was a separate social and cultural sphere with its own structure and calling, grounded in the ordinances of God's common grace. Thus, the conception of election to a divine destiny for Afrikanerdom received firm theological support from Kuyperianism.

Kuyperian Calvinists rested their version of the Afrikaner civil faith upon God's sovereign activity in electing the Afrikaner People as a separate national entity within the manifold personal, cultural and social ordinances of his creation. Neo-Fichteanism went further. According to this social philosophy, represented most prominently by Dr Nic Diederichs and other Afrikaner academics who returned from graduate study in Europe in the 1930s to start the Afrikaner National Student Union (ANS), the nation takes priority over all other spheres of life. For neo-Fichtean nationalists 'humanity is not the highest value, but rather the nation. So-called humanity can be served only through the nation and the individual can find himself only in the nation' (*Wapenskou*, April 1935). The nation is defined in terms of single-minded devotion to a common culture. Political commitment, race, even patriotism, are insufficient for the realization of the nation, unless they are undergirded by love and service to a culturally defined spiritual calling. A national culture involves not merely the acceptance of certain values, but also the struggle to realize those values; not only a common faith, but also communal action.

> A nation is one because its members feel united in their common attitudes to the same values. Furthermore, their unity is no rigid, static unity but a living, moving, growing unity, a unity of direction and struggle . . . Like any other spiritual being, a nation must continually struggle to remain itself, continually to conquer itself and regain itself. . . .The cultural history of a nation is the process along which this self-realization takes place. . . .But nations are not historical entities in the sense that history created their unity. Their unity is supra-temporal and grounded in the common ideal world of values (Diederichs, 1936: 36-41).

For Kuyperians, then, the nation shared equally with the other spheres of creation in God's cosmic ordinance. For neo-Fichteans, on the other hand, the nation stood supreme under God.

While Diederichs's analysis of the nation was not actually idolo-trous, Stoker said, it 'houses the danger of deification of the nation' (*Volksblad*, 25 April, 1936). Despite his reservations, however, Stoker declared himself ready to co-operate with the neo-Fichteans in fulfilling the calling of all true Afrikaners to keep Afrikanerdom pure and united in expectation of the republican eschaton (Stoker, 1941: 274-79). To this end an Afrikaner unity committee under the chairmanship of Professor L. J. du Plessis, issued a declaration in June 1941 signed by representatives of the FAK, the OB, the RDB, and the three Dutch Reformed Churches, which spelled out clearly a Christian-National revision of the civil faith which was accepted by Kuyperians, by neo-Fichteans and even by liberal nationalists like Malan:

> The state must be genuinely Free and Republican and Christian-National. It must acknowledge as basic the eternal legal principles of the Word of God, the clear direction of the development of our ethnic history, and the necessary application of this past to modern circumstances.

> The constitutional system must not be cast in a foreign mold. It must break away from all which is false or damaging to the People in democracy as it is here known, and must make possible a powerful government built upon the concepts of People's government of the South African republics, with necessary application in an industrial state for furthering the interests of the People. No inroads may be made upon the freedom of conscience and independence of the social spheres which are grounded in creation unless state policy as laid down is being undermined.

> Far-reaching social and economic reforms must be undertaken. Exploitation of Afrikanerdom by any financial power must be ended. The riches of the land must be powerfully developed in service to the People and in order to ensure a worthwhile living standard for every member of the People. The backward position of the Afrikaner in various professions must be eliminated. Education must rest upon a Christian-National foundation, and the maintenance of the mother tongue education must be ensured. The Afrikaner, as the original exploiter of the land, must be confirmed in his citizenship, and protected against domination by any who will not extend their fullest loyalty to the country. His rights must receive absolute protection and be guarded at all times (*Transvaler*, 13 June, 1941).

This anticipation of a republic, based on the eternal principles of God's sovereignty and yet conforming to both the Afrikaner past and an industrial future, managed a workable marriage between the various warring secondary revisions of the civil religion. At least until the achievement of the Republic, a measure of co-operation between the different philosophical factions could be expected under the rubric of Christian-Nationalism. Some such version of the civil faith was thus normative for Afrikanerdom during the 1940s – and indeed until the achievement of the Republic in 1961. Disagreement and conflict between Liberal, Kuyperian and neo-Fichtean Afrikaner Christian-Nationalists was played down in the interests of political and cultural unity. The 'granite face of Afrikanerdom' after 1948 was thus based upon political exigency and a common civil faith rather than basic agreement upon social philosophy. All could agree that a republic must come, but the precise nature of that republic and a post-republican policy for Afrikanerdom would necessarily lead to compromise or division in the ranks of Afrikanerdom.

VI

Spelling out some of the various secondary revisions of the civil religion current before 1948 helps to dispel any misconception of a static doctrinal system which my initial exposition might have implied. There were, however, completely different versions of the civil religion operative in the 1930s and 1940s. These were genuine transformations of the sacred history rather than secondary revisions of the basic symbols. One of these, which we shall call the 'militant' version of the civil religion, had been current among certain sectors of Afrikaner opinion since the failure of the 1915 rebellion. Instead of emphasis upon the sufferings of Afrikaner innocents, this rendition saw the whole sacred period as a series of glorious revolutions against British tyranny. Stress was laid upon the fighting at Slagters Nek, rather than the executions which followed; the Great Trek was seen as a successful revolution; and the battle of Majuba mountain became the central sacred event. The exploits of Boer war guerillas such as de Wet and de la Rey were stressed in preference to concentration camp atrocities; and Jopie Fourie was seen as a great man of action rather than the final martyr.

As early as 1936, N. G. S. van der Walt (later editor of the official OB newspaper) gave vivid expression to this militant faith:

We shall never get a free republic in the true meaning of the word with constitutional methods. Armed force is essential, in the first place to command the respect of the English-speaking element so that they will be willing to be assimilated by the Afrikaner; in the second place to weld the Afrikaners together again; and in the third place because I do not believe in the bloodless way; a sacrifice must consist of blood (van der Walt diary, OB archives, Potchefstroom University, entry for 24 January, 1936).

This alternative version of the civil religion received public circulation after 1934 in the Potchefstroom Nationalist newspaper, *Die Republik-ein*. After the outbreak of war in 1939, this romantic call for action became the official civil faith of the Ossewabrandwag (OB), a proto-Nazi Afrikaner organization which had its origins in the Oxwagon Trek of 1938 and blossomed after was was declared in 1939. (cf. T. D. Moodie, 1975: 190-93, 208-33). Professor Cronje gave clear expression to it in a speech at the grave of Jopie Fourie in December 1942:

> We have come to declare that we as Afrikaners will remain true to the ideal for which Jopie Fourie struggled and died, namely the freedom and self-determination of the Boer nation. That ideal is not only our goal but also our measure. All which will further the realization of our freedom-ideal is right and good; everything which stands in the way of the realization of that ideal is wrong and bad. So judged Jopie Fourie. So do we judge (*Vaderland*, 23 December, 1942).

Certain single themes in the mainstream civil religion were also trans-formed in response to exigencies perceived by the Afrikaner elite in the 1930s. Most important of these was the theme of the *Tweede Trek* (Second Great Trek) which developed in response to the rapid urbaniza-tion of Afrikaans-speaking South Africa before 1948, and which feared racial equality and class conflict in the great cities as threats to Afrikaner unity and Afrikaner exclusiveness. The *Tweede Trek* theme was a favourite of the neo-Fichteans, but it was given popular expres-sion in an oxwagon centenary speech at Blood River by Dr Malan:

> Where he too must stand in the breach for his People, the Afrikaner of the new Great Trek meets the non-white beside his Blood River, partly or completely unarmed, without the defenses of river bank or entrenchment, defenseless upon the open plain of economic equalization. . . .[Divine power] was intended to go out from that sixty percent of South Africa's white population who are flesh and blood of the exhausted trekker struggling in the city. Unite that power purposefully in a mighty salvation-deed *(reddingsdaad)* and then the future of Afrikanerdom will be assured and white civilization will be saved (Pienaar, 1964: 177, 129).

We have said that fear of the black masses was not a central theme of the classical Afrikaner civil religion. By 1938, however, it seemed that not only white civilization but the very existence of Afrikanerdom was threatened by racial equality and class conflict. Henceforth 'white civilization' and 'Afrikanerdom' were equated and the full thrust of the civil faith would be marshalled in support of racial discrimination.

On the other hand, one final transformation of the civil faith which needs special mention is the doctrine of *apartheid*, or separate development, which attempts to deal rationally and morally with racial discrimination in South Africa. This is the doctrine by which each tribal/language group in black South Africa is said to have its own national integrity in order that each might best develop along its own lines. In a famous speech in Parliament in 1959, the Minister of Bantu Affairs laid out clearly the moral justification of this doctrine:

> [The doctrine, he said] rests on three main basic principles. . . . The first is that God has given a divine task and calling to every People in the world, which dare not be destroyed or denied by anyone. The second is that every People in the world, of whatever race or color, just like every individual, has an inherent right to live and to develop. Every People is entitled to the right of self-preservation. In the third place, it is our deep conviction that personal and national ideals of every individual and of every ethnic group can best be developed within its own national community. Only then will the other groups feel that they are not being endangered. . . . This is the philosophic basis of the policy of apartheid. . . . To our people this is not a mere abstraction which hangs in the air. It is a divine task which has to be implemented and fulfilled systematically (*Hansard*, 18 May, 1959: 6001-6002).

The influence of the doctrine of *sowereiniteit in eie kring* in its Neo-Fichtean Christian-National form must surely be obvious. 'We grant to the Bantu', said the Minister, 'what we demand for ourselves' (col. 6023).

Much of the civil religious enthusiasm of committed Afrikaners after political victory in 1948 was devoted to making this doctrine a basis for policy. Aside from the unconscious arrogance implicit in the policy's paternalism — Afrikaners know better than blacks what blacks ought to demand — there are two further contradictions which have emerged in the course of twenty years of application of separate development policy. The first stems from the fact that the Afrikaner civil religion, for all its stress upon language-group identity, depends on a deeper assumption of white racism. Although the civil faith was inspired by a deeply anti-English animus, it never questioned the more fundamental postulate that whites must rule in South Africa – although certainly these white rulers should be Afrikaner and republican. The policy of separate development has always been torn between its ethnic protestations and the racial assumptions of white South Africans. There is thus a contradiction between ethnic theory and racist practice which is almost always resolved in favour of the latter.

A second fundamental contradiction is implicit in the whole notion of identity as it has been developed in South Africa. Afrikaners maintained their identity by a process of symbolic and ritual sacralization of their ethnicity, but their identity was also ensured by their pursuit of political power. Nor was the acquisition of political power accidental to the civil faith – their political eschatology placed it at the very centre. The separate development proposal that black satellite states be given political independence recognizes the problem, but it overlooks the fact that a majority of the inhabitants of 'white' South Africa (the Bantustans aside) are black and coloured. Any suggestion that these people be given political rights where they live or work is seen as a threat to Afrikaner (or white South African) identity. Identity, then, is at root a matter of power.

The rise of a black consciousness movement based upon race rather than language amongst the urban black elite seems to the outside observer but a logical extension of the theory of separate development. But the political implications of a black consciousness 'civil religion' are anathema to South African whites. The Afrikaner identity has been sustained by a drive for power. Black consciousness in South Africa has been suppressed (after an initial hestitation) because, on the basis of their own experience, Afrikaners believe that a move for black identity will ultimately lead to black power. Separate development is then shown in its true colours – a pluriformity of identities with an Afrikaner monopoly of real power.

VII

The future of the Afrikaner civil religion is now seriously in question. The economic prosperity which accompanied political power (cf. Sadie,

1975) has led many Afrikaners to doubt the necessity of continued vigilance against the English. The republic, which was finally achieved in 1961, was liberal nationalist rather than Christian-Nationalist in its constitution and yet Dr Verwoerd (a leader of the Christian-Nationalist faction in the 1940s) was able to say after the republican referendum that 'the English-speaking and the Afrikaans-speaking sections have become like the new bride and the bridegroom who enter upon the new life in love to create together and to live together as life-mates' (Pelzer, 1966: 427). Increasingly since 1961, National Party leaders have urged rapprochement with the English.

With the achievement of a republic, the diminution of expressed anti-English sentiment, and the growth of economic well-being the Afrikaner civil religion has begun to lose its central thrust. At the same time, inhumanities in implementation of separate development policy (especially the increase in migrant labour) and its theoretical and theological contradictions have led to decreased support from the Dutch Reformed Churches (T. D. Moodie, 1976: 158-66). Brutal suppression of the black consciousness movement has exposed the racist assumptions of separate development policy.

Whether the Afrikaner oligarchy's awareness of the need for a new white identity in South Africa will lead to a new, explicitly racist, 'South African' civil religion, remains to be seen. Certainly it does not yet exist. Nor is it likely to occur until Afrikaners display some willingness to share political power. Any such devolution of power, however, would threaten the old 'Afrikaner identity' which remains sacred to many ordinary Afrikaans-speaking voters. Also, a new ideology of white co-operation would threaten the elaborate institutional network based on the old Afrikaner civil faith (cf. Thompson and Butler, 1976, article by van Zyl Slabbert). A new South African civil faith cannot be realized by preaching alone. The old Afrikaner identity and its institutional supports would first have to be demolished and dismantled at the grassroots. This is not a price that most Afrikaner leaders are presently willing to pay. The Afrikaner civil religion which emerged out of years of struggle cannot easily or quickly be dismissed from the political arena.

NOTES

1. Calvin *does* speak of the intermediate election of Israel, but as a particular case, a precursor of the covenant of grace, which is applicable only to the election of individuals (Calvin, III, 21: 5-7).

2. At Slagtersnek on the eastern frontier of the Cape Colony in 1815 a small group of Boers rebelled against the established authority, which by this time was British. Six of them were executed. For more detail regarding the Afrikaner sacred history see T. D. Moodie (1975: ch. 1).

3. Jopie Fourie was an officer of the South African Defence Force who mutinied in the rebellion of 1915. He was executed on the orders of General Smuts.

4. Dr D. F. Malan was a minister of the Dutch Reformed Church (NG), who resigned to become editor of *Die Burger*, the Cape National Party newspaper. He eventually became a Member of Parliament and the leader of the Cape National Party as well as Minister of the Interior in Hartzog's cabinet after 1924. In 1933 he went into the wilderness rather than join the Hertzog-Smuts coalition (cf. T. D. Moodie, 1975: ch. 7). He emerged in 1940 as leader of the reunited National Party and thus became the first South African Prime Minister with purely Afrikaner support.

5. Verhage (n.d.: 41-46) deals briefly with the sense of paradox in Langenhoven's faith. Langenhoven himself is the Poet Laureate of Afrikanerdom.

6. 'White civilization' was shared by English and Afrikaner and any threat to the white man's dominance was feared by both white groups alike. The Afrikaner civil faith made a narrower, cultural appeal, although white racism was taken for granted throughout.

7. On 16 December 1838, during the war with the Zulus which followed the Boer invasion of Natal, a Boer commando swore to keep the day holy if God would grant them victory. During the battle which followed the Zulu forces were completely routed. However, the day was not celebrated on a wide scale until 1881.

8. At the outset of the first Anglo-Boer war in 1881 the Boer forces under Paul Kruger gathered at Paardekraal to reaffirm the Covenant of 16 December, 1838. The British forces were defeated on Majuba mountain soon afterwards and the Transvaal Republic regained its independence.

9. The *Helpmekaar* (Help Ourselves) movement was founded as a defence fund for those Boers who had rebelled and been defeated and arrested in 1915. Most of the financial support came from the Cape.

10. This theme is most fully developed in Durkheim (1965: conclusion), and Durkheim (1953: ch. 4). Zolberg's (1972: 183-207) is a sensitive development of the theme of the French civil religion, although he neither uses the term 'civil religion' nor refers to Durkheim.

11. 'My stone and that of my wife lay there too, and I know the feeling that gripped us that day when the fierce covenant of brotherhood, of sacrifice and of religion was sworn with prayer and tears', wrote one old man remembering Paardekraal in 1931 (*Vaderland*, 10 February, 1931).

12. Half of those who had been *veldkornets* between 1839 and 1870 became members of the *Volksraad* between 1845 and 1880 (Trapido, 1973: 57).

13. Like *veldkornets* in the South African Republic or elders in the Dutch Reformed churches, if prosperity *does* come the way of a *Broer* it is no doubt believed to be well deserved.

14. I not argue, of course, that Klopper or the Broederbond conjured up the sacramental ferment in 1938. They were quite as surprised at the intensity of the enthusiasm as were ordinary Afrikaners. Priests celebrate sacraments, they do not create religious ecstacy. Similarly, civil religious ferment is spontaneous and *sui generis*, but it seldom, if ever, occurs without organizational and ideological preparation.

15. The Broederbond did not create the civil religion. However, the influence of the Broederbond as bearer and sustainer of the civil faith cannot be over-estimated. It is perhaps necessary to emphasize that I do not deal at all in this chapter with the political effect of the Bond. In matters political it was definitely overshadowed by the National Party despite interlocking memberships. I ought perhaps to mention that the Party (at least in the 1940s and 1950s) was also oligarchal in organization (the signs are that it still is). Malan was wont to speak of *leierskap-in-rade* (leadership-in-council).

16. For a fuller discussion of the very complicated question of Dutch Reformed theology and church politics see T. D. Moodie (1975: ch. 4).

17. I mean by Neo-Fichteanism what Kedourie (1960) calls 'nationalism'. The nature and origins of South African Neo-Fichteanism is more fully discussed in T. D. Moodie (1975: ch. 8).

REFERENCES

AUERBACH, F. E. (1965) *The Power of Prejudice in South African Education.* Cape Town and Amsterdam: A. A. Balkema.

CALVIN, John (1961) in John T. McNEILL (ed.), *Institutes of the Christian Religion,* translated by Ford Lewis BATTLES, Philadelphia: Wesminster Press.

DAVENPORT, T. R. H. (1965) *The Afrikaner Bond.* Cape Town: Oxford University Press.

DIEDERICHS, N. (1936) *Nasionalisme as Lewensbeskouing.* Bloemfontein: Nasionale Pers.

DU PLESSIS, L. J. (1942) *Jeug en Toekomsstaat.* Stellenbosch: Wapenskou.

DURKHEIM, Emile (1953) *Sociology and Philosophy.* Glencoe: The Free Press.

——, (1965) *The Elementary Forms of the Religious Life.* New York: The Free Press.

DU TOIT, J. D. (1962) *Versamelde Werke*. Johannesburg: Dagbreek Boekhandel.

FREUD, S. (1900) (trans. 1955). *The Interpretation of Dreams*. London: Hogarth Press.

HANCOCK, W. K. (1962) *Smuts: The Sanguine Years*. Cambridge: Cambridge University Press.

KEDOURIE, Elie (1960) *Nationalism*. London: Hutchinson University Library.

KLEYNHANS, W. A. (1966) *Volksregering in die Z.A. Republiek: die Rol van Memories*. Pretoria: van Schaik.

MALAN, D. F. (1911) 'Taal en Nationaliteit' in *Wij zullen handhaven*. Studente Taalkonferentie, Stellenbosch, 6 and 7 April. Bloemfontein: De Vriend.

MOODIE, T. Dunbar (1975) *The Rise of Afrikanerdom*. Berkeley: University of California Press.

——, (1976) 'The Role of the Dutch Reformed Churches as Legitimating Factors in the Rise of Afrikaner Nationalism', *Social Dynamics*, (2).

MOODIE, Meredith A. (1976) Unpublished research findings on the formation of national identity in South African elementary school children.

MULLER, Tobie (1913) *Die Geloofsbelydenis van 'n Nasionalist*. Stellenbosch: Afrikaanse Taalvereniging.

NEL, B. F. (n.d.) *Ons Jeug en sy Nasionale Vorming*. Bloemfontein: Nasionale Pers.

OELOFSE, J. C. (1964) *Die Nederduitse Hervormde Kerk en die Afrikaner Broederbond*. Krugersdorp: N.H.W. Pers.

OPPERMAN, D. J. (1949) *Die Joernaal van Jorik*. Cape Town: Nasionale Pers.

PELZER, A. N. (1966) *Verwoerd Speaks*. Johannesburg: Afrikaanse Pers.

PIENAAR, S. W. (ed.), (1964) *Glo in U Volk: D. F. Malan as Redenaar, 1908-1954*. Cape Town: Tafelberg.

SADIE, J. L. (1975) 'Die Ekonomiese Faktor in die Afrikanergemeenskap', in H. W. VAN DER MERWE, *Identiteit en Verandering*. Cape Town: Tafelberg.

SMIT, F. P. (1951) *Die Staatsopvattinge van Paul Kruger*. Pretoria: Van Schaik.

STOKER, H. G. (1941) *Die Stryd om die Ordes*. Potchefstroom: Calvyn Jubileum Boekefonds.

THERON, H. S. (n.d.) *Die Kerklike Byekorf: die Ontstaan, Werksaamhede en Organisasie van 'n Gemeente*. Cape Town: N. G. Kerk-uitgewers.

THOMPSON, L. M. and J. BUTLER (1976) *Change in Contemporary South Africa*. Berkeley: University of California Press.

TRAPIDO, Stanley (1973) 'The South African Republic: Class Formation and the State, 1850-1900', in *The Societies of Southern Africa in the 19th and 20th Centuries*, no. 3. London: University of London Institute of Commonwealth Studies.

UNDERHILL, E. (1962) *Worship*. London: Fontana Books.

VATCHER, W. H. (1965) *White Laager, the Rise of Afrikaner Nationalism*. New York: Praeger.

VERHAGE, J. A. (n.d.) *C. J. Langenhoven, die Volkskunstenaar*. Cape Town: Nasou.

ZOLBERG, Aristide (1972) 'Moments of Madness', *Politics and Society*, Winter.

12

IDENTITY AND SOCIAL COMMITMENT

David F. Gordon
Florida Atlantic University, USA

Gordon contrasts two Jesus People groups in a major midwestern city in the USA. The one (JPU) separates the converts from the world and from his social ties. Members are encouraged to give over all their possessions to the group and to spend 100 percent of their time living and working with the group in common residence. The other (JPS) reintegrates the convert into the world and its social ties. Its members meet two or three times a week, but do not engage much in witnessing to those outside. They often discuss how to get along with others, such as relations and fellow workers. Gordon finds that the pre-existing relationships of the members to society determine whether the particular group will integrate or segregate.

Yet in both instances Jesus provides the overarching, unifying framework legitimating the personal, group or social identity. The new identity is all the more compelling because the Jesus People believe that it has been given to them rather than chosen or earned by them.

INTRODUCTION

Any identity is anchored in a set of social relationships. It is these social relationships which provide the meaning that is attached to a particular focus of identity. Part of that meaning is a spelling out of the implications which the identity has for the individual's life. In Berger and Luckmann's terms the social relationships also provide a 'plausibility structure'. These relationships are most critical when a person has changed identities or is converted. According to Berger and Luckmann,

> To have a conversion experience is nothing much. The real thing is to be able to keep on taking it seriously; to retain a sense of its plausibility. *This* is where the religious community comes in. It provides the indispensible plausibility structures for the new reality (Berger and Luckmann, 1967: 158).

In a religious conversion or a change of religious identity, the religious community can provide several things for the convert in addition to plausibility and meaning. The religious community is often responsible for provoking the change of identity in the first place and is often responsible for providing the interpretation of an experience as a conversion. In this chapter the focus is primarily on the plausibility and meaning provided by the religious community. The relationship between religious identity and the religious community in the context of two Jesus People groups is examined. I spent approximately two years observing these groups and participating in many of their activities. Toward the end of this period approximately forty depth interviews were tape-recorded with members of the two groups.

One of the groups, which we shall designate as the JPU, is a commune of approximately ninety members living in a major midwestern city. The other group, the JPS, is a non-communal group of approximately thirty members located in a suburb of the same midwestern city. Although members of both groups have adopted the same personal identity focus — Jesus — the implications of this identity for individuals' lives is different in the two groups. In the case of the JPU the religious community operates to separate the convert from the world and from his former social ties, whereas in the JPS the religious community operates to reintegrate the convert into the world and his social ties. In both cases the individual's relationship with Jesus provides the rationale and legitimation for the action taken.

THE JESUS PEOPLE IDENTITY

As Mol (1976) points out identity locates an individual in society. A given identity may then be sacralized or, in other words, made compelling, legitimate, and lasting. Being a Jesus Person locates the individual in a hierarchy which runs from God through Jesus, through the worldwide Christian movement, through prominent national Christians, through prominent regional and local Christians, through the elder(s) of the Jesus People fellowship, through brothers and sisters in the fellowship who have been Christians relatively longer, and finally to the individual. A somewhat parallel hierarchy runs from God and Jesus through civil (not necessarily Christian) authority, through parents, through the husband to the individual. These hierarchies provide identity foci at several levels going from the cosmological through social and group to the individual.

One reason that this particular Christian identity is so compelling is that it simultaneously locates the individual at each of these various levels. Each identity focus gains reinforcement and legitimation from the others. The search for personal identity becomes intertwined with God's will and with the fate of the world. During a meeting of the JPU one of the young men told the group that when he first came into the group he only wanted to solve his own problems. Now that he has been there for a while, though, he feels that it is really real and he is most interested in doing what God wants him to do. Another member of the group said, on another occasion, that he had realized he was preventing Jesus from returning by not walking with the Lord as closely as he should. This was because Jesus said He would return when His church was in order. The elder of the JPU explained to the group one day that the cross symbolizes the vertical relationship with God and the horizontal relationship with people. The vertical relationship with God must be in order before the horizontal with spouses and families can be.

Each of the above examples illustrates the interdependence between personal identity and a different identity focus. In the first example membership in the religious group has drawn the individual's attention away from his personal problems. In the second solving personal identity problems becomes a prerequisite for the ultimate unfolding of history and the development of the worldwide Christian community. The third example indicates that personal identity is crucial for establishing proper ties with family members.

The overarching framework which unifies the connections among all of these identity foci is Christianity. Evangelical Christianity, the Bible, the nature of Christian conversion, and belief in an unchanging god all lend authority and legitimacy to this identity. A member of the JPU told me.

When I was in the peace movement I was always looking for peace and joy and love and there never seemed to be any. I'd come home at night and it just didn't seem real, it just didn't last. You know it says in the Bible that if you build a house on sand that when the wind and the water come it will blow away. But if you build a house on a rock, when the wind and the water come it will stand firm. When I heard about Jesus it just blew my mind that something came before and then just went on into eternity. It blew my mind that I could be grounded into that rock. That rock transforms you. The authority runs right through your whole being. I had always believed that there was a truth, a rock, that you could grab hold of and that wouldn't change, but I was never able to find it until I found Jesus.

He went on to say that he had searched for order in the world and couldn't find it, had searched within himself and couldn't find it, and finally found it in Jesus.

The relativization of values and beliefs which confronted the Jesus People as they matured is overcome by locating themselves within the Christian system and by relying on the Bible, each other, and God for guidance. Many expressed dissatisfaction with the chaos of belief outside of Christianity. A discussion during a JPS meeting indicates the importance of the new behavioral guides. Marge said,

I'm really excited about what we're discussing because lately when I feel like I don't know whether I'm supposed to be doing what I'm doing I just pray and ask God and He tells me.

Kate added,

This gets back to what Sue said earlier about Verse Six. When you have Jesus you're sure about what you're doing. Without Him you're always going back and forth back and forth like the waves coming in. And there's nothing worse than that, than being unsure about what you're supposed to be doing.

Another reason that the new identity is so compelling is that Jesus People believe that this new identity has been given to them rather than chosen or earned by them. Since this 'gift of grace' is bestowed by God it obviously is not created by man as are all other religions and beliefs. One of the JPU members told me that in all other things the person tries to bring about his own happiness. He said that the only genuine happiness is that given by God, and there is nothing that we ourselves can do to receive it except to be willing. Salvation is given as a gift despite the fact that we do not deserve it. A typical comment by Jesus People is that this is the first thing they have ever 'been into' that has seemed increasingly real as time has passed.

The single most important characteristic of the Jesus Person's identity is that he or she has a personal, intimate relationship with Jesus, and through Jesus with God. It is this relationship rather than belief or membership which defines one as a Christian. According to one member of the JPS,

> Jesus was a person, not an historical figure who lived and did such and such, but a person. Jesus is a person, and unless we know him personally we aren't going to be living a true Christian life. In order to do what God wants us to be doing, we have to be able to hear Him when he talks to us. But we can't hear Him unless we know Him.

During a meeting of the JPS the elder told the group,

> Don't let people call you a label, and most importantly don't think of yourself as a label that differentiates you from a brother. . . . So don't think of yourself as a Pentecostal, and don't think of yourself as a Charismatic, and, sorry Dave [a reference to me], don't think of yourself as a Jesus Person. You're a child of God and that's all you need to know. There are groups now that call themselves Jesus People that are into everything under the sun; so you don't want to ally yourself with a lot of what is going on.

The relationship between the individual and his or her primary focus of identity is one of identification in a Freudian sense, Jesus (and at a more advanced stage the Holy Spirit as well) becomes a love-object which is emulated and incorporated into the individual's personality. It then becomes extremely important for the individual to behave in a manner pleasing to Jesus. Failure to do so involves betrayal of Jesus as well as a certain amount of self-betrayal. One of the young men in the JPS told the group of his failure to follow through on something God had told him to do. He said,

> So finally this week, just a couple of days ago, I did what God told me to do a year ago. And I just felt so different. I felt like a weight had been lifted off of me, like something that was inside of me was suddenly taken out. And this morning worshipping here is the most blessed I've felt in a long time. So I just want to tell you that if God tells you to do something don't wait a year to do it, don't wait at all.

The importance of obedience to God is indicated by the fact that this experience is described in terms usually used to describe a conversion experience. Failure to obey produces a great deal of anxiety and guilt. In addition, fear of failure to obey produces anxiety.

How can the individual be sure what God's wishes are in a certain situation? How can he be sure he is following God's wishes rather than his own? These concerns were often expressed by members of both groups. During a meeting of the JPS the elder answered the first question by saying.

> That's where the church is really important. If you're really confused and don't know what to do in a certain situation, if you have other people around who know you that can sit down with you and tell you where the hangup is.

Guidance and interpretation of this type are a large part of the reason many of the Jesus People expressed the desire to be with other Christians once they were saved.

A believer distinguishes between God's wishes and his own in two major ways. One is through prayer. If the desire to do something persists after prayer it is assumed that the desire is from God. When this fails or the believer is in a hurry the elders of the group are consulted. It is presumed that God would not tell the elders one thing and the believer another. A member of the JPU told me that if you don't belong to a group God can tell you to do something and if you don't do it no one would ever know that God told you to do it. He continued, 'But when you have an elder over you he can mediate between you and God and make sure that you follow God's commands.'

The religious community, then, is crucial in guiding and approving individual behavior and in allaying the anxiety which would exist without this guidance. This problem is particularly salient in a situation where the focus of identity is a personal relationship and hence is open to a variety of personal interpretations. We now turn to an examination of the role of each group in interpreting the Jesus People identity. As we shall see these interpretations differ in a major way.

DIVERGENT CONSEQUENCES OF
THE JESUS PEOPLE IDENTITY

The two Jesus People groups under discussion are similar in many ways. In terms of beliefs and religious doctrine they are almost identical. Both believe that the Bible is the literal and revealed Word of God. Both believe that Jesus is God and the Son of God, that he died for man's sins and was resurrected. Both believe that the only way to salvation (and to avoid eternal damnation) is to accept Jesus as one's personal savior. Further steps in becoming a strong Christian involve submitting to a spiritual elder and a body of other born-again Christians, being baptised by water, and receiving the baptism of the Holy Spirit. This last step involves praying for the Holy Spirit to enter one's person. The individual then has more power to witness and to live a Christian life, and he usually receives 'gifts of the Spirit' such as speaking in tongues. In addition both groups oppose smoking, drinking, using drugs, and extra-marital sex. Authority, both secular and spiritual, is to be obeyed unless it obviously goes against the will of God. Both groups are critical of mainline Christian churches which are seen as dead, superficial, and formalistic.

Both groups believe that the highest service they can render to an individual or to society is to convince them to accept Jesus. While the JPU carries out this duty directly and aggressively, the JPS carries it out by example, if at all.

Historically, both groups were founded by evangelistic individuals for the purpose of winning souls. Both were heavily influenced by the Jesus Movement, and both were founded at approximately the same time. In fact, the two groups cooperated in holding rallies and concerts in their early days.

In terms of the social characteristics of the members the groups are also very similar. The median age of both groups is 21 years. The median education for the JPU is 12 years and for the JPS is 13 years. Median length of membership in the group is one year for both groups. Based on a response rate of less than 50 percent in each group the socio-economic status of members' families is almost identical. Similarly, there is no difference in the ethnic composition of the groups.

Despite the considerable similarities between these two groups there are also considerable differences. The difference which concerns us here involves the effect of the group on the individual's attachments to the rest of the world. The JPU operates to sever these attachments while the JPS operates to re-establish and strengthen them. The respective groups have these opposite effects despite the fact that both groups provide a common identity for their members. The JPU group itself demands a higher level of commitment from the individual and correspondingly cuts him off from other commitments to a greater extent.

The most obvious example of this difference is that the JPU is a communal organization while the JPS is not. Those joining the JPU are encouraged to give over all of their possessions to the group. Once they become members they spend 100 percent of their time living and working with the group in a common residence and sharing food, clothing, and responsibility with others in the group. As one of the older members of the group told me, 'This is a leave-everything-behind ministry.' In the JPS a member merely pledges to submit himself to the elder. The group meets two or three times a week and attendance at meetings is encouraged but not necessary; otherwise members' lives continue unaltered.

The difference between the two groups manifests itself in many of the group practices. Those entering the JPU are required – at least for a time – to abandon talents they possess. Musicians in particular are forbidden to use their talents as are those with other skills such as writing, crafts, and so on. These talents may or may not be used again once the individual's commitment to the group has been established. Often those with no prior experience are assigned to positions in the group over those with prior experience. In the JPS, on the other hand, the talents of members are sought out and encouraged. If someone who is performing a function in the group leaves the group, that function often ceases. For example, the Bible scholar in the group left and thereafter Bible studies ceased to be held. In the JPU someone else would have been pressed into service.

The members of the JPU wear more distinctive clothing than those in the JPS although they do not have uniforms as do some religious groups. The JPU men typically wear flannel shirts, jeans, and boots while the women wear blue denim floor-length dresses and skirts. Both sexes wear their hair long and straight and many of the men have beards. Those in the JPS are indistinguishable from others their age. In addition, the JPU has a number of cars and buses which belong to the group and all of which are painted bright red and white with huge letters spelling 'Jesus' on each side.

Another JPU activity which promotes separation is witnessing (Mol, 1976). For the JPU witnessing is a major, well-organized group activity. Members are divided into teams and dispatched to the major areas of congestion around the city such as the downtown area, the airport, the rapid transit system, and shopping malls. Members then attempt to engage passers-by in conversions about Jesus and hand them a copy of the group's newspaper which is printed as a witnessing tool. The JPS on the other hand has no organized witnessing activities. Members occasionally are encouraged to witness but on an individual basis with people they know. On these occasions differences between the witnesser and witnessee are downplayed as much as possible.

The major difference between the two groups in this regard, however, is in the area of relationships with others, especially families. The JPU encourages members to establish relationships within the group while the JPS encourages members to retain relationships with those outside the group. Members of the JPU see each other on a daily basis and often form close ties with one or two other members of the group. This tendency is discouraged as much as possible so that the individual will have a wider attachment to the group. The elder told a meeting of the men, 'So you should get to know as many people as you can and benefit from all of them.' In contrast to this members of the JPS often know only two or three others in the group well. For example, one member told me he sees his closest friend in the group once a week.

In the JPU discussions often revolve around proper and effective witnessing techniques, such as how to recognize that someone is not really interested so as to avoid wasting too much time on them. In the JPS a common topic of concern is how to get along with non-Christians with whom the members of the group must interact in their daily lives. These include friends, families, employers, co-workers, and fellow students. In the case of parents, husbands, and employers members are taught to submit and obey. In the case of other non-Christians they are taught to live by Christian principles and teach by example.

Those in the JPU, when interviewed, said that they could not imagine any future outside the group. They had no ambitions or expectations of doing anything else. For those in the JPS, however, discussions of college plans and future occupations were common.

In the JPU members are taught to make decisions independently of their parents while in the JPS members are taught to submit to their parents' wishes. Parents of those in the JPU in particular often object to their children joining the group, which they see as a radical, hippie group. Another major conflict occurs when members decide to marry one another. The elder of the group discussed a member who got married against his parents' wishes:

> Phil's parents didn't want them to get married. But Phil finally just stood up and said, look, I love Nancy and we're going to get married. That caused Phil to break away from his parents and to really grow up. It says in the Bible that a child shall leave his parents. I can't think of anyone in our ministry whose parents were really overjoyed about them getting married.

In contrast the JPS believes that their task is to get parents and children back together. One of the girls stopped attending meetings because her father objected. The group regarded this as the proper action on her part. During a discussion of the children of God the elder told the JPS,

> Their policy of separateness means that they are not in submission either to their parents or to the government. So their pride has led them into disobedience which is leading them into perversion. They separate kids from their parents instead of getting them back together the way we do here.

Much of the group's discussions revolved around relationships with parents and how they can be improved. One member of the JPU who had previously been a member of the JPS said that the latter group was 'off the wall on submission to parents'. She saw this as the major difference between the two groups.

Two possible explanations can be given for these differences between the two Jesus People groups. On the one hand the members of the groups could self-select themselves on the basis of whether or not their ties with family and other lines of activity had already been broken. On the other hand the groups themselves could be responsible for either breaking or reinforcing these ties. On the basis of the interviews with members of both groups both explanations seem to hold with the first being the most important. Most of those who joined the JPU had already broken their family ties, had physically moved away from home, and had quit either school, their jobs, or both. Once in the JPU their status as being unconnected with the society was affirmed, legitimized, and sacralized. Relations with parents often improved after a period of time, but only when the parents accepted the independent status of their children as born-again Christians. A good example of this is Lisa. Lisa had been saved at an early age and both her parents were committed Christians. When Lisa was a sophomore in high school her parents got a divorce which she said really 'freaked her out'. Lisa began drinking and hanging around with a drug crowd. When she finished high school she moved into the city from the surburb where she had lived with her family. She became a singer with a rock band, lived with a guy for four years and got saved again when a friend sent her a copy of *The Late Great Planet Earth*, a book written by a Christian about the End Times. Shortly after this Lisa encountered one of the JPU members in a park and eventually joined the group. Lisa said she now gets along with her stepfather — who she used to hate — and gets along with her parents even though her father objects to her religious commitment.

The common elements which emerge from the JPU interviews are loss of a parent through death or divorce, antagonistic relationships with parents, an adolescent reputation as a promiscuous or bad person, as an outcast or loner, heavy drinking and/or drug use, a period of separation from the family preceding involvement with the JPU, and a search for order and acceptance. The few exceptions to this pattern joined the JPU as the result of having close friends or siblings who joined ahead of them.

Those who joined the JPS typically had not left home, jobs, or school, but were having difficulties with their parents. Joining the JPS often made things worse for a time, but the group's belief in submission to parents eventually led to a reconciliation with at least one parent and usually with both. In this case the group functions to adjust relationships between members and society rather than to separate them from that society. Here the group is facilitating and affirming its members' prior identities. A good example of this is Don.

Don grew up in a Baptist church which his whole family attended. He stopped going to church when he reached high school. Don was rebellious and always fighting with his parents and getting in trouble at school. When he was a sophomore his girlfriend got saved and began talking to him about it. Finally Don got saved too. He met some of the members of the JPS and started attending their meetings. He has continued attending for periods on a regular basis and then not attending for long periods as well. Since he has been saved Don has gone to his father for advice and told him he is willing to follow his wishes. His father was puzzled by this at first but they now get along very well.

Another member of the JPS said,

> Jesus has really done wonders in my life, especially with my father. My father and I never got along, and he's an alcoholic so my mother has sort of been the head of the family. . . . Anyway I had all this bitterness in my heart for my father . . . and I never could have gotten rid of that bitterness myself. But do you remember the teachings we had on submission last winter? Those teachings really changed things . . . I began submitting to my father after I submitted to God and to the elders.

Still another girl in the JPS told me that even though she had been a born-again Christian previously she had never thought about submitting to authority until she started attending JPS meetings, which was the first time she had really heard about it. She said that recently, quite suddenly, she felt that it was important and wanted to submit to some authority.

The common elements which emerge from the JPS interviews are a fundamentalist Christian background, a falling away from commitment to God and to parents, continued involvement in school and/or jobs, and a renewal of the original commitments.

The JPU, then, emphasizes location in the hierarchy running from God through the religious community to the believer while the JPS emphasizes location in the hierarchy running from God through government and parents to the believer. Neither group operates to transform the individual's relation to social groups and lines of activity but rather operates to legitimize a pre-existing relationship or relationships. The JPU, like its individual members, is isolated from the community. Its location in a multi-ethnic, lower-class urban area allows the group to maintain this isolation and group autonomy. The JPS, like its individual members, is integrated in the community and must adjust to it. Sunday night meetings were discontinued, for example, because as the elder said,

A lot of people are tired, people, and had to hire baby sitters and that's not right. And others of you have to be at work and things like that, so we know that Sunday night is, what we're doing on Sunday night is really a hardship.

The suburban setting with its relatively small, homogeneous population would be much less tolerant of a large number of young people living communally and espousing a somewhat deviant belief system.

CONCLUSION

We have seen that being a Jesus Person provides identity at the personal, group, and social levels. Within this identity, however, individual religious communities provide interpretations emphasizing varying degrees of integration with the surrounding non-Christian society. While accepting the same set of religious beliefs and morality one group may separate its members from society while the other integrates them into society. Based on the data collected from two Jesus People groups, the pre-existing relationships of the members to society determine whether the particular group will integrate or segregate.

The individual's position vis-à-vis society and family is not radically altered. Rather, it is placed within a framework of meaning which is supported by close, intense interaction with others who share a similar position. Perhaps this helps to explain why many in the groups find being a Jesus Person more real than previous identities they have had.

REFERENCES

BERGER, Peter L. and Thomas LUCKMANN (1967) *The Social Construction of Reality*. New York: Anchor Books.
MOL, Hans (1976) *Identity and the Sacred*. Agincourt: The Book Society of Canada, Limited.

NOTES ON CONTRIBUTORS

Taufik Abdullah was born in West Sumatra in 1936. He has an MA and PhD in History from Cornell University, New York. Since 1963 he has been on the staff of the National Institute of Economic and Social Research and since 1974 has been director of the Indonesian Institute of Sciences (LEKNAS-LIPI). He is also chairman of the Southeast-Asian Studies Program, and vice-president of the Southeast-Asian Social Science Association and chairman of the Indonesian Association for the Advancement of Social Science. His publications include: 'Modernization in the Minangkabau World' in C. Holt, B. Anderson and A. Siegel (eds.), *Culture and Politics in Indonesia* (1972); *Sejarawan dan Kesadaran Sejarah* (Historians and Historical Consciousness) (1974) and editor of *Islam di Indonesia* (Islam in Indonesia) (1974) and *Pemuda dan Perubahan Sosial* (Youth and Social Change (1974).

Max Assimeng was born in 1939 in Eastern Ghana. He completed his undergraduate studies in sociology at the University of Legon, Ghana, in 1964 and obtained a DPhil. from the faculty of social studies at Oxford University in 1968. He is currently senior lecturer in sociology at the University of Ghana in Legon. Dr Assimeng's publications include: 'Status Anxiety and Cultural Revival' in *Ghana Journal of Sociology* (1969); 'Religious and Secular Messianism in Africa' in *Research Review* (Legon, 1969); 'Sectarian Allegiance and Political Authority: The Watch Tower Society in Zambia 1907-35' in *Journal of Modern African Studies* (1970); Social Life in Ghana (1974); and 'Traditional Life, Culture, and Literature in Ghana' in *Conch* (1975).

S. Gopalan was born in India in 1935. He has been awarded the degrees of MA (Madras, 1956), MLitt (Madras, 1958), PhD in philosophy (Madras, 1965), and PhD in religion (McMaster University, Canada, 1977). He is currently reader in philosophy at the Dr S. Radhakrishnan Institute for Advanced Study in Philosophy at Madras, India. His publications include: *The Hindu Philosophy of Social Reconstruction; Social Justice: An Axiological Analysis; Tradition: A Social Analysis;* and *Outlines of Jainism.*

David F. Gordon was born in 1947 in Evergreen Park, Illinois, USA. He graduated from Grinnell College in Iowa and did postgraduate work in the department of sociology at the University of Chicago. His PhD thesis was a comparative study of identity and structure in two Jesus People groups. He published an article, 'The Jesus People: An Identity Synthesis' in *Urban Life and Culture*, 1974.

Bert L. Hardin was born in 1939. He completed his study of sociology and social psychology in the USA at the University of Arkansas and obtained his masters degree in 1969. He has since been involved in scientific research at the University of Tuebingen where he is presently employed as a *Wissenschaftlicher Angestellter*. In 1975 he obtained his *Doktor der Sozialwissenschaften*. His major areas of interest include the sociology of science, sociology of religion and the sociology of medicine. Dr Hardin's publications include *The Professionalization of Sociology. A Comparative Study: Germany – USA* (1971) and various articles on the sociology of medicine in German scientific journals.

Robert Kenneth Jones graduated from the University of Hull, studied the sociology of education at Oxford University and obtained a PhD in the sociology of religion at Lancaster University. He was senior lecturer and head of sociology at Kirkby Fields College of Education, Liverpool, 1965-70, and staff tutor, north west of England, Open University, 1970-75. Until recently he was director of studies and head of social studies at Ulster College in Northern Ireland. He is author of *Sociology in Medicine*, and has published articles in a number of journals including *Philosophy, Sociology, Sociological Review, Modern Churchman, New Society, Human Relations*. He is currently working on a study of psychiatric admission and categories of ideological affiliation.

Guenter Kehrer was born in 1939. He studied social sciences at the University of Frankfurt am Main and Tuebingen, obtaining his PhD in 1965. From 1965 to 1971 he was *Wissenschaftlicher Assistent* in Tuebingen and has since been employed as *Universitätsdozent*. His major fields of research include the sociology of religion and social ethics. In 1970 he was awarded the *venia legendi* for sociology of religion and social ethics by the University of Tuebingen. His publications include: *Das religiöse Bewußtsein des Industriearbeiters* (1967);

Religionssoziologie (1968); *Dogma und Politik* (with Feld et al.) (1973); *Das Jenseits der Gesellschaft* (with Dahm and Drehsen) (1975); and articles in various German scientific journals.

Frank William Lewins was born in Melbourne, Australia, in 1941. In 1976 he received a PhD from the School of Social Sciences of La Trobe Unviersity in Melbourne. He is now a lecturing fellow at the Australian National University. Dr Lewins' PhD dissertation on *The Australian Catholic Church and the Migrant* will be published as a book in 1978. His published articles include a number on ethnicity and Catholicism in the *Australian and New Zealand Journal of Sociology* and in Peter E. Glasner (ed.) *The Contemporary Australian Parish and Ministry* (1975).

Johannis (Hans) J. Mol was born in 1922 in The Netherlands. He is professor in the sociology of religion at McMaster University, Hamilton, Ontario, Canada. He is also the president of the Research Committee in the sociology of religion of the International Sociological Association for the 1974-78 quadrennium. In 1961 he obtained his PhD at Columbia University in New York. His major works include: *Churches and Immigrants* (1961); *Race and Religion in New Zealand* (1966); *The Breaking of Traditions* (1968); *Christianity in Chains* (1969); *Religion in Australia* (1971). His most recent book, *Identity and the Sacred* (1976), is a sketch for a new social scientific theory of religion.

Thomas Dunbar Moodie was born in 1940 in Cape Town, South Africa. He holds a PhD from Harvard University and was until recently professor and head of the department of sociology at the University of Witwatersrand, Johannesburg. He is now professor of sociology at the Hobart and William Smith Colleges, Geneva, New York, USA. His publications include *The Rise of Afrikanerdom* (1975).

William Shaffir was born in 1945 in Montreal, Canada. He received his doctorate in sociology from McGill University in 1972 and is currently an associate professor in the department of sociology at McMaster University in Hamilton, Ontario. He has published several articles about chassidic Jews and has written a book on the chassidic community in Montreal. Dr Shaffir's present research is a study of the socialization and professionalization of medical students at an innovative medical school in Ontario. During his sabbatical year in 1978-79, he intends to study the organization of several chassidic communities in Israel.

Braj Sinha was born in 1943 at Monghyl in India. He obtained his PhD from McMaster University in Canada in the year 1976. His wife Manju Sinha was born in 1950 at Khaspur in India. She has an MA in Sociology from McMaster University in Canada and is currently working on her PhD dissertation. Before coming to USA Dr Sinha taught at Vikzamshila College, Bhagalpur University and B.N. College, Patna University in India. He is currently teaching at the College of Wooster, Ohio, USA. His scholarly works include: *Time, Self and Transcendence: the Indian Perspective*; and *Surdas' Story of Rama: A Critical Analysis* (co-authored with Professor Edmour Babineau of the University of Moncton, New Brunswick, Canada). He has also contributed to a number of International symposiums and conferences.

Jan M. G. Thurlings was born in 1927 at Tegelen in The Netherlands. In 1960 he received a PhD from the Catholic University of Nijmegen. He is currently professor of empirical sociology in the social science faculty of the Catholic University at Nijmegen. His publications include: *Het sociale conflict: van psychologische naar sociologische benadering* (Social conflict: from psychological to sociological approach) (1960); and *De wankele zuil: Nederlandse katholieken tussen assimilatie en pluralisme* (The tottering column: Dutch Catholics between assimilation and pluralism) (1971). He has also published several articles.

NOTES

NOTES

NOTES

NOTES